2 BEST AMERICAN GAY FICTION

Edited by Brian Bouldrey

Best American Gay Fiction 1996

Wrestling with the Angel:
Faith and Religion in the Lives of Gay Men

By Brian Bouldrey

Genius of Desire

2 BEST AMERICAN GAY FICTION

Edited by Brian Bouldrey

Foreword by Bernard Cooper

LITTLE, BROWN AND COMPANY

Boston New York Toronto London

First Edition

The characters and events in this book are fictitious. Any similarity to real persons, living or dead, is coincidental and not intended by the authors.
Copyright acknowledgments appear on pp. 312–314.

ISBN 0-316-10298-9 (hc)
ISBN 0-316-10299-7 (pb)
ISSN 1088-5501

HC: 10 9 8 7 6 5 4 3 2 1
PB: 10 9 8 7 6 5 4 3 2 1

MV-NY

Book design by Julia Sedykh

Published simultaneously in Canada by Little, Brown & Company (Canada) Limited
Printed in the United States of America

This book is for the "awfully archival"

Don Osborne

CONTENTS

FOREWORD: **THEY STAND APART**

by Bernard Cooper

I discovered it on my parents' bookshelves, wedged among the popular paperbacks of the time — *Bridge on the River Kwai, Alfred Hitchcock's Mysteries* — and slid it out with great trepidation, holding my breath. I remember the murky glow of a streetlamp on the cover, and beneath it the silhouettes of two men engaged in a furtive negotiation. A shared match flared between them, providing just enough light to see that they were dressed in trench coats; or perhaps I imagined these details in order to give definition to an otherwise unimaginable act. The jacket copy touted Dr. Hailsham's credentials and suggested that only a trained psychiatrist, a man whose years of clinical experience had hardened him to the shocking deviations of human lust, was qualified to guide an innocent reader through the strange, nocturnal world of the homosexual.

I opened *They Stand Apart* and read that homosexuals were able to identify one another "with a simple glance." The glance I imagined fixed on me was anything but simple — it was piercing and clairvoyant, a look that claimed me by saying, *You are one, too.* The author's assertion haunted me for months and caused me to scrutinize, with paranoic intensity, a greeting from the brown-eyed milkman or a nod from the junior high school janitor. Did they see me for who I really was? Would their glance expose me? It never occurred to me that, if this theory were true, it would also allow me to recognize others who shared my longing; it promised only a kind of indictment, locking me more deeply into what, ever since I was old enough to imagine a future, I imagined as a future of secrecy and loneliness.

Another book I pulled from my parents' shelves was *The Hidden Persuaders,* by Vance Packard. In his examination of subliminal advertising, Packard claimed that if you looked closely enough, you would find, say, the image of a fornicating couple hidden in the ice cubes of a bourbon ad, or a shape suspiciously like an erect penis and testicles airbrushed onto a bottle of aftershave, or the word *sex* faintly written across the hood of a sports car. The book contained illustrations of subliminal images found in magazine ads, and I spent hours staring and squinting and turning the book this way and that, mesmerized by Packard's oddly Freudian premise: the world around us is riddled with hidden enticements and meanings, most of them sexual.

By the age of thirteen, these two reading experiences — a tawdry exposé on homosexuals and a treatise on subliminal imagery — shaped my view of the world: afraid that a simple glance would mark me as an outcast, I lived a guarded and vigilant adolescence, aware of all the unwitting sexual signals in my own and others' voices, dress, and gestures. The most innocuous act — the way you walked or held your pencil or raised your hand in class — could betray you, leave you open to ridicule and shame.

This need to be observant, along with the busy but isolated imagination of one who is forced, as Dr. Hailsham would have it, to stand apart, are two of the earliest and most important factors that led me to the writer's life. I consider it no small stroke of luck that the side effects of repression have turned into precisely those qualities — a combination of watchfulness and inwardness — that have made self-expression possible, that have allowed me to give voice to experiences and perceptions that once remained nameless. My guess is that this, or something like it, is true for many of the writers in this fine anthology.

I am forty-five years old, and though I long ago dismissed that book cover, with its faceless men and dank atmosphere, as one more pitifully inadequate representation of gay life, it is not necessarily a false one. We often *do* recognize one another at a glance, establishing an instantaneous link in our personal histories, a look that presumes we have moved through the same maze of confusion and doubt in order to come to terms with the nature of our desires. We often *do* meet or acknowledge one another on city streets, perhaps inventing some excuse to initiate contact and — is there anyone who has not wished for this? — alleviate our loneliness and bodily solitude.

For me, writing short stories has meant finding the words that will bring those two silhouettes to life, that will illuminate their faces with something brighter and more lasting than a match. They are men who have come to each other out of lives that can be made vivid and rich and convincing through language. They are characters whom the fiction writer can honor (though they needn't always be likable characters) by giving them what Flannery O'Connor called "weight and extension," a certain posture or nervous habit or set to their jaw that arises from the very core of character and makes their presence on the page both tangible and memorable. And finally, refusing subjugation to the author's will, these flat and shadowy men might, after several drafts, become autonomous, acting and speaking for themselves, behaving in ways that surprise a reader because they have surprised the writer as well.

Writing short fiction is arduous. Lifetimes must be distilled into a form that is both self-enclosed and larger than the sum of its parts. Paradoxically, the narrative must lead to a conclusion that seems both inevitable and unpredictable. The specific rules of composition change with each story, and the process, in retrospect, is as elusive and difficult to explain as a dream. Each word is a cell, embodying character. Each character lives out, in some jumble of joy and despair, strength and frailty, what the writer knows, or strives to know, in the act of setting words to paper. "We tell ourselves stories to keep ourselves alive," says Joan Didion. And so gay writers are doing just that, in our varied and inexhaustible ways. Too many of us find ourselves in a world whose narrative is ill fitting. We try to set the story right, to make it more reflective of the lives we lead. We work to master our craft, to enrich the story of the given with other, more challenging versions. Here are twenty-one of the best.

INTRODUCTION

Ethan Mordden, quoted last year in a review of Stephen McAuley's lovely novel *The Man of the House,* said, "A people as chosen as gays are must erect a ghetto not so much for segregation as for concentration: to learn what gay is."

Ghetto is a word that was first used in medieval Venice, where the Jews were required to live within a walled area and, while allowed to come and go during the day, were locked in at night. The ghetto was permeable, to a point. Historical documents tell us that the Jews didn't mind. Compared to the way other Europeans treated Jews, the Venetians were tolerant. And the walls afforded a certain amount of protection. One comes to love one's prison, after a while. In fact, *ghetto,* the Italian word for foundry (a foundry had once stood on the place where the Venetian Jews were relocated), sounded a lot like the Hebrew root for "cut off."

I live in a ghetto, too, San Francisco's gay ghetto. We're constantly debating in our little gay cafés and gay dinner parties and gay club meetings whether gay is a culture. And while our lingo does have its gender-bending pronouns ("smell *her*"), shorthand ("No fats. No fems."), and even an extensive slang lexicon that requires a decoder ring, if not a dictionary ("She think she velvet, but she wet and wild"), would "homophonics" be considered a separate language?

Language is often the key to a culture. Where would the Basque country be without it? How has Hebrew contributed to building the state of Israel? How did Franco come down hard on the Catalonians if not by discouraging them from speaking Catalan? Language is used to create art and literature. This anthology, for instance, is a ghetto. However much the reviews of last year's edition pointed out that the *Best American Gay Fiction* series is a good source for anybody who wants to find out what is going on in gay literature, the fact is, these books contain stories about and for gay men. If a straight black woman picks up one of these anthologies, it's done in the same spirit that I pick up an anthology of black women writers — to see how somebody else lives; curiosity; a field trip.

I'm reminded of a talk show conversation years ago (a Letterman-type show, not an Oprah-type) in which a fussy, articulate white actor was sharing the guest spotlight with a slouching, phlegmatic African American rapper. In the middle of the conversation, the white actor broke down: "God, I hate rap!" he shrieked. "I hate the noise, I hate the words, I hate that repetitive beat, I hate . . ." He went on and on, offering dozens of aspects of rap that bothered the hell out of him. There was an uncomfortable silence as the host tried to pick up the pieces. The audience sat in stunned shock, and the rapper began to rise out of his slouch in order to respond: "But hey, man," he said, carefully, calmly, "it's not *for* you." That's a troubling truth I have wrestled with for a long time: Who cares if I don't like it? Who cares if I don't think bodybuilders are attractive? In *The Rocky Horror Picture Show,* Dr. Frank-N-Furter tells Janet Weiss, who doesn't like the artificial man the doctor has created for his sex toy because he has too many muscles, "I didn't make him for *you.*"

Frank-N-Furter, rap stars, gay writers, we are all constructing our private clubs and ghettos — not just for survival, but for pleasure.

Thinking back on what Mordden said about erecting a ghetto, I wonder if we haven't learned what gay is by now. What happens when the ghetto no longer has a purpose? Will the sandstone walls around it melt away? Will we stay behind them in an uneasy detente with the rest of American society? Or will the pleasures we create assure persistence of the ghetto? Which comes first — the ghetto or the culture?

The queer ghetto is not like the African American ghetto or a Chinatown. Many gays are white men, a group of people who have culturally dominated western civilization for two thousand years. Sure, we get bashed, we chafe under terrible laws, both religious and civil. Who knows how much discrimination has impeded HIV research or added to the deaths of gay men afflicted with AIDS. But the way the gay movement has progressed, for the most part, is through the law, through an implicit belief that both the law and the government that made the law do work, and are worth improving. Gay men are working daily to chip away at the ghetto they love, their own separate language, their own difference.

Gay men live in a ghetto, but many of them (not all) have the luxury of slipping out of the ghetto and looking like the pervasive American culture. We "pass." We also have our hand in many important arenas, making decisions for the country. In a speech delivered at a fund-raising dinner for the San Francisco Public Library's Gay and Lesbian Collection, Andrew Sullivan pointed out to The Rest Of The Country that they should watch out for gays and lesbians: "We write your textbooks, your laws, your history." And that's just the beginning. Gay men are lawyers, doctors, teachers, politicians, academicians, scientists. People with power. Because we often pass.

It's a goal heavily debated in the gay ghetto, this passing — drag queens even hope not to be "clocked." And if you're not too much of a sissy, perhaps you can sit at a judge's bench, a newspaper editorial desk, a congressional committee, or any of those other seats of power, usually off limits to marginal populations — women, African Americans, Latinos, sissies, transvestites. At times gay men are put upon. At other times, we are putters upon. We have our own literature about it, too — if only we'd just act straight, says Bruce Bawer, we'd get a place at the table.

What we have is a porous ghetto. In the stories of this collection, that porousness is shown often: Michael Nava's gay judge lives a daylit life as a husband and a father. Alan, the boy in Tom House's "The Chicken Man," gets an erection thinking about a man while lying on his stomach in front of the family television; he can't get up without exposing himself. But a sexy woman is on the screen, and his father mistakes Alan's dilemma for a heterosexual problem — Alan passes. Dale O'Keefe, in Scott Thomas's "Mainframe," is a middle-aged computer specialist whose homosexual life is deeply hidden, perhaps even from himself. Paul Lisicky's adolescent narrator passes as straight among his straight buddies as they torment the town fag; only the town fag knows the narrator's real identity.

The gay man is split down the middle, a mishmash of public and private activity. We are exceedingly good at being public figures, whether we pass or not. We've learned how to act in public, either acting normal or putting on an act. This is all to cover or contrast with the private life, what happens behind closed doors, between the sheets. By making public changes, we believe, we will be treated better. Most of our law, at any rate, is built upon the enforcement of good manners and taste.

Living by the rules of diversity is much more difficult than making the rules. The criteria for what is considered "good" can be as different as the various people we live among. How can we praise excellence when excellence seems so relative? Can there be a set of rules that governs all of, say, literature? Is Edmund White's *The Beautiful Room Is Empty* as vital, on its own terms, as the hip-hop ebonics of James Earl Hardy's *2nd Time Around?* And could they sit side by side in an anthology like this and maintain their own integrity, be judged on their own terms?

When you read the stories collected here, you will marvel at the variety of voices and forms. You will also see a lot of what is called multicultural. The 1996 edition was thin on African American, Latino, Asian, and other nonwhite representatives. The work just wasn't out there. This year, the publishers of gay fiction made up for lost time. Some of the best stories in this collection were written by African Americans (Gary Fisher's "Red Cream Soda"), Latinos ("My Son, My Heart, My Life" by John Keene), Filipinos (R. Zamora Linmark's "Blame It on Chachi"), and Asian Americans (Russell Leong's "Phoenix Eyes" and Kolin Ohi's "A Backward Glance"). These stories are outstanding not only for showing readers a new world, but for technique and craft, style, subtlety, wit — all the things we love in good writing.

What is in the future? The late David Wojnarowicz, whose work is featured in this book, wrote in an earlier book, *Close to the Knives,* that America was too big to be all-inclusive. He called for a "tribal" society, a balkanized nation of small groups that care about their own people and do not even pretend to get along. When I look at the truly balkanized countries — the Balkans, for example — I furrow my brow in disagreement. If tribalism means a clean, well-lighted space for hatred, then I don't want to split up the union. I don't want us all to retreat to our separate tribes and put up walls rather than tear them down. To give up, in a way.

In *Best American Gay Fiction 2,* you'll see examples of chinks in the wall — Karl Woelz's "Port Kansas" is the story of a gay couple escaping from New York to the backwater neverland of a small college town. Andrew Holleran's Lark is an aging gay man in a tiny

Florida community who is looking for community when it all seems to have died away. In both Woelz's and Holleran's fiction, the characters have once lived in the ghetto, and have left it for a new kind of home. I think a continued porousness is a better answer, a chipping away at the ghetto so that wedges can be driven, until one day the walls can come tumbling down.

This does not mean I don't say *vive la différence*. When the Bible calls for the lion to lie down with the lamb, most Christians interpret that to mean that the lion must become lamblike, giving up its fierce instincts. "But," says G. K. Chesterton, "that is brutal annexation and imperialism on the part of the lamb." How can we preserve the qualities of diverse living (both in the gay subculture and in the culture at large) while being entirely inclusive, recognizing all the differences in a unified way?

It's important that gay men realize that even if the walls of the ghetto were to come down, there would be little reason to fear that the lion would become lamblike. Not with writers like Kevin Killian, D. Travers Scott, and Ishmael Houston-Jones, for example, creating fine writing about the differences, even in the ghetto, among us. A great comfort can be found in Dale Peck's *The Law of Enclosures,* a novel that has very little to do with being gay but which has with every word a gay sensibility, a gay point of view.

Each gay person springs from a family and forges his or her own identity in addition to that familial identity. Every family is a kind of ghetto, with a dialect and customs of its own. Gays leave their homes and join other communities, and somehow become members of several ghettos concurrently — family, race, religion, sexual orientation, second family. That is why this anthology shows how our ghetto speaks several dialects.

This is also why gays are accustomed to binding differences up, reconciling them. How else could we have gay Republicans? The gay identity is about being more than we seem, and about growing into ourselves, often overcoming the obstacles or limitations of our births. The ghetto for gays can remain vital only to the extent it permits difference, self-invention, and diversity.

If there is anything that I would like this anthology to be, it is a reflection of real diversity, a kind of ghetto without walls, a sign that the ghetto may one day melt away, and that its necessity, as Mordden calls it, will cease to be.

Brian Bouldrey
April 1997

2 **BEST**
AMERICAN
GAY FICTION

Andrew Holleran

IL PARADISO

HE TAKES A LOCKER when he gets to the baths — after driving faster than usual to put sixty miles between himself and Becker quickly — though he knows this disappoints; mature men, he suspects, are expected to bring money — take a room — while the young need merely a five-dollar locker, their beauty being their contribution. He doesn't care. The minute the door closes behind him, he feels a sense of relief, as if this is where he can obliterate the memory of that embarrassing scene more quickly than anyplace else. The foolishness of his obsession, the inappropriate quality of his courtship, the lunacy of even imagining for a moment that Becker was his soulmate, are clearer with each step he takes down the corridor to the locker room. I was a fool, he thinks, a vain, deluded, old queen. Only here, he thinks, as he passes a clump of men at the vending machine, everyone is even older than I am. In the afternoon there are always men older than himself, retired, on disability, or taking a long lunch; men who have come here by bus, who have to be home at night with their families, or who don't want to stay out late. He is younger than they, at least. This is the Hour of the Manatees, and it will be till shortly before five o'clock; till then he's young — a beneficiary of this ruthless system in which men who refused to consider older gentlemen when they were young now have to use the same standards on themselves. He who lives by the sword, he thinks as he walks down the hall, dies by the sword. The baths in the afternoon are like the games in the Colosseum; only here the gladiators cry, "We who are about to die want you!"

The television used to be downstairs; one could watch reruns of *Laverne & Shirley* while appraising the men entering and leaving the steam room through the glass doors beyond. Now the television is upstairs, in a sort of theater; the ground floor contains only gym equipment and lockers. On Friday afternoons they set up a table with free pizza. On Tuesdays once a month they administer tests for HIV. It's such a clean, well-run, civilized place; he's always been, and always will be, grateful for its refuge. Even now when his face still burns with the memory of Becker at the urinal. I used to go to the baths, he thinks as he opens his locker and unties his shoes, because it was a refuge from the bars; you didn't have to speak, or play games, or pretend you were interested in whatever topic you dreamed up to start a conversation with the man you wanted. I used to go to the baths because it was the most honest form of communication there is: My body wants your body. Does yours want mine? Like his mother, he values honesty. ("How are you?" people would say to her, on long distance, as he held the telephone to her ear. "I'm paralyzed," she would say. "How are you?") He used to go to the baths because it cut through all the games and affectations, the pretense, the tedious peregrinations of seduction. Now he goes because he has no place else to go. Now he goes because Time is passing, Becker's told him to get lost, and in two months he will have even less hair than he does now. The indignities of loss, he thinks as he removes his pants and puts them into the locker. Indignities Becker will not have to deal with for some time. Life is an Indian giver that takes back everything it gives you. I am approaching that peculiar time, that psychological stalemate, he thinks as he pauses for a moment in his underwear (a look he feels turns people on), when a man is too old to be pursued, but too proud to pursue. The trap of Vanity. The tomb of Pride. Lined with mirrors like the one at the end of this locker room — a mirror he used to check his appearance in but that he now ignores, because he's worried the sight of his reflection would cause him to dress and go home, if not lose consciousness.

Going to the baths has become almost as difficult as walking down the sidewalk in New York. But he goes anyway, because the baths are always a throw of the dice. No matter what happened the last time, he thinks, the next will be different. Even Becker cannot deny him that. As at the boat ramp, there is no predicting, no pattern. How could there be, for something as irrational as sex? *Abandon logic, all ye who enter here* should be written above the doorway. He no longer even understands it himself. Or knows what is expected of him by the men who are now drifting through the locker room (on the pretext of visiting the vending machine) to examine the new body. That's the mantra of gay life, he thinks: *Show us your meat.* Like the Sodomites demanding that Lot show them his houseguests. Instead, waiting till the locker room is empty, he removes his underpants with the celerity of a quick-change artist, then wraps a big blue towel around his loins, makes sure the knot will hold, and walks away as a man with a white handlebar mustache passes and stares at him.

The stare is comforting, even if it's not Becker's, and even if he has no idea what it means. Each person who walks into a bar or baths, he thinks, is an enigma — a complex accretion of longing, disappointment, desire — a personal history that cannot be narrowed into anything so tiny as a look, or even a sexual gesture. Yet that is what we do when we come to these places, he thinks — reduce ourselves to body parts. Only now my outside no longer resembles my inside. Outside I am somewhere between what Sutcliffe used to call a Dried Arrangement and an Unwrapped Mummy. Outside I look like a retired marine drill sergeant — a man who has just spent six months training drug agents at a jungle camp in Ecuador. People with rings in their nipples and shaved heads stare at me. Inside I am a mess.

He has no idea what Becker saw when they met. Perhaps Becker slept with him that night simply because he was there. He cannot be sure. That's why he's come to the baths; although even here he's lost his ability to discern his role. At the baths, because he no longer looks in mirrors, all he has to go on is the mirror of men's eyes, so often averted these days. He's left that time of life when one person looks at another and each knows immediately, clearly, wholeheartedly: *Yes*. There's a certain defensiveness, a craven apology, in offering himself now. He hates it. Driving to the baths in 1983 was like going to Valhalla, he thinks as he walks down the hall. Going to the baths in 1995 is like driving in to have his tires rotated and oil changed.

In other words, he thinks, I've become my father. That's what he did his last decade of life, when the only reason for an excursion away from the house seemed to be car care. The day the oil needed changing, or the tires rotated, was a day of purpose, action, excitement. The others were spent on the porch, turning cards over in a game of solitaire: a man in prison, the prison of retirement. Ernie is right to keep going to the boat ramp, he thinks as he walks toward the stairs. You have to stay interested in something. You have to keep going out, no matter what. Look at my friends left in New York, plunged in depression, hunkering down in their tiny apartments till the plague is over, which it won't be before they die. Better to be cheerful, to live. My own mind is a septic tank, he thinks as he climbs the stairs. I can't hope to be happy here in this black mood. Empty your mind of its misery and shit, he thinks as he enters the lounge upstairs. Flush your mind, like a toilet, and smile!

This he does, but the four men watching *Oprah* in the lounge are too busy arguing about whether or not Michael Jackson will beat the sex rap to notice. Oh, Becker, Becker, he thinks, throwing himself down in a chair. A moment later he gets up and walks down the hall of rooms, which lately has begun more and more to resemble the halls of his mother's nursing home; only through these open doors, he sees men lying in towels upon narrow beds — in the nursing home, he sees odd shapes of both sexes, connected or not connected to a call button, propped up or not propped up in hospital beds, often calling, "Nurse!" But one thing the occupants of both sets of rooms seem to have in common, in his present state of depression: They all need help.

Every two months Lark reads in the newspaper another article about our need to be touched; that's all he wants. He no longer knows what others want from him. "After forty," Ernie told him, "all men are looked on as daddies. Your trouble is you don't want to be a daddy." Right, thinks Lark as he walks downstairs. The sight of a real child walking hand in hand with a real father makes me melt — but to impersonate a marine sergeant, a football coach, the pop they never had — forget it! I'd rather pretend I'm a German shepherd.

He doesn't really want the young anyway; and in point of fact all he gets is men his age or older who have let their figures go. Manatees. The young man with black hair and tattoo, a leather cord around his neck, who wakes up from his debauch the night before and leaves his room to dunk himself in the pool, can live without him. The two old men he steps between in the showers both say "Hello," however.

There are four of them, in various shades of silver: men with rounded shoulders and white hair, standing motionless in the showers, like elephants beneath a waterfall in some Cambodian forest — bull elephants, ancient and wrinkled. He would no more consider sleeping with them than he would with the patients in the nursing home. Even though the man with white hair on his left has, he can plainly see, bone structure that made him gorgeous when young. Which means the man on his left also ignored older men in his youth, received his share of admiration, of being desired (though the share is never enough), and endured the gradual disappearance of interest on the part of others, the gradual spread of invisibility, limb by limb, feature by feature, till now — even though he stands beside Lark, letting the warm water course down his shoulders — he has no corporeal value whatsoever. He is a ghost. One of many. Since, in the afternoons, men like him, in various shades of gray and white, with bodies obese or trim, with small cocks or big cocks, all come — for warmth; not just the warmth of the steam room, but the warmth of other human beings; including one handsome hoar-frosted Father Time who stands naked in the middle of the wet area, an enormous sausage hanging between his legs, staring at Lark as if to say, This has always got me what I wanted before, why not now? (Because, thinks Lark, repeating his cruising mantra, it's not the penis, it's what the penis is connected to.)

The point is, thinks Lark as he washes what's left of his hair, one does not so much reject the old when one goes out as ignore them — which is the most complete form of ostracism — the way whites make blacks invisible. Sometimes the old can't be ignored. In the seventies, he often found himself on the steps of the St. Marks Baths, in the red-lighted darkness, waiting impatiently for some old man to put his foot carefully on the next step down, afraid to fall; and Lark would wonder how he dared hold everyone else up, when that cute blond with the mustache had just gone downstairs and was probably lying in his room with the door open. Hurry up, hurry up, he shouted at the old man silently. Why do you come here at all? What on earth are you doing in this place?

Now he knew: company. The sight of other men's bodies. The off chance that something might happen. The sounds of love-making that sometimes carry through the walls of a cubicle upstairs.

Even Lark stops to listen to these five minutes later, in a cluster of other men who stand there enthralled by the gasping "Yes! Yes! Yes!" they hear repeated over and over again, as two bodies collide with the wall; and Lark is reminded that even now, in the age of the virus, people are still Doing It.

He is too proud to linger long at such concerts and too crushed by Becker — he pauses for only a second, a wry smile on his lips, refusing to look at the old man who smiles at him on the basis of this auditory bond and grabs Lark's genitals, hoping to take advantage of the reflected radiance of the two men grunting, groaning, and hissing beyond the slender wooden wall. Lark instead disengages and keeps walking, as if he is above all that — until, on a dimmer, darker hallway, when no one else is around, he becomes stock-still listening to another set of faint hisses, gasps, and garbled murmurs: proof that, if he is too afraid, too disillusioned, too hopeless to engage in such a surrender, others aren't. Nobody knows now what bargain someone else has made with the situation. And the moment he hears one of them rise up and put his hand on the doorknob, he springs like a gazelle around the corner, as if the sounds are not, at this point, the sweetest in the world — thinking, as he moves on, I am now one of Them. One of those men who linger in the hall, listening to other people screwing.

And so he walks past other doors, thinking, Nice stomach. The Hour of the Manatees is never exclusively that: a few young men taking the day off lie patiently in their rooms, waiting for the opportunity to cash in on their beauty. He used to want to climb such a stomach with his tongue, scale it the way rock climbers ascend cliffs, but now he thinks, What is the point? What is the point of any of this? My God, he thinks, I am finally, more than twenty years late, arriving where I knew I should have been in 1972: I can no longer have sex with strangers. (I have to be introduced.) I no longer want to have sex with someone if it doesn't mean anything.

And then an old man rounds the corner. This man is tall,

skinny; he has a caved-in chest and protruding belly, like someone with malnutrition. His ribs show beneath the skin. His head is birdlike, gaunt, with a beak of a nose, silver hair across a balding scalp. It is astonishing that he should come here and actually hope to have sex. He looks the way Lark's father looked when he was eighty-nine. He looks the way Lark will look if he ever reaches that age. He is, this bony, tall, cadaverous man with sagging flesh, so pitiful that Lark thinks, That's right! Push the envelope! See how old you can be and still go to the baths! Set new frontiers for the rest of us to come!

Let's face it, he thinks, we are all packages. An assemblage of elements. The traditional three are youth, beauty, cock. When you have all three, you are a god. When you have two of the three, you still do okay. But when you have none, you are in trouble. Perhaps I should think in terms of export, he thinks. Perhaps I should go to Japan. The baths in Kyoto, after my mother dies, a room with one piece of her furniture to remember her by — a vase, a figurine — my hair completely hennaed. The children of Nippon will shriek when they see me.

Or just quit, he thinks. Admit defeat. Like an opera singer who knows she can no longer perform certain roles. I am approaching entropy. I now get only the ones the ads say *need not respond:* fatties, fems, drug addicts. Thank God for all three. Thank God for the ones who still look, who still say, "Good evening." Thank God for Compromise Sex! Hell is the inability to love, said Dostoevski. Hell is the inability to touch Beauty, thinks Lark. Beauty is out of my reach. I'll take *willing.* Though I am less and less willing myself. Which is the better reason not to have sex, he wants to ask the attendant putting clean sheets on a mattress in a room he passes, HIV or meaninglessness? Maybe HIV provides meaning — that's what Roy said when he got it, at any rate: "Now my life has some structure."

Whatever the reason, Lark can no longer predict what happens to him here — he's lost a sense of himself. So he sits down on a bench in the locker room, a wraith, a wreck, and waits for someone else to tell him what his problem is. "What do you see when you look at me?" he wants to say to one of the Manatees.

Instead he gets up, when the Hour of the Manatees comes to a close and several of the white-haired old men open their lockers to dress, and walks down the hall, past the room of a tall, skinny young man with a crew cut and a crucifix around his neck and a bottle of poppers on the table. For a second Lark's eyes meet his; for a half second Lark pauses and holds the glance; then the youth averts his eyes while a sneer deforms his lips — a sneer that carries the caption: Don't even *think* of parking here! Lark blushes as if he's just been slapped on the face. I must be careful, he thinks; I must remember my place. An aged man is but a paltry thing, a tattered coat upon a stick. The supercilious shit!

He falls in behind a short, beautiful Cuban with curly hair and an aquiline nose who walks on the balls of his feet, as if trying to increase his height, and follows him upstairs, far from the sneering beanpole, and sits down to watch Deborah Gianoulis and Tom Wills deliver the same news they are reciting to the patients in the nursing home seventy miles to the west — a universal ritual, he thinks, like the mass.

The beautiful Cuban slumps in a chair in the front row, while a man older than Lark, pink-faced and porcine, stands against the wall masturbating under his towel as he watches the young man. Sleeping Beauty, thinks Lark. The Cuban is not really sleeping, only closing his eyes to eliminate the embarrassment of his admirer, who refuses to recognize the deportment, the expression, of all these young men who know older men are looking at them — young men who simply endure it, the way travelers avoid flies when going through a marketplace in Sierra Leone; something they have to put up with, but don't like. I know how you feel, Lark thinks, how you regard and edit us out, the silent onlookers, the Greek chorus to your search for Love, because I too once wore that expression. I too endured and ignored the looks of older men. I too once was annoyed to find only the old when I checked in. I too knew I had what they wanted — Youth and Beauty, the self-sufficient oxygen pack that enables you to traverse this cold and lonely planet; whereas we, the old, with only a dwindling supply, must eventually suffocate and die, while the young continue to explore.

The Cuban suddenly stands up and leaves the room. The old man against the wall, still fiddling with himself, glances over at Lark, as if to say, Will you be my valentine instead? But Lark stands up and exits the lounge too.

That particular man is always obnoxious, thinks Lark, as he walks down a dark, cool hallway — the other Manatees are all models of rectitude, restraint, reserve. So much so that when he goes downstairs, he realizes that most of them are gone. The Hour of the Manatees is over. The lull between it and the Invasion of the Virile has begun — a strange, unpredictable period when anything can walk through the door: people who want to get an early start on their evening, men just off work, or the Regulars.

The Regulars are people who seem to live here. One in particular is never not here when Lark comes; he's decided the man must have an arrangement with the owner, a secret room upstairs. Lark calls him Coach, a potbellied, bald man with a fat penis, who rents only a locker, and then goes around choreographing group sex in the steam room or bathrooms as if he were running around a large gym supervising basketball games. The other Regulars include the Bartender, a lean man in his thirties with an enormous dick, who brings with him an overnight bag containing hair care products and stands in front of a mirror in the locker room spraying his hair — once long, now worn in a Dorothy Hamill cut — and then goes to the steam room, where he shaves his groin on a tiled ledge while the others there gape; the Telephone Lineman, a big, beefy man with thick black hair all over his body and tits so big it looks as if he could give milk; the Mean Cold Queen, a gaunt man with a shaved head and an expression of discontent so deep Lark cannot imagine what would please him; the Kid, a slender, white youth of indeterminate age, who has black hair so thick it forms a sort of cloud around his head and a voice Lark has heard only once — when the Kid asked in a nasal, clogged whine if he could change the television channel; and the Hippie, a frankly effeminate man with a ponytail and bleached-blond mustache who seems to move around the halls without touching the floor — who glides, slides, floats, zooms, cigarette in hand, making wisecracks and being friendly to people. "Cute bottom," he says of a man dressing at his locker, as Lark sits there waiting. "Nice feet."

All of these people are at the baths almost every time Lark goes; and because they are, he refuses even to nod at them. Only the Kid was an exception to this rule. He looked so skittish, frightened, timid, nerdlike, Lark thought him anything but a Regular the first time he saw him; but when he paused one evening before the room in which the Kid lay, the Kid shook his head ever so slightly, and Lark, stung, moved on. So Lark pretends to ignore him now; devastated by the Kid's superiority, he watches the boy come in, go to the steam room, select whom he wants, and disappear. (The functional disappear at the baths almost immediately: They are having sex. The dysfunctional remain in view, sitting in the TV lounge or on a bench in the locker room, like Lark — a penitent in the street before Santiago de Compostela, asking only the pity of the passersby.)

After an hour, the Kid emerges, returns to his locker, and dresses — while Lark sits there still, thinking the Kid must be wondering why Lark never seems to meet anyone or have sex. Lark wonders the same thing; or rather, he expected that one day he would envy the young their smooth skin, their beauty, but what he never thought he would envy was their ability to find all this significant — to feel desire. I can no longer access Lust, he thinks, as the Kid checks out. I can no longer pretend that brief ecstasy is adequate.

Because I grow old, I grow old, he thinks, I shall wear the bottoms of my trousers rolled. I do not dare to eat a peach, much less beg to suck the Kid's fat cock.

He sits there instead like a man who has stumbled into a suburban racquetball club, watching Coach scamper past with yet another trio he has put together in the steam room. He sits there watching them walk by, go into rooms with one another, talk among themselves, laugh, nod, and sometimes smile at him. He thinks: Sex *is* like racquetball. Especially when you've divorced it from the procreative function. It *is* like going to the gym — you may not feel like working out beforehand, but you always feel better afterward. Because the skin needs to be touched. Esalen says this is good. The Church says it is bad. Tennessee Williams said, "Each time I pick someone up on the street, I leave a piece of my heart in the gutter." It's true, he thinks. There is a cost to this. There is a constant, cumulative cost. Slutty is as slutty does. Then why, he wonders, is this man smiling? Coach trundles past with an overweight, sexy young man who looks like a football player and has obviously begged Coach to let him suck his dick. And Lark watches them go into the toilet opposite the weight room on the first floor.

Wittgenstein told us not to ask certain questions, thinks Lark as he listens to them lock the door — metaphysical questions, questions of angst — because they have no meaning. I am doing the same thing with sex, he thinks as he sits there on the bench in the locker room; I am trying to freight it with meaning. I am trying to make a connection with another man that will justify my life, will make all that has gone before and is going on now worthwhile. And I cannot, I can only collide with their bodies; I can only lick a stomach, suck a dick, and maybe — this I would really like — embrace, if I am lucky. Though the way I want to embrace, he thinks, I cannot. I want to embrace the way a father enfolds a son.

Except these are not my sons, he thinks. These are my family, perhaps; the band of men on whose embrace I have relied the past two decades. Only that embrace is now becoming harder to obtain: a scary prospect. And it's all my fault. I'm not what you think, he wants to tell the black youth with an earring who stares at him as he goes by: I'm a self-loathing queen who carries an image of a younger self within him. Like the men in San Francisco John met at parties for PWAs, who would show him photos of themselves when healthy — photos that made John weep when he told Lark about them afterward. John, who is now almost certainly dead, though Lark cannot bring himself to call his family in Massachusetts to find out. Why remind them? Why bring the subject up again? They lived with it for six horrifying years.

Maybe that's it, he thinks — having sex with these men here would be like spitting on his friends' graves. Too many have died, too many have suffered, for sex to be casual again or what it used to be. "The first time you heard the Tomb Scene from *Aida* is not the five-hundredth time," Sutcliffe said one evening. "It's different."

It's more than different, thinks Lark. It's sacrilegious. Though none of the dead — the ones who lived the Tomb Scene — would agree with that; they'd want to have sex. Certainly Eddie. His favorite line was Auntie Mame's: "Life's a banquet, and most poor fools are starving to death." "I'm so glad I was born in America with a big, fat dick," Eddie said one night, as Lark sat in his bedroom happily watching him dress for Flamingo, "and not on some garbage mound in Egypt!" But you were, Eddie, you were, thinks Lark. Or you might as well have been, toward the end. The virus made us all third world. And changed absolutely nothing otherwise. Even though the moment it began, everyone thought, Everything will change now. Change utterly.

At first he thought it meant the end of the sex, and with that, the end of gay life; then he thought gay life would be humanized somehow, that all this suffering would make gay men nicer to one another. It didn't. If Joshua were to come back from the dead right now, he thinks, all I could tell him would be "They've got fat-free ice cream now, Joshua. Totally fat-free!" (And that would not be enough for Joshua, who used to sit there, guiltily spooning Häagen-Dazs right from the carton after his gym workout, and saying in the dreamy voice of Katharine Hepburn in *Stage Door,* "If only eating ice cream made your penis bigger." Well now, he thinks, there's penile enlargement surgery; that doctor in Los Angeles is opening franchises.) Otherwise, things are pretty much the same, as far as human nature goes, except the fact that a lot of people have been depressed on some subconscious level. (Would Prozac have saved Joshua? he wonders. Odd, how all the drugs people took illicitly in the sixties are now prescribed.) With total strangers, it's still the hunt, the hunger, the horrendous haughtiness of queens. Because, as Dr. Johnson said, no man is a hypocrite in his pleasures. We don't sleep with people to be nice, he thinks. AIDS changed nothing in that respect — the rest is just the same. What else could it be, he wonders as he watches Coach and the young football player emerge from the toilet, smiling.

The Regulars he will not sleep with, and the men who want him — the Manatees — he does not want, so he sits on the bench in the locker room, smiling at Coach when he goes by, watching people go up and down the hallways of rooms without meeting their eyes. Look at the eyes, one of his lovers told him years ago when Lark asked him how he assessed people, the eyes. He cannot. Now it's the eyes that tell you if someone has AIDS, he thinks, remembering Eddie, in 1983, before many people even knew what it was. "It's a look in the eyes," Eddie said, and Lark heard those words, thinking, The same visual acuity that enables him to design rooms, furniture, clothes, now lets him ferret out PWAs at Studio 54. Different uses for the eyes. At the baths, he never looks at anyone's. He's afraid of what they will see in his. He looks at their stomachs, their chests. When he is seated on the bench, that is just what passes in front of his eyes; it's perfect. He should leave, but he doesn't; he stays for the Invasion of the Virile.

The Invasion of the Virile begins not long after the departure of the Manatees. He sits there and watches the young come around the corner of the locker room, at the very start of what will be a long night for them. It's so odd, he thinks, when not only the doctors but the men at the baths are younger than you. They run to the wet area like puppies, shaking the water from their hair as they come back from the steam room and shower. This foreign race — the clientele the baths manager desires — the ones the attendants give free passes to when they go out to the bars on fishing expeditions. He watches them all come in: the shy, the downcast, the merry and bright, even a short-haired man in black shorts, black tank top, black baseball cap, and black shoes — a young clone, a fashion victim, an ACT UP trickle-down he watches undress. His chest is hairy and black, Lark thinks, while mine is hairy and gray. The man slams the locker shut with a bang, looks back at Lark with a smoldering, mean expression that withers him on the bench, and walks down the hallway to the steam room. Lark stands up, pricked by the man's contempt, and goes up the hallway to see what the young man passes up.

What the young man passes up is something Lark thinks will do very nicely: a man he has seen here before, who walks down the hallway now, fully dressed, towel and key in hand, and weaves groggily toward Room 186. He is drunk; Lark sits down on the rowing machine in a corner of the gym and watches.

Sometimes this man is bombed when he gets here, and sometimes sober — when sober, he is prim, cold, intellectual; he sits in his room smoking with one leg drawn up against his chest, exposing a large thigh Lark finds intimidating. When he is drunk, lying naked on his pallet, he turns into a Christ lying on the sepulcher by Mantegna. The man is now in transition. He has just come from the bar. Through the open door, Lark watches him undress, lie down on the bed, and fall asleep with the door still ajar. Moments pass. Then, like a vulture that can feed only on dead things, Lark enters the room carefully, and quietly closes the door behind him so the Food will not awaken — just as he sat by the telephone after lunch as a child, guarding the nap his father took when he came home from work. He stands there, making sure the man is truly slumbering, and then, ever so gently, begins to lick his thigh.

This is much easier than the reality of another man, fully awake, with his needs, idiosyncrasies, tastes, and snobberies, the dreadful competition of sex, the fact that they have both done this little dance many, many times before and it has not freed them. The failure of another man to meet Lark's dreams is so great, what he wants from another person is so incommunicable at this point, only someone asleep will do. A man who looks, as this one does, like a farmer, or a coal miner in a sepia photograph taken years ago: long, lean, Scotch-Irish, altogether beautiful. A ghost. Because a real person could not possibly understand, he thinks, what is in my heart, the large accumulation of grief. Fifty-seven miles and one hour and twenty minutes from home, all depression vanishes in three licks of a tongue, and Lark is thinking, as his lips graze on the surface of the flat white stomach, I bring you gray skies, a light rain-soaked breeze, the sound of wind in the trees, the translucent panels on either side of Becker's door late at night, the care with which he raises his daughter, and the gazebo he's building out back. I bring you his long, lean torso, not unlike yours, and the thunderstorm that drove him, his daughter, and his boyfriend from the beach back to a town I cannot find Love in but that I live in anyway.

I bring you all the desire for Love that town engenders in me, including the young high school student who bought cigarettes in the Jiffy as I was filling out my Lotto card just yesterday — about five feet eight, brown curly hair, a thin mustache, a perfect butt, an upper body that was a slab of milk-white muscle. I bring you his faded blue jeans, and the butt beneath his white football jersey as he walked away across the parking lot and I glanced through the glass doors, compelled to look at him. I bring you the woman who sold me my Lotto card as she asked the young man with the thin mustache whose upper body was a slab of milk-white muscle, "How do you think we'll do?" and he replied, "Okay, I hope," and

I wondered if she, in her twenties, desired him, in his teens, and whether sex did not make everyone in this town as bananas as myself, and no doubt Becker. I bring you all the handsome men in that town besides Becker, including the two policemen standing in uniform by the road as I returned from the convenience store, and the mother and the small boy who stopped at the bin at the public beach to put in their newspapers to be recycled. I bring you the tall, skinny, black-haired young man who works at Publix, and his colleague with straight brown bangs across his forehead, in camouflage T-shirt and faded jeans, as he talked to the supervisor with an earnest, supplicatory expression.

I bring you Becker in his jeans and black T-shirt the time I saw him standing in Produce with the cabbage held like a basketball in his right hand. I bring you his enormous hands; the way he smokes a cigarette; his grave, leaden, melancholy voice; the fact that he too must admire the stocky, cheerful bag boy who scooped up a small blond toddler running amok and returned her to her mother before beginning to bag my groceries. I bring you the beefy, blond father getting out of his car outside in the parking lot, with a blond son on his arm, saying, "You'll be all right, you'll be all right," with the majestic calm of someone who is no longer afraid himself of what frightens three-year-olds.

I bring you the young man mowing the lawn of the electrical cooperative as I drove by. I bring you the long, soft luxury and peace of a summer afternoon in an American town where goods and services are distributed efficiently among the populace, and extremes of wealth and poverty are not noticeable. I bring you all the bag boys, the football players whose pictures are already taped on the window of the drugstore in preparation for that most priapic of seasons, and Becker, who lends his beauty only once to mortals, myself included.

I bring all this to you, the soft gray afternoon in town, sixty miles to the east, through neon and strip mall, gas station and supermarket, an ocean of moving metal; to you, the soft flesh beneath my lips — *not* the stomach of the boy at the Jiffy buying cigarettes, *not* the desire the older woman felt when she inquired about the chances of the football team, *not* my hopeless, humiliated love for Becker, but something close to it — yes, even the love of my parents, the deaths of my friends, and what still survives, my love of summer afternoons, the whole erotic force that makes me come here to discharge my desire, like something ricocheting off someone else, so stupid, so pointless, so neurotic, but all I've got. I bring you this, he thinks, and takes the penis into his mouth.

And the man lifts his head gently and says, "Do you have poppers?" as Lark feels the penis he has enclosed in his mouth begin, miraculously, to swell. And all sadness and regret fall away.

Eventually even this must end, however; and when his ministrations have brought the corpse to life, when a marmoreal hand reaches out to grab Lark's own penis, he separates himself from the ghost, rises, wraps his towel about him, and, holding the tainted saliva in his mouth, leaves. Then he rinses his mouth out with the red mouthwash in the bathroom and decides to go home. Time is running out. This is not the solution. He goes upstairs anyway and watches a rerun of *Roseanne* beside a handsome, talkative Jamaican with a shaved head and earring. Then a movie about a suburban killer on USA. In America, he thinks, Love means having someone to watch television with; but when the Jamaican gets up, says, "I'm going to do one more cycle," and leaves, Lark realizes the friendliness was after all just that and nothing more. Nothing more, nothing more. What I'm facing, thinks Lark, is the Void.

The Void means I believe in none of this anymore. I'm ashamed of being gay, of being old, of being ashamed of being gay and old. How stupid. I resent the men at the baths for no fault of their own — I resent them because they're not my friends, because they're men in Jacksonville. Hardly their fault, he thinks, yet on some level I hate them for it. What a recipe for mental health. And he gets up and walks into the dark maze of hallways that is the only place he feels safe these days, safe and still and peaceful.

It's so peaceful that when he sees, down one of the most obscure, least traveled hallways, a young man lying on his bed smoking a cigarette in bright light, he stops, like a traveler coming to a hut in the forest, and the young man waves him inside. He is not particularly good-looking: The curly hair of a permanent is receding already from his forehead; his lips are thin, he wears glasses, he starts talking the moment Lark enters the room and does not stop. But Lark is grateful to be taken in, out of the storm, and happy to listen, with a detached, avuncular air, to the young man's explanation of why he's here — a bartender he is in love with, six years younger than himself, who comes here sometimes before work and sometimes after, and won't return his phone calls. He's obsessed. In fact the young man himself — managing a Hardee's on Blanding Boulevard — is about to be fired from his job. "I'm missing work because of him, and you know what? I don't really give a shit."

At this point Lark sits down on the edge of his bed, and then, when the man moves to his side, he accepts the invitation to stretch out beside him. There they lie for several minutes while Lark, psychiatrist manqué, asks his companion questions about the bartender that lance the boil of obsession, and Lark listens patiently, happy to be hearing about somebody else's unrequited love, even smiling at the more painful details. Misery loves company, he thinks, as he rolls over on top of the manager of a fast-food franchise, lays his head on the mattress next to his companion's, and slips his arms underneath his back.

Oh God, he thinks, I could lie here forever, this feels so good! It's always felt so good, this connection, this embrace. It's like finally plunging into the water after a long, hot car ride to the ocean as a kid. It's like finally rushing into the waves, naked, free, joyous at last. It's all the thoughts I cannot express, and all the things I cannot say, and all the feelings I cannot act upon, and all the sadness, all the failure, all the grim reality wiped out in a single electrical spark — my body's warmth against his body's warmth, raising each a few degrees. It may be only temporary comfort, the current may be cut off in a few minutes, the sea may dry up, but for now — even if it has no meaning — I am happy, he thinks; and the common woe of heartsickness, the solid grace of this man's body, his embrace, weld their torsos together in a sticky, sweaty glue, till Lark stops listening to the actual words being slipped into the air between puffs on the man's cigarette, and does not even care when he stops talking altogether.

Then there is a silence, during which Lark sighs, and begins ever so gently to stroke with his thumb the backside of the man's right ear; at which point, the man says to Lark, "Honey, you need a pet."

Lark lifts his head like a man awakened from a deep sleep and says, "What do you mean?"

"I mean you need a pet," the man says. "I mean, you're holding on to me like I'm the puppy you just got for Christmas."

Lark leaps up. He laughs. He knots his towel. He says, "Well, I've got to get home and feed my real dog. Good luck with your friend," and leaves the room, pausing to adjust the open door — enough to let passersby know the man is Receiving, but not a quarter inch more, which would mean Slut — and takes the stairs two at a time. I'm needy, he thinks, as he dashes to the locker room. They can smell it. Like Richard Friel, toward the end. "Richard is a very needy person," Sutcliffe warned Lark. Not good to be needy. An open wound. Got to get out of here, he thinks, as two men his age round the corner with cardboard cups of coffee from the vending machine, talking loudly.

Old friends who lived in Washington, D.C., in the seventies but now live in different cities, the two men sit down on the bench while Lark opens his locker. They reminisce about a party one gave at which Roberta Flack was hired to sing. The tall man asks the short one, as Lark takes his clothes out, where a friend at that party is now. "Boyd lives in Kentucky, on a farm," says the other man. "Every day around five o'clock he buys a six-pack, gets in the Jeep, and starts driving the back roads, hoping he'll meet some fourteen-year-old." (Oh God, thinks Lark, that's it! That's simply all there is!)

"Does he still have his hair?" asks the tall man.

"Yes," says his friend, "but it's all on his back." And they burst out laughing.

It's all about hair. And cock, Lark thinks, when the two men glance at his genitals as they walk past him into the hall, suddenly silent with the seriousness of this chance to view the sacred item.

"Good night," says the youth when he checks out.

"Good night," says Lark, as the boy buzzes him through and he finds himself in the warm parking lot.

Tom House

THE CHICKEN MAN

ALAN'S FIRST adventure, happening about the middle of March, frightened him a great deal. In fact, he thought afterward that if back in February, when he had begun hitchhiking home from St. John's, the Chicken Man with the long coat had picked him up, instead of the friendly carpenter-man, he might never have tried it again. He thought, too, that perhaps he wouldn't have accepted the ride in the first place if it hadn't been for the rain, and for the fear that no one else would stop, as wet as he was and as gray as it was getting. For the car had been going in the opposite direction, and had nearly passed by before the driver, catching sight of him, brought it to a screeching halt in the middle of downtown Bay Shore; then once the man rolled the window down, and Alan was able to see him more clearly, his impression was one of disappointment, and even revulsion: he was his father's age, or older, and wearing an old-fashioned, private-eye style hat, and as he extended his long arm into the rain, pointing a finger sternly at Alan, as if to hold him there until he could pull the car around, Alan remembered what the carpenter had said, about not jumping right into every car that stopped, and making *character assessments,* because it did seem unusual to him, and maybe even a little bit dangerous, for a person to make a U-turn like that in the middle of Main Street.

"I'm all wet," Alan said through the crack in the passenger window, and perhaps he would have gone on to say, *No, thank you,* or, *Listen, pal,* if the man hadn't leaned across the seat and pushed the door open so forcefully: "Get in," he said.

As Alan took his place inside, positioning his sports bag on the mat between his feet, and making an attempt to brush the drops of rain from the water-repellent nylon, he noticed how big the man's galoshes were below the hem of his overcoat, and how long his legs seemed beneath it, and finally, as the car pulled away from the curb, and there was the loud sound of water spewing up from the tires and hitting the fenders, he looked up at his face, and saw the startling shape of his nose in stark profile against the dusky light from the driver's window: it jutted right out — like a fin, or a little cleaver.

"Thank you for picking me up," he said, but the man merely turned to look at him, and didn't say anything, and then Alan realized what it was besides the nose that was so striking about his face — he had no sideburns, and no hair at all on the portions of his head that he could see, just a kind of pink, goosey skin everywhere; and then as Alan asked the man how far he was going, and he replied, "Oh, don't you worry!" in a loud, cackling voice, the name came to him, *Chicken Man.*

"Are you going as far as East Islip?"

He shook his head. "I'm going past there!"

"Past there?"

"Isn't that what I said?"

"But you were just going the other way before. Weren't you just going in the other —?"

"What direction? I'm not going in any direction, I'm going to East Islip." Then he mumbled another word, which could have been *smarty,* Alan thought.

"Excuse me?" he asked faintly — too faintly perhaps, because the man turned to him and said, *"Excuse me?"* in a soft, lisping voice, and it was plain to Alan — as he looked to the windshield, and to the wipers frantically sheeting the water away — that the man was making fun of him.

"What are you doing out hitchhiking, young boy like you?" His voice was softer when he said it.

"I'm not that young," Alan said.

"Yes, you are; you're a young little boy."

"I'm fourteen; I go to high school."

"What are you doing out hitchhiking?"

"I missed the bus."

"Yeah, you missed the bus. That's a lot of crap."

Alan looked at him, unable to conceal the surprise he felt, for that seemed a sudden, rough thing to say, and all the more so for the new soft tone. "I did miss it."

"What are ya, out looking for trouble?"

"No."

"Ya out lookin' for trouble, you'll find it."

"I'm not looking for any —"

"Don't tell me."

Alan turned to his window, and to the passing brick facade of the Long Island Savings Bank, dim yellow lights illuminating its stark white columns and double doors, and his heart was beating faster now, for he didn't understand why the man should be angry with him, or why he should say he was looking for trouble, and it was that, the bullish way he kept insisting, that brought to mind his Grandpa Daly, how he would always stick to his opinions no matter what anyone said, no matter what the facts. "Nope, nope,

nope," he would say; "I'm tellin' ya," his mother would try to reason with him, she would slap her hand down on the table, and though Alan imagined slapping his own hand down, and raising his voice above the man's — "Dad," his father would plead; *"Laura,"* his father would threaten — he wondered if it wouldn't be better to keep quiet now, and to let the man go on ranting, his voice softer one instant, louder the next, about boys and trouble, and then just as he decided it was, he heard the man say the word *crazies,* and listened closer. How did he know he wouldn't get picked up by one someday, huh? How did he know that? "Ever hear of the guy who slams the door on boys' hands as they're getting out of the car?"

"What?" Alan said.

The man was grinning beneath his hat. "He waits till they're gettin' out and *wham,* slams the door down on 'em. Big bag of fingers he's got in his car."

"No," Alan said — to the man's laughter, and to the image in his mind of the bloody hands, the bloody bag, and all the fingers falling *chop chop chop* to the rubber mat. It was a horrible story to tell, a horrible thing to laugh at, and he wondered, as he crossed his arms and tucked his hands beneath them, if it was true, and why the man had told it all in the present tense — *waits, slams,* as if it were still happening; and then to think of all those boys, what must their hands look like now? He shook his head, he didn't want to imagine hands without fingers, and he didn't want to think of the expressions of pain on the boys' faces as they emerged from the car, pressing handkerchiefs to the wounds.

"You're all a bunch of hoods!" he yelled, and Alan jumped, glancing warily at the man's narrowed eyes, his thin, twitching lips.

"Hoods?" he said, his mind filling absurdly with images of The Fonz and *Happy Days,* boys with greasy hair and leather jackets who smoked cigarettes and cut out of school. "I'm on the honor roll," he told him; it was the only line he could think of to prove the kind of boy he was.

"The honor roll?" The man laughed a short bursting laugh, then his voice became serious again. "Oh, so you think you're a Rhodes Scholar."

"A what?" Alan said. "What kind of scholar?"

"A Rhodes Scholar! Road, road! Rrm rrm rrm rrm rrm. Nah." The man made to pat him on the shoulder, and Alan winced away. "I'm only kiddin'. I know you're a nice boy. You're a nice boy, right?" The hand reached up higher, as if to ruffle his hair, and again Alan recoiled until it dropped to the seat. "Little goody two-shoes never does anything wrong, that's you."

"No," Alan said, and then he said it again, understanding, suddenly, that maybe he wasn't anymore — nice or good — now that he missed the bus and hitchhiked home, because it *was* wrong to do that, wrong, he realized, because of men like the Chicken Man, and men who slammed doors on boys' fingers, and men who were crazies, and if only he hadn't gotten into the car in the first place, if only he could have said, *No, thank you.*

"Nice boy."

Alan saw the man's pink, long-fingered hand — the hand of a man his father's age, an able hand — reach for his left knee; then he could feel its clawlike clutch locking in and squeezing, and his first impulse was to move his leg, and to push the hand away, but instead he froze, for fear of what the man might do if he tried. And so it remained there, for what seemed a very long time, before the grip tightened further, and the man swung Alan's leg back and forth, and then he let it go. Immediately Alan turned toward the door, angling his legs away from the grinning face, the wiggling fingers, and in the instant before the hand reached for him again, and slapped at his thigh, and at the inside of it, little stinging slaps, he had the terrible thought that perhaps the man had been talking about himself before, perhaps *he* was the one who slammed the door on all the fingers.

"You like that, don't you?" His voice was filling the car. "That's what kind of boy you are!"

Alan shook his head, trying to shoo the tears that rushed to his eyes, and struggling to bring himself to move, to object in some way to the grabbing and the slapping, and when the words finally did come, *"Please don't hit my leg,"* they weren't much more than a whisper, and the man laughed.

"Please don't hit my leg," he said, in the wispy, singing voice, then he was yelling again. "What are you, some kind of pansy? You're not a little pansy, are ya? Little tap on the leg? That's not so bad, is it? Up — oh, he's gonna cry. Yes, he is a little pansy, look at him start to cry."

Alan could feel them — two tears, three — loosed and warm and running down his cheeks, and he covered his face with his hand.

"Wise up, kid." He slapped Alan's thigh. "It's a friendly tap on the leg, between men."

Alan kept shaking his head. "No," he said, trying to assume a louder, firmer voice, and then finally to push the hand away, and his palm butted up against the hard bones of the man's wrist. "Let me out."

"What?" he said, grabbing at Alan's arm, and pulling his hand away from his face, and Alan could see, then, through the wash of tears, that there was a new, frightened look in the man's eyes. "Out?"

His breath came in fits. "Let me out," he said again, pulling back his hand, and looking out the windows — to the drenched sidewalks of downtown Islip, and to the string of oncoming head-lights, and the traffic signal at Brentwood Road, changing from yellow to red.

"You don't have to get out of the car, I'll take you home."

"Please let me out, *please."*

"What ya gettin' so upset for?"

Alan felt about for the door handle, raising his right knee to hide his hand as much as he could. But when his fingers found it, and curled around its cold metal lever, the car was still rolling, the slick black pavement still whizzing by beneath his window, and

then the man was calling him, and telling him to stop crying —
"Here," he said, "hey kid, look at this."

A succession of rapid, indistinct impressions accompanied the
shouldering open of the door, the grabbing of his bag, the stag-
gering to the side of the road: chiefly, the bright flash of the overhead light, and the image of the man's hand jiggling it up and
down — pink, fleshy; the sound of rain and of cars moving in the
rain; the wet moving asphalt beneath his feet; the cold drops pelting
his face and hair and hands.

"What are you doing, kid?"

With all his fingers, Alan jumped to the sidewalk, and watched
the man shake his head and lean over the seat to yank the door
closed; then as the light switched off again and the car sped away,
he saw his tall darkened shape shifting and leaning forward, his left
hand pulling down on the brim of his hat.

In a moment, there was the glare of headlights, a station wagon
pulling over to the side of the road, a woman with brown, pulled-
back hair rolling down the passenger window. "Are you okay?" she
said, and Alan, moving toward the car, looked past her, within the
shadows of the interior, to a darker-haired man at the wheel, and to
two children in the space behind the backseat. "What happened?"

"That man —" he said, but his voice was trembling, and he
wasn't sure what he could say to her.

"You need a ride somewhere? You want us to take you home?"

He stood dumbly a moment, then nodded, and the woman
twisted around to unlock the back door. The two girls stared up at
him as he climbed in, and the woman spoke to them in sharp
words, and told them to behave; then the man pulled the car back
onto the road, and she faced front again, revealing, above the hood
of her raincoat, the beginning of a thick braid.

"We saw you jumping out of the car," she said, glancing across
at the man; Alan saw the back of his head nod. "Did he try to hurt
you?"

"He wouldn't let me out."

"He wouldn't let you out of the car?" She spun around, eyes gleaming in the dim light. "Who was this man?"

"I don't know," Alan said. "I never saw him before. He kept grabbing me. He grabbed my leg."

"Your leg?" She looked beyond him to the girls, her eyebrows knitting. "Were you hitchhiking?"

"Yes," he said, "I missed the school bus," and when her expression didn't change, he added, "He hit me."

"What?"

"On the leg; he kept slapping it and shaking it, like this." Alan shook his fist over the empty seat beside him, and there were giggles from the back; "Whoa-oo," the girls said. Yet the woman continued to look at him that way, with her eyebrows knitted.

"He shook it like this," he said, moving his fist faster.

"Well," the woman said, "are you okay? Did he do anything else?"

"Else?" Alan thought an instant, his eyes wincing at the memory of the pinkish, wrinkled skin. "No."

"You do look pale."

"I'm okay," he said, wishing, suddenly, that he wasn't, that he could have fallen and scraped himself on his hand or elbow, and then he could have held that up somehow, and pointed to the cut, the blood. Instead the conversation gave way to the usual questions and arrangements, and after the man indicated that he knew where Secatogue Avenue was, the woman insisted they drop him off at his house. That wouldn't be necessary, Alan told her. But it was raining out, and he had had a bad experience. No please, Alan said, the corner would be fine. Finally she shrugged, *"Okay,"* and when she didn't look at him after that, he leaned back in his seat, wondering what it was she was thinking about him, and if there was something he might say to change her mind, and then he became aware of the girls again, and glancing over his shoulder, saw that they had toys spread over the carpeting, little plastic letters; the smaller of the two was trying to place a *K* before the *MA* in the middle.

"Don't put it there," the bigger girl said, pushing her hand away.

"Yes."

"No." She pushed the hand away again, and leaned closer to the little girl's ear. "That doesn't make a word," she whispered, glancing at Alan, and when he looked down at his folded hands, and at the wet cuffs of his coat, it was the long, wiggling fingers he saw, clutching around his wrist, he could feel them tugging at him, and prying his hand from his face, and he squeezed his eyes shut, and tried to think some other thought, see some other image, and then just when it seemed he wouldn't be able to come up with one that could displace the memory of the Chicken Man, he opened his eyes, and found himself focusing on the back of the new man's head, and on the outline of his jaw and cheekbone, dusted with the faint reflections of the road. And though the outline seemed pleasant enough — there was nothing harsh or hairless about it, no sudden, startling shapes — Alan still wasn't sure what the man looked like; for he had only spoken the one time, to say he knew the street, and he hadn't turned around to say it, but had simply looked up at the rearview mirror, offering but a glimpse of his right eyebrow, the bridge of his nose, and so it was mostly his hair that Alan perceived, how dark and wavy it was — it looked dark enough, in the brief light that spilled through the car as they passed the East Islip Movie Theater — dark and feathery and soft, as if it would feel very soft in one's hand.

Alan imagined the woman had felt the hair, that often she would walk over to the man while he was reading the paper in the TV room and comb her fingers right through it, that her fingertips had grazed over his scalp and down the back of his neck. It must be a very private thing to feel, he thought, a person's scalp, and wondering, then, if he had ever felt one that wasn't his own, he raised his hand quickly, and raked it over the back of his head. But his hair was wet now, his fingertips cold; to really run one's hand through someone's hair, it should be dry, one's fingers warm, and it was difficult, too, if one was combing the fingers and feeling the fingers comb at the same time, to try to imagine what it would be like just to do the one, or just to feel the other, and then as the man turned suddenly to the woman and said, "Must've been some kind of queer," and the woman shook her head slowly, Alan found his profile — revealed, as it was, in near silhouette — so strikingly handsome that it sent a little pang zipping across his stomach.

When he got to his house, he unlocked the storm door and the big wooden door as quickly and as soundlessly as he could, then raced upstairs, not calling, *"Hi, Mom!"* until he had reached the landing. At once he shut his door and locked it and took off his wet clothes, and hung them on hangers in the closet to dry; he yanked down the window shade and flicked off the light and pulled off his damp undershirt and underwear, and his skin, too, felt damp, as he lay down on his bed and thought of the man coming up at last, the paper finished.

Hi, honey, Alan would say, sleepily, his mass of thick brown hair loosed now from the braid and spreading over the pillow. *Hi,* the man would say, feeling his way to the desk chair; then as he hung his clothes, article by article, over the back of it, Alan would be able to make out the side of him by the light from the crack beneath the door, and he would be able to see, when the man bent over to slip off his underwear — not wiggly, not pink or fleshy — the smooth length of it standing out straight, the extra blackness around it as he approached the bed, lifted the sheets, and there would be the feeling, then — the warmness, the unimaginable incredibleness — of the man's bare stomach touching down on his, the man's bare thighs on his own bare thighs, and there would be the brushing of lips over Alan's neck, the brushing, wet tip of his tongue, and the man would whisper how much he wanted to make love to him, and he would slowly push his legs apart and slide inside — there would be a place for him to slide inside — and he

would go softly and tenderly at first, softly, slowly, and then . . .
but before Alan had time to imagine how the man's motion would
crescendo, and how, in a fit of pleasure, they would cleave to each
other for the final, galvanizing moment — it happened, in four
measured spits, three deep breaths, and right away he wiped himself
and pulled on dry clothes and stole across the hall to flush away
the tissues, and then he raced back to his room and locked the door
again and slipped his clothes off again and lay back down. *Where
were we?* he said, positioning the pillow — now damp from his
actual, still-wet hair — lengthwise beside him, and, *Ah yes,* the part
where they would be lying next to each other, quietly entwined,
where he would rest his head on his husband's chest and say, *I can't
stop thinking about that boy and what that man did to him in the
car.*

He seemed very shook up.

Indeed. Would she have said *indeed?* And he seemed *like such a
nice boy.*

Must have been some kind of queer.

Alan shook his head slowly, and hugged the man tighter, thinking, just then, how this was the best kind of love, what they had.

I hope he's okay now.

I think he's just fine, the man said, kissing up at his cheek, and
as he did so, he gave him a special, winking look, as if he knew
who Alan really was.

Then occasionally that evening — in the TV room, for instance,
during the first set of commercials for *The Bionic Woman* — bits of
the afternoon came tumbling back to him: terrible, tumbling
glimpses, and he glanced across at his father, and at the raised face
of the *Newsday,* wondering what reaction he might have if he could
see, as clearly as Alan did, the Chicken Man in the long coat, if he
could hear the loud, cackly voice say, *That's the kind of boy you are!*
What expression would his features take on if he could know that

the man had touched him and slapped him? Would they grimace, or look disgusted, and would the disgusted look be directed at Alan in any way, as if it were he who had done something wrong? Alan shook his head, to chase the thought away, but it wouldn't leave, and so he shook his head a second time, and a third, and then just as he felt his worries escalating to a kind of panic, he heard the bar of music signaling the restarting of the episode, and looked back at the screen, back to the familiar characters and the simple logic of the story, and felt the tightness in his stomach loosen somewhat, however tentatively; for minutes later, during the second set of commercials, his thoughts returned to the imagined grimace, and his legs began to swing a little, his breath to quicken until, just as suddenly, the profile of the handsome station-wagon man jumped to mind, diverting his attention back to the fantasy he had begun in his room — but before the man had come upstairs now, before he had finished his paper, or had even started reading it. For this would be the time of day when they sat on the couch together, the man's arm stretched across the top of it, his fingers tapping at the Naugahyde just inches from the back of Alan's neck; perhaps they would even stroke his neck, and Alan could turn, and gaze across the couch — this he did, ignoring the call of the music bar — and as the fantasy spread over the next segment of the episode, he began to call the man *Chris* for want of some other name, after which the picture of him in Alan's mind — dark-haired, silent — would alternate with the more familiar one of the blond boy who sat across from him in homeroom, and though at first the switches were sudden and unsettling, after a while it didn't seem to matter to him which particular image held sway; in either case the situation remained the same: both the older and the younger Chris liked *The Six Million Dollar Man* better than *The Bionic Woman,* and yet they sat beside him anyway, watching it, because it was Alan's favorite show, and then when Alan picked up one of the red throw pillows and got up with it, to lie on his stomach on the round, similarly red area rug, either of them followed. *Okay if I join you?*

Alan shrugged, letting him nestle alongside, letting him toss an arm across his back, a leg across the backs of his legs, and then he imagined, too, a gentle nuzzling at his neck — the side of his neck farthest from his father — the boy's nose, the man's lips; he wants Alan to turn his head, is very insistent; *Sweetheart,* he whispers, *look at me.* Yet Alan waits a moment more, grinning at the TV set; finally he complies — he has wanted all along to comply — resting his right cheek on the pillow; superimposing, over the tangled fringe of the rug, over the dusty, metal tip of the couch leg, Chris's wide, tender gaze, his waiting lips, and at the instant he imagines them touching his, he closes his eyes, and tries to feel what it would feel like, tries to move his own tongue in circles within his closed mouth; their kiss deepens, their bodies draw closer, and Alan pushes his hips down against the rug, first his right hip, then his left, he hears the shuffling of the newspaper, hears Chris say, *Come on, let's go upstairs.*

Now? he says to him. *Don't you want to see the end?*

I'm not watching it, are you?

No, he admits.

Come on, then. He holds out his hand.

I can't, Alan says.

You can't? This without hiding the disappointment in his voice.

I can't get up like this.

Like what?

Alan presses his hips against the rug again, and Chris smiles knowingly.

Me, too, he says, looking down at his own fly, and Alan was about to look down at it, also, about to imagine the kind of bulge it would be making in the corduroy, when he heard his mother say, "On the floor like that," and looked up.

"Huh?"

She was standing in the doorway in her robe and curlers, her right index finger wedged inside a paperback; *Interview with the*

Vampire the cover read, in blood-colored letters. "You're falling asleep on the floor again."

"No, I'm not."

"Yes, you are. Go to bed if you're tired."

"I'm not tired, I'm wide awake." He propped himself up on his elbows to show her his eyes, how open they were.

"Don't tell me that, you were just out cold."

"Mom, I wasn't. I was resting my neck, it was a commercial."

"You were just out cold. Go on up to bed."

"I'm watching a show."

"No, you're not. Go to bed."

He breathed out, and slapped the rug.

"Al," she said, looking past him.

His father shook the paper. "What?"

"He's falling asleep on the floor."

Alan swiveled his head, stretching his eyes even wider; and his father — slender-nosed, with dark receding hair — stared blankly at them from behind his black-and-gold reading glasses; then he frowned, and glanced up at his mother. "He's not asleep."

"He was just a second ago."

"I wasn't," Alan told him.

His father shrugged. "He says he wasn't asleep," and his mother shook her head, then, retreating from the doorway.

"Don't come crying to me when you wake up with a stiff neck," she said, and as her footsteps padded down the plastic runner in the dining room, and across the kitchen linoleum, his father rolled his eyes and returned to his sports articles. Then it was several moments later, after Alan had gotten up for the couch, that he saw him glance from behind the paper, first at the red pillow on Alan's lap, next at the TV and the clip of Lindsay Wagner running down a street, her hair streaming, breasts bouncing; his father's face smiled, then — Alan thought he saw it smile — before it disappeared again behind the newsprint.

David Wojnarowicz

FROM THE DIARIES OF A WOLF BOY

I'M STILL a piece of meat like something in the Fourteenth Street markets swinging from stinking hooks in the blurry drag queen dusk. Maybe a hundred dollars to my name, no place to live, and I can't hustle anymore. I'm trying to keep my body beyond the deathly fingers of my past but I'm fucked up bad never learned shit, how to create structures other than chaos. I'm attracted to chaos because of all the possibilities and I don't have to choose any of them or die frozen inside one but right now all I know is that I am tired, bone and brain tired. I woke up in this guy's bed in the middle of the night and realized not a whole lot had changed since I got off the streets. He was an alcoholic doctor I'd known on and off over a handful of years and he let me live with him for the last couple of weeks cooking me upper-class meals in return for me fucking him legs over my shoulders like a video stud. He could have gone on forever like this but the distinct sensation of being made of glass, of being completely invisible to him, was growing and curving like a cartoon wave. I feel so fucking dark I don't even have the energy to throw myself off a building or bridge. Now he's starting to come home slam-down drunk banging into walls moaning and crying falling down murmuring: Fuck me my lovely. I told him one night he needed some help and he responded by bringing home a hustler from West Street and I ended up sleeping on the living room floor.

The doctor takes me on a week's vacation in his station wagon up to the coast of Maine. No license but I'm driving the almost deserted interstate north. I haven't slept for about two days and feel sort of drugged, the hypnotic lines of the dawn's highway wavering like an unraveled hypnotist's disk. It's kind of beautiful the foliage on the shoulders still illuminated by the tungsten lamps blip blip blip. The doctor vaguely woke up and his hand drifted over the armrest between us and slid over my leg slowly back and forth till I got a hard-on. Then his sleepy fingers unbuttoned my trousers and he leaned over taking my dick in his mouth. There was a car way ahead of us and another way behind; beacons of headlights were circling the hills and the sky was turning still and black, night being pushed up through the sky over the car by a quiet surfacing day. My whole body stiffened with my hands on the wheel. I had a hard-on for thirty miles moving my hips up and down finally shooting into his mouth, surprised as a lone car overtook us and sped past causing me to realize I'd slowed down to fifteen miles per hour.

He rented a motel room somewhere on the breezy oceanside. An oddly beautiful coastline but I knew this was temporary so I didn't let myself buy into it. I went for a walk while he slept and climbed through the craggy rock postcard views among postcard families and vacationing heterosexuals, drifted away from the sand and up onto this mammoth asphalt parking lot bordering the motel. This guy, young and handsome in an indefinable way, with short brown hair, a pair of dark shorts that revealed muscular legs slightly browned from weather and sun, a ruddy color to his forehead and cheeks and nose, coasted up on a bicycle and stopped short a distance away checking me out. I was walking under this long canopied bench area so I sat on one of the empty seats, folded my arms over the back of the bench and laid my head on it staring at him sideways. He rolled a little closer and dismounted, standing next to his bike, hands thrust deep into pockets for a while. He finally moved toward me one more time then tossed back the hair from over his eyes, a boyish gesture suggestive of a remote past, school days, something that still makes me weak in the knees. He said: Hey, hello. I straightened up and said: How's it going? He gestured okay with his head and then said: Where do ya go for fun around here? I told him I just got into town and didn't know nothing. I felt that blush in my chest as we talked stupid talk never quite revealing our queerness to each other but somehow wordlessly generating volumes of desire like some kind of sublanguage that makes you want to splash into it even with all its tensions. He continued loose conversation watching me closely for reactions to his coded words and then finally seemed to abandon it all and said: You want to get together later? We made a date for 11 P.M. at the same spot and I walked away wondering how to handle the doctor.

The doctor started drinking after dinner and I encouraged him to go to bed. He finally fell asleep around 10:45 and I slipped from between the sheets, put on my clothes, and fished the room key out of his pocket, every movement noiseless until the barely audible click of the door. I walked to the bench area overlooking the ocean and stood around. The night was heavy, the water indiscernible in the darkness. The tide was way out so it was just this screen of grainy blackness that contained the rushing hollow sounds of waves crashing way out there. Every so often a lone car would swing to the lot, its headlights illuminating one patch of ocean in a field of circular light, and beyond that I could see the low caps of broken waves spreading in toward shore, lit as if by luminous microbes. I walked down to the sand into the darkness to see how far I could go before I touched water, leaving behind the cars turning round and round and the windows of the motel along the beach with rectangles of burning orange light and the flap of banners and flags as the staff hoisted them on poles for the holidays.

I got close to the water's edge when an old ghost of a man materialized with his open palms stretching out toward me. I heard a murmur: Want some action? I turned and walked to the opening of the bay along the coastline, climbing the boulders to the back end of the parking lot. Walking to the bench area two local toughs — *Hey yo!* — came up fast behind me their arms dangling at their sides like whirligigs. Both were kind of sexy but dangerous. One guy with close-cropped hair and a red face said: Any women out here tonight? Then they came up on me on both sides spinning their heads from looking for witnesses. I became as charming as possible: Cigarette? As they took one a car spun in the lot illuminating all of us and I took that moment to tip toward the headlights and lose myself among the parked cars. I circled back to the benches and the young guy I'd met earlier was sitting on the hood of his car. He told me to get in and we drove out into the town, parking behind a deserted bank and walking through the streets looking for a bar. He wanted to drink some beers. His name was Joe and he was in town for the naval reserves, a two-week training with a few days off in between.

There were no regular bars around just a couple of queer joints with heavy cover charges and pounding disco, so we ended up walking a couple miles down a dark road talking about ourselves and the distances we'd been. We turned back to his car. The gear-heads were out in their pickup trucks whizzing around the curves of the small streets. One truck sped by a club we were approaching and white ugly distended faces blew out of the side windows: *We hate queers!* I turned to him: Let's go somewhere. Okay? Yeah, he said: We really should. There's got to be a place we can just sit down and have a drink and talk. I was wondering if I had this guy wrong; if that's all he wanted was talking company. I was already drawn in by the movements of his chest and belly beneath his shirt, his arms and the outline of his thighs in his trousers. I turned to him in the darkness behind the bank and said: Well, what I really meant was that I want to lie down with you at some point. Tonight. In fact the sooner the better; I can't stay out all night. He laughed: For sure for sure. We got into the car and I was feeling nervous. He startled me by reaching his arm out, encircling my neck and pulling my face over his. His mouth opened slow and he kissed me for a few seconds. He drew away leaving his hand curved around the nape of my neck and smiled, leaned back in for another kiss, and then drew away again. He patted me on the leg and turned the key in the ignition.

He had this shitty piece of plastic that he'd fashioned into a tent strung between two trees in a forest of firs. It was some rarely used campground way up in the hills, no lights just dirt roads among the trees. The car twisted its way along illuminating a pitched tent or rusting trailer. He finally swung in between some trees and came to a stop snapping the headlights off. He left his door open a bit softly casting light on nearby trees. His tent billowed in the slight breeze.

We stood in the dark kissing for a while, then he went to the back of the car and got an old sleeping bag out from the trunk and spread it under the tent. He closed the car door extinguishing the interior light and turned on a tiny flashlight, lying on the ground between us. We struggled to get our clothes off we were so blasted from a bowl of pot he produced as we drove up the hillside. We were trying to pull off our pants standing on one leg, tipping over and making crashing noises in the bushes. I was completely disoriented but he grabbed on to my arm pulling me into the opening of the tent his skin so warm. We couldn't stop tasting each other's mouths, changing back and forth in different positions, lying on top of each other, moving down and licking each other's arms and bellies and chests. At some point I was hovering over him in a push-up position leaning down drawing my tongue over the wet curves of his armpits when an intense light swept over the tent. I felt like we were in the path of a searchlight. A lot of noise, shouts, and the slamming of car doors. I froze with my mouth on his chest and then the light disappeared.

At about two in the morning he dropped me off outside the hotel and we exchanged addresses. I entered the room as quietly as I could and saw the doctor still passed out in the bed. I had that rude perfume of sex all over me and needed to take a shower. I passed through the darkened room into the bathroom and closed the door, stripping off my clothes and hitting the light switch. I was in front of an enormous mirror that reflected an image of my pale white body covered in dozens of thick red welts. Mosquitoes. Everywhere. I took a hot shower, soaped off, and finally crawled into bed without waking the doctor. The next morning the welts were gone. Everything was casual and we left the motel and drove up the coast.

My life was falling apart. A hustler moved in and I spent a week's worth of nights on the living room floor. I scavenged for leftovers in the refrigerator rather than sit for sullen meals at the dining table. I'd wake up early and leave for the day coming back only after the doctor and his boy were asleep. He left me a couple of angry letters taped to the refrigerator saying he didn't like the ghost routine and that he thought I should give him his set of keys back. I'd been writing Joe for a while and asked if I could come up for a visit. He wrote back saying he had a four-day break coming up the next week. I called him long distance and he gave me instructions to some small town in Massachusetts and said he'd meet me at the bus station. I packed a small shopping bag and left without saying anything to the doctor. I didn't know what I was doing or where I was going I was just leaning into a drift and sway that I hoped would set me down gentle. I walked around the streets until five in the morning around the East Village and sat on a bench near St. Mark's Church watching dawn coming up. A pale, depressed queen sat down next to me and eventually invited me to his place nearby. It was a filthy room in a tenement with lots of dirty bed sheets and clothes. I stayed there a week till I caught the bus to Ludlow.

He met me at the station and drove to some queer bar on the outskirts of a city. We stood in the dark near a cigarette machine and hardly spoke, grinning at each other and sucking on cold bottles. Later he drove us back to his apartment complex where he shared a small place on the second floor with his brother. We went for a walk in the back fields and woods down a dirt road where a fat 'coon kept trying to beat the cars to get across. We followed rusting steel railroad tracks long ago abandoned, reddish brown and swallowed up by the dense undergrowth. We pushed through thick nets of trees and bushes catching our feet on vines past a house with a howling yard dog behind a storm fence, through some forest with a steep incline tumbling toward a river. Further on we came to tracks that continued on a trestle bridge which went over small rapids that merged into a vast smooth curve suddenly broken up on more rocks creating a whooshing spill toward the west. Watching the trees dipping down toward the banks we were forty or fifty feet up in the air tightroping these tracks with nothing but rotting steel stanchions holding us up. There were sounds of left-over fireworks somewhere in the distance, huge bullhead clouds, some rosy from the disappearing sun, others dark and bruise-colored drifting heavily overhead. We sat on a girder, the water rushed below giving us the sensation that we were moving at high speeds through the quiet and dying world.

He pulled a little bowl of pot from his pants and lit up. I had a difficult time not staring at his arms and torso, he left his T-shirt back at his place. I was falling, like from the portal of a plane way up in the skies. He had the kind of sexy grace that you want to swim in, currents warm and breathing. In those years I fell in love easily: gestures of an arm, the simple line of a vein in the neck, the upturning of a jaw in dim light, the lines of a body beneath cloth-ing, the clear light of the eyes when your faces almost touch. We talked about flying saucers, whether it's some kind of psychic reality for those who claim abduction or whether it's some kind of psychic schism that people have experienced. I was slowly leaning toward him and without any reason suddenly kissed his bare shoulder. He kind of wigged, pulled back in vague shock: Uh uh. Don't ever do that. There's people around here.

Two days later at around midnight he stepped out of his bed and squatted next to where I lay on a sleeping bag on the floor of his room. He was wearing shorts and he pulled his dick out the leg part and bounced it against my lips. We hadn't mentioned sex since I arrived. We got into something quiet and slow, came, and then he slid back into his bed and fell asleep.

I was feeling dislocated, my money was going to run out fairly quick from fast-food meals and occasional beers. The feeling of dislocation was really about dreaming too much in this guy's move-ments. There was nothing ahead of me but a return to the streets of New York unless there's something called love but it probably doesn't exist except in the mythologies we're fed in the media or by lying to ourselves over time. It's not only the urge to climb inside someone's skin and fuse in the rivers of their blood; it's wanting to leave the face of the planet, our bodies rolling against each other in the cool spacious sky. But this guy couldn't verbalize anything that touched his sexuality; he had a look of pain when I strayed near words so I slid back into my solitary drift and waited till his hands began to move toward me.

We were going to go swimming so he lent me a pair of cutoffs which I put on, slightly self-conscious about my hospital-white legs. His legs were darker, sturdier, that's what I recall about first meeting him on the windswept coast, late afternoon beneath the flapping canvas awnings and the lines of his muscular thighs and calves. We were in his two-door car stopping outside of town to pick up a six-pack and then onto the interstate. We went many miles further, finally swinging onto this small asphalt road, then onto an even smaller road that climbed up through trees and into hillsides. He was picking up some kid who wanted to come with us. (Telephone call: Is your mother home? Well, then, meet us on the rock near the road.)(Hanging up the phone: He's really worried about his mom or sister seeing him going out with other guys.) We pulled onto this fucked-up asphalt strip that rolls vertically up another hillside, made a curve and there's this young kid maybe seventeen sitting on a large white boulder lodged in the green lawn. He looked vaguely Indian, and he also had muscular legs, a baby-hair mustache almost transparent on his lip. (Later that evening: Yeah I met him outside a bar in Springfield. They carded him and he had to stay outside. We camped out in his backyard a couple times . . . Yeah I slept with him once. The first night I met him we talked for a long long time. He didn't have a ride home so we got in my car, ran out of gas the needle on empty just outside his home. His mother works in a hospital, father dead. We spent the night in his house no one home.)

*   *   *

Down by the lake right off the road in a dirt patch we parked with the windows open and a slight breeze easing through. The kid was rolling a meticulous joint on a cardboard cover of a shoe box; gypsy moths, hundreds of them, beat soundlessly against the trunks of trees, some flying over into the windshield of the car, climbing inside, around the dashboard, on our legs, leaving behind a blond powder. Someone's ugly poodle, hairless, almost gray skin, was tied to a tree shivering in the tall grass. We could hear sounds of splashing and ripple currents drifting nearby. I was smoked up to the point of getting stupid. I got out of the car and drifted to the water's edge. I walked ahead of them into the lake with my eyes focused on the horizon like a happy zombie, steady, smoothly upright, I moved forward into the dreamy nothingness with the waters riding up around my waist and further up around my chest, shocking my armpits, I was far from shore without my glasses; everything took on that indistinct look like water cascading over a window, just wobbly form and light and color. Without my glasses color seems to fade because there are no true lines to contain it, it mixes with things and rides outside its surfaces, no density to anything in the world but what I feel beneath my feet.

I dive in the water and swim for the longest while beneath its surface slow and quiet. I'm aquatic, surrounded by silence, everything gray beneath my eyelids, feeling like I'm aware for the first time of my arms and hands and kicking legs and what they all mean. I lie sideways on the water's surface seeing pale bodies of strangers moving waist high on the shoreline far away.

In the shallows of the lake I walk on my hands, digging into the sand. Further out it's silt so soft and deep you know it's black and rich; my feet sink up to the ankles. It's a texture that's like the inside of a body when your fingers go wandering. I pull smooth objects to the surface, some kind of freshwater mussels. He's doubtful when I tell him so I toss one to him and he's amazed. Later he holds it against the top of a wooden fencepost and slams it with a rock cracking the shell to bits, which he pulls apart revealing tan flesh. I pick up my little camera off the backseat and take his picture. He gets embarrassed: You just take a picture of me? Yeah, I said. Just of you talking. (Not of your beautiful chest which I'd love to spit on and rub my dick over.) The car radio is on and the announcer says: The worst riots in England in memory; worst civilian damage since World War II.

Later we drive the kid back home, up the small darkening road of the hillside into the blue shadows of evening. The house is softly illuminated from behind by a back porch light. The kid gets agitated: Uh oh . . . my mother's probably home . . . uh . . . just let me off here and if ya can turn around in someone else's drive . . . I didn't leave that light on . . . she's probably home. We say good night and he whispers: Joe . . . call you later in the week. He turns and runs across the lawn disappearing into the shadows of the porch, screen door squeaking and the bowwow of a dog.

His brother has buddies hanging out in their apartment; they might spend the night since it's heading toward the weekend. He wants sex with me really bad all of a sudden. He's trying to get a motel room so we're on the interstate driving miles and miles. Finally he spots a Holiday Inn. I wait in the car as he goes inside to register. I'm sitting there for a long time feeling this melancholy circle around me. Couldn't tell exactly what it was, part of it I guess was being outside New York City in a slow place with air and grass and bodies of water to lie down in. Some of it was the growing tension leaving soon almost broke and no place to live. Death was a smudge in the distance. I don't know what exactly I mean by that but lying down inside this cradle of arms in my head was sometimes all I wanted. Sometimes I wonder what planet I got dropped off from; what foreign belly did I get birthed from. This shit is painful, it's like being on a raft way out in the middle of a sea completely alone.

I wave my hands in front of me, I know I'm not invisible, why are my thoughts so fucking loud? I'm lost in a world that's left all its mythologies behind in the onward crush of wars and civilization, my body traveling independent of brushes with life and death, no longer knowing what either means anymore. I'm so tired of feeling weary and alien, even my dreams look stupid to me. They belong to another world, another century, maybe another gender that fits the codes of all this shit. I don't know.

He comes back visibly upset, swings into the car through the driver's open window, slumps back: Shit. How could I be so fucking stupid? The clerk asked me if I lived nearby and I told him where and he goes: We have a policy not to rent to nobody who lives within a thirty-mile radius of here.

He was upset. I put my hand on his leg and said: Look, don't let the asshole get you down. So what? Let's look for another place or else forget it and go for a ride. (I really wanted to try to fuck him.) We drove onto the highway again and rode for a while in silence. He pulled into a Ramada Inn. He got a room. Everything was calm again. He took a six-pack of beer from the trunk along with a carton of photographs and albums from his days at sea. It was a standard motel room with double beds and cheap thick white curtains, a sink with glasses wrapped in wax paper and a color television with air conditioner humming behind it.

We're sitting on one of the beds, our shirts off, shoes and socks lying scattered across the floor, our legs resting together and stray hands smoothing down each other's sides and chests. We're looking at his notebooks filled with Kodak pictures of faraway places and naval scenes of boy sailors passing the equator. Mop wigs and overloaded halter tops and string skirts and underwear of different colors. Some of the photos look like a drunken fashion show with sturdy-legged guys with balloons or cloth tits beneath their T-shirts, sort of like a hula nightmare but more sexy. In other pictures they're dressed like canines, on all fours with sheets of paper and cardboard curved and strung around their faces with Magic Marker lines drawn like grinning dogs. One Filipino guy has a white T-shirt with a pirate's skull drawn on his chest. Another guy is dressed like a hound dog bitch with eight fat papier-mâché tits dragging on the deck. There were other pictures of him with all his friends, bare-chested waist high in a foreign sea with delicate pink and white flowered leis around their necks. I put my hand casually on his butt and he jerks away. Anyone ever put their hands on your ass? I ask. He makes a disgusted noise: That's fucking gross; I'd never put my dick in somebody's ass and I'd never let somebody try that with me . . . makes me sick to think about it. Same way I'd never be in a relationship with a guy, maybe a girl but never a guy . . . it just ain't . . . uh . . . normal . . . it just doesn't make any sense. I don't mind playing around here or there but not a relationship. . . . No way.

Sometimes I wish I could blow myself up. Wrap a belt of dynamite around my fucking waist and walk into a cathedral or the Oval Office or the home of my mother and father. I'm in the last row of the bus, the seven other passengers are clustered like flies around the driver in the front. I can see his cute fuckable face in the rearview mirror. I lean back and tilt my head so all I see is the clouds in the sky. I'm looking back inside my head with my eyes wide open. I still don't know where I'm going; I decided I'm not crazy or alien. It's just that I'm more like one of those kids they find in remote jungles or forests of India. A wolf child. And they've dragged me into this fucking schizo-culture, snarling and spitting and walking around on curled knuckles. They're trying to give me a damp mattress to sleep on in a dark corner when all I really want is the rude perfume of some guy's furry underarms and crotch to lean into. I'll make guttural sounds and stop eating and drinking and I'll be dead within the year. My eyes have always been advertisements for an early death.

R. Zamora Linmark

BLAME IT ON CHACHI

EDGAR RAMIREZ is a faggot. Mrs. Takemoto knows it. She's always telling him to stop putting his hair behind his ears.

"And cut your hair, Edgar," she says. "It's getting long again."

Edgar Ramirez is a faggot. Christopher and Rowell, the fifth-grade bulls, know it. They're always tackling him in flag football.

"A flag for a fag," they say. "Fag flag."

Edgar Ramirez is a faggot. Nelson and Prudencio, the other fifth-grade bulls, know it. They're always shooting him with their slingshots or tripping him each time he walks by swaying his hips hula-style.

"What, cannot walk without heels?" they say.

Edgar Ramirez is a faggot. Caroline, Judy-Ann, and Maggie, the Hot-to-Trot girls, know it. They're always fighting over him because he looks like a Filipino John Travolta.

"Edgar, you wanna come over my house?" they ask at the same time. "We can play Chinese jacks," Caroline says. "We can read my *16* or *Teen Beat* magazines," Judy-Ann says. "We can listen to my Peaches & Herb tape," Maggie says.

Edgar Ramirez is a faggot. His mother and father know it. They're always grounding him because he spends all his money on life-size John Travolta or Shaun Cassidy or Scott Baio posters. And pins them up on the walls, ceilings, doors, in his father's workout room, and next to the altar.

"Anak, go to confession," his devout mother says. His father doesn't say anything. He just grabs the gardening shears and chops at Edgar's hair until he's bald, or burns the posters and shoves the cinders down Edgar's throat.

Edgar Ramirez is a faggot. His friends Katrina, Vicente, Loata, Mai-Lan, and Florante know it. Even Edgar himself knows it.

"Since when, Edgar?" Katrina asks.

"Ever since I saw my father naked," he says.

"So what are you going to do about it?" Vicente asks.

"Nothing," Edgar says. "Nothing."

Blame my parents. They started 'em. First I was Totoy.

"Go give Daddy a hug, Totoy."

"Come, Totoy, come kiss Daddy bye-bye."

"No, Totoy, that's bad. Yes, Totoy, baaaad. Only Mama can do that to Dada."

"Yes, Maaama."

Then one evening, while we was watchin' *Happy Days,* the episode where Chachi kiss Joanie for the first time, my father wen' call me all my names and other names too, just like I one schizophrenic or somethin':

"Totoy-anak, don't sit too close to the TV or you'll go blind," my father said. "Edgie, I said not to sit too close to the damn TV before you go baaalaaind! Punyeta, do you want me to turn the TV off? Don't but-it's-Scott-Baio-Dad me, Edgar. Move it before I smash your head," he said. "Move, or else. What, Edgardo? What, Totoy, what did you say? Who taught you that f-word, Edgar? Answer me, Edgardo 'Totoy' Cabanban Ramirez. I said, answer me. Okay, you wanna play deaf, go play deaf in your room. And from now on, I don't want to hear anymore Scott Baio or Chachi from your filthy mouth. Do you want your classmates to start calling you a fag? A mahu?"

At school the names they call me always come with one nudge or one punt, usually from the Filipino O. J. Simpson and Kareem Abdul-Jabbar wannabes, like Christopher Lactaoen, Rowell Cortez, and Prudencio Pierre Yadao.

"Eh, you guys, check out that Fag, Edgar."

"What, Mahu, what you starin' at?"

"No act, Panty, before I give you one good slap."

"What, Bakla, you like beef right now?"

"C'mon, Homo."

"Right here, Sissy."

"Edga's ooone faaag. He like suck one diiick."

I swallow the names like the vitamins I gotta take before I go school. The pink-colored pills my mother stuffs in bananas cuz they supposed to make me grow big and strong. But when Christopher them start gettin' outta hand with the names, and their nudges start for turn to bruises, I roll up my sleeves and turn into the Queen of Mouth and Sizes.

"You guys think you so so tough, so so hot cuz you the youngest ones in the Kalihi Valley JV football team? Win one game first before you guys start actin' all macho. No shame or what? Why not pick on your own size, Tiny Tims? That's right. You guys are small, and I mean small, like the vienna sausage your mothers fry every mornin'. I know mine's bigger than yours. C'mon, pull down your pants. What, scared? Scared cuz mine's bigger than the three of you put together? Bust 'em out then. C'mon, no need be shame. Bust out those teeny-weenies. What, gotta have one microscope for look at your botos? C'mon then, prove how big and strong you really are. What you guys waitin' for? Bust 'em out so we can put you guys in *Real People* with Sarah Purcell. No, even better, *That's Incredible!* and have Fran Tarkenton introduce you guys as the junior jocks with microscopic cocks."

PROOF #1: QUEEN OF ICE PACK & CURAD

In the courtyard, I the Sham Battle Queen to re-enact what Florante calls the Fall of Bataan. Feelin' elegant in my Dove shorts I wear like one French-cut bikini, like Cheryl Tiegs in *Sports Illustrated,* I skip to the battlefront with one red ball as my tiara, and pose as Queen of Atomic Words.

"Eh, everybody, everybody, I got one story to tell. Once upon a time there was two boys and a bathroom. One day, an angel named Edgar spotted them jerkin' each other off. They was goin' at it like cats and dogs. For real, I no kid you guys, brah. If you no like believe, go ask Prudencio and Christopher what they was doin' yesterday after school between three and three-thirty at the C-building bathroom.

"Eh, fuck you, too, Christopher-wanna-be-Kareem. I got better stories for invent than watchin' you and Prudencio jack each other off. With my own eyes and ears, brah, I saw and heard everythin'. Shit, even Helen Keller can hear all that moanin' and groanin' you guys was makin'. Prudencio, no be givin' me that stink-but-innocent look, like you don't know what the hell I stay talkin' about cuz I saw you, dumbass. When I heard noises comin' from one of the stalls, I wen' climb up the urinal for check out the view. And the view I got was better than the Pali Lookout. With my own brown eyes, I saw you, Prudencio Pierre-my-Cardin, goin' down on Christopher and makin' all that drownin' sounds. How did it taste, Pierre? So mahulani, I tell you."

I drop my ball to try for catch the rubber grenades attackin' from all sides, but they stay comin' at me at a hundred miles per hour to sting my face like one swarm of bees. I duck, of course, but as usual, I end up runnin' straight for the clinic where Mrs. Sugihara christen me Queen of Ice Pack and Curad.

But the next day, I march back to the court in my skimpy PE clothes for be the I Shall Return Queen.

PROOF #2: QUEEN OF CONTRABAND BOOKS & WHISPERS

"Hey, Katrina-Trina, here's Judy Blume's *Wifey*. You better not mark it or show it to everybody else like you did my *Forever*. What you mean 'no'? You such a liar, Trina. Had your red pen marks all over the ne-ces-sary parts. Next time, just take notes, or better yet, circle the page number. No have to damage my books. Expensive, you know, especially now cuz of in-fel-lay-tion. You no watch Walter Cronkite or what? What you mean only the price of oil goin' up cuz of the OPEC guys? Now it's more worse cuz of the American hostesses in Iran. See now, I lost my thought of train. Oh yeah, damagin' my books. Yesterday, I found this book in Honolulu Bookstore. The Adult Section, of course. Where else? The Children's? Anyways, it's triple worse than *Forever* and *Wifey*. It's super-perverted. There's fuckin' in almost every chapter. And the way she describe the guy's dick is so unreal I can almost see it. No, you no can read 'em now. Finish *Wifey* first, but you better not mark that book, or else you never goin' see *Looking For Mr. Goodbar*."

After school, before I turn into the Queen of Wide World of Sports, I stay in the utility room playin' Rejuvenation Queen for

Mr. Campos, the custodian of the century. He say I make him young again. I tell him he make me feel so so mature. I lie, of course, cuz I no can tell him I rather do the splits for his young son who drive one mean-assed white bug with a bad stereo that vibrate throughout the valley. He's such a hunk. Like a cross between Dirk Benedict and Sly Stallone.

PROOF #3: QUEEN OF AFTERSCHOOL GYMNASTICS & DONNA SUMMER

"Eh, you guys ever seen one Filipino Nadia Co-ma-nee-chee? C'mon then, let's go to Loata's house cuz he get the best clothesline for swing on. Trina, you got your tape or what? No, not the Peaches & Herb tape. I tried to do the uneven bars to 'Shake Your Groove Thing.' That's only good for floor exercises. Bring the one, you know, the one, the theme from *The Young and the Restless*. It's more better, more a-pro-pri-yate."

On afternoons when I no can be the Queen of Clothesline Gymnastics, I the Queen of Disco Divas.

"Katrina, you think I can pass for Donna Summer? What you mean, 'Gloria Gaynor'? Fuck you, Trina. I no look like Gloria Gaynor. What you mean cuz I get one afro. Eh, girl, my hair ain't no afro. It just look like one. What you mean Donna get one afro too? Fuck, Trina, you talkin' bubbles. Donna no more afro. The word is full, Trina, not afro. Eh, at least I no look like one white monkey like Alicia Bridges, like somebody I know. That's right, Trina. You look like Alicia Bridges. Maybe you guys twins, ah? No get all habuts on me, Trina, you the one who started it. Besides, who's the one who always tell me I sound like Donna Summer, especially when I sing 'Bad Girls'? No tell me Florante cuz he no even listen to disco. What you mean he does? For your information, Trina, Florante listen to kundimans, not disco. Big difference, you know. And no tell me was Vicente or Loata, either. Eh, if you like stay my friend forever, no start twistin' my words around and make like I the one who's at fault, okay? Okay. C'mon then, play one song already so we no make ass when we enter *America's I Love the Nightlife* dance contest. The judges strict, you know. They professionals, that's why."

PROOF #4: QUEEN OF DANCE FEVER

"Vicente, try feel my face. Smooth, yeah? Shut up, Trina, I talkin' to Vicente, not you. And don't ever tell me that I scrub my face, Trina. The word is d-fo-lee-yate. At least I no use SOS like somebody who get one a-bray-sive face. Anyways, Vicente, you ever tried playin' footsie under the table? You know, foot-c. That's what the haoles do in the movies before they oof. Like this. Shit, Vicente, you supposed to enjoy it. You supposed to re-c-pro-cate. Never mind, already, you not as smart as I thought you was. Eh, Katrina. Trina? Trina, fucka, no fall asleep on me. We next, you know. You ready for blow 'em away or what? You better make sure you got the steps downpacked cuz I no like make A, like the last time. Screw this one up, Trina, and I goin' find somebody else for be my dance partner. Just remember, first comes the sunshine, then the moonlight, then the good times, and then, the boogie. You got it? Better be, bumblebee."

PROOF #5: QUEEN OF CATECHISM, ROLLERWORLD & VIDEO GAMES

"Who says I hate my mother for makin' me go catechism class? You guys just jealous cuz I goin' straight to heaven. How I know? Cuz Father Pacheco told me so. He said, 'Edgar, my son, you keep doin' whatever you're doin' and you won't need to take the test when you get to Him.' Why, just cuz I go catechism, you think I goin' turn like one of them Jehovah Witnesses? Screw you guys, you never ever goin' find me knockin' on your door just for tell you

for twenty cents that you goin' burn in hell cuz you masturbate.
Forget it. I worth more than that. You really like know why till this
day, I still go catechism? Cuz Mr. Lee, my cathechism teacher, is
one fox, that's why. And after every class, he take us Rollerworld,
Farrell's, and to the movies. And we no gotta pay anythin' cuz he
overly rich, plus he get one nice car. That's why I go to catechism.
Last week, in fact, we went for see *The Amityville Horror,* and after
that, he took us to the new Mitsukoshi building down in Waiks
where we spent all his money playin' Galaxian and Space Invaders.
That's where I saw the baddest hapa-babe I ever seen in my entire
life. Now, all God gotta do is answer my prayers."

At night, after playin' Queen of Hail Mary, I stare at Scott Baio
thumbtacked on my door with the valley breeze flappin' his pants.
I slip between the cream-colored sheets and under the blue comforter my mother wen' order from Fingerhut, the one with the
alphabets, then I flick off the lamp. In the dark, I feel the big letters
and I start for write my name and all the names people call me.
Faggot. Mahu. Queen. Bakla. Queer. Cocksucker. Dicklover. Even
though most of the names are who I am and what I do, they say
'em with so much hate, like I ugly or somethin'. But I not ugly. I
might be mean, but that's cuz I need for be strong when they tryin'
for put me down and make like I the one ugly cuz I not like them.

I close my eyes hard

and Scott Baio stay kissin' me I kiss him back

I feel Mr. Campos' chapped lips, his pomaded hair and greasy
face

my father peepin' through the keyhole, murder in his eyes I tell
Mr. Campos for get off me Quick

get off me get off me

I wake up like I no can breathe. Like my father was chokin' me.
I stay sweatin' like I the one who got the DTs and not him. I
change my clothes and jump back into bed

*   *   *

I in one white bug cruisin' around Waikiki with Mr. Campos' son. We stay listenin' to Donna Summer's *Bad Girls* eight-track tape He steer the wheel with one hand and smoke Kool Milds with the other I move my Nadia legs slightly apart, like one perfect V Then I fling my head back and my arms out and make pretend I Nadia after a perfect landing He throw the cigarette in the air I catch his hand as it slides between my legs I play with his fingers

We in the old Pali Road It is pitch-black and dead quiet I put his thumb in my mouth and suck it like one Sucrets lozenge The car move at caterpillar speed until it veer to the side of the road

I see the tree where Morgan hung himself I see Morgan's ex-girlfriend laughing I scared

No be I hea I take care you

He eject the tape for play my all-time favorite Peaches & Herb song, "Reunited" He massage the nape of my neck

I fall back he climb on top of me
he press his lips we dry-kiss for long time
my mouth slow
ly
his tongue in one circle after circle I fall
in' with each circle
full raw new like Chachi kissin' me
for first time.

Kevin Killian

A CONSCIENCE CALL

KIT TOOK the 47 bus to where it lets you out at the entrance to the seedy warehouse district where Sam now made his home. After their break-up several years ago, Sam had retreated to this cheerless, empty interzone, where all you saw was people smoking crack or hauling giant slabs of debris into artists' live-work lofts to make public art for the walls of the new Yerba Buena Center downtown. It was three o'clock on a Tuesday afternoon, a brisk wind blowing trash and dried leaves down Eleventh, messy wet sheets of newsprint slapped with the names and 900 numbers of nude men. Smell of creosote in the thin air.

Kit wanted a beer so he rapped sharply on an unobtrusive black door on the alley next to the auto body shop, with a star of glass carved in it. The face of Rover appeared in the center of the glazed star, as though he were the host of some TV program, squinting at the light, then popping out of sight. Rover was a sly, fox-faced white man of about twenty-two, the bartender or manager here. The door swung open silently, and Rover pulled it shut behind them with a bang. From a dark anteroom they passed through a heavy rubber curtain to a bar the size of a small closet. The smell of gin and cleaning fluid.

"What brings you to this part of town?" Rover asked.

"It's the company," Kit said, hardly smiling. By using a measured approach to expansion, devoid of advertising and relying instead on word-of-mouth references, this sex club had garnered a large market share in its home region. "I'm paying a conscience call on an old boyfriend, dude, who lives around the corner."

Rover's sharp nose sniffed in disapproval.

"If he's sick, I don't blame you." He poured Kit a large glass of some Balkan beer. "Some of these sick guys can get *awful dour.*" A rubber curtain parted and a flurry of commotion erupted from the room beyond; huge puffs of dust, like tumbleweeds, blew across the floor at top speed. "Having fun, girls?" Rover called out. Then he swiveled back to Kit. "We have a guy who is hella sick and keeps hobbling in and wants to watch; I tell him, why? You are just putting the crimp on the others' style! This place is for the healthy." He pointed to a large heart-shaped box, heaped with condoms of assorted sizes, that sat on the bar next to a jar of sweet and sour pickles. "They both gather dust as far as I can see, because condoms are just about as popular as pickle chips." He shook his head, gulped his beer. "And plus, when you put a pickle chip on your dick at least you can still feel sensation."

Kit nodded, checked his watch, and then put down his empty glass, nodded again and moved on into the larger room, where a tape of some insistent industrial music was chugging away, and a red strobe kept darting and slanting until everyone in the room looked like Diane Keaton getting stabbed to death at the end of

Looking for Mr. Goodbar. Her herky-jerky movements, her awkward stumbling and trying to catch at the furniture. Except these guys were having fun, Kit noted with a sudden lift in his heart.

An hour later, he stood in the sunlight, on Sam's doorstep, hesitating. Remembering how he used to want to see Sam. How he longed for him. God, that was so long ago. Sam lived in a third-floor walk-up on this quiet diminished street, around the corner from Club Rover.

"I think I know that guy Sam," Rover said. "But he never comes in here, I guess he knows he wouldn't like it here. He's got dignity, he ain't the type to make other guys feel like shit just because they're young and healthy and want some fun."

"I remember him from ACT UP," said another guy. This was Ladd, one of the neighborhood's visual artists who came here to shower. "He was wicked handsome, made my boxers like this wet swamp, but now he just walks like a ghost. Like he's dead already. I was in the corner store last month and I felt this voice talking in my ear, and it was him, but I couldn't see a mouth talking, or any body, it was like Sam was invisible. But his cigarette was glowing and steady and he was carrying a big bag of cat food and a copy of the *Star,* the one with Nicole and Paula were like in this cat fight over Ron Goldman, and how they had to keep it out of the trial."

"You never heard much about Ron Goldman," said Rover.

"Oh he must have been gay, don't you think?" Kit said.

"Because he was doing tables at Mezzaluna?" Ladd was skeptical. "They say there are some straight waiters, I think, in Milwaukee, was it? Someone was telling me! I heard he was castrated and they found his cock stuffed down his throat."

"And they couldn't bring it forward at the trial," Kit said. "Too true, Danny saw the autopsy photos."

"And Paula used to be some kind of knife thrower in some Japanese carnival," said Rover. "That's what didn't come out at the trial. They called her the Little Ginza-matic, but you think the jury knew that? I don't think so, my friend!"

Ever go to visit a sick pal, and you think you're doing them such a big favor, and you're like this big martyr, then when you get there he's surrounded by others? Hell is crowned with such disappointments; even with the best will in the world you'll still feel utterly unappreciated if your noble gesture's only one of many! So, when on Sam's landing Kit saw all the signs — the ugly signs — that Sam had company already, his lip curled and he felt like turning back, going home to Danny, who was probably wondering where he was anyway. Sam had always one group of friends who were almost equally attractive, though in different ways, so sometimes when they all got together, Kit thought of them as the "Village People." Who he kind of remembered from the Disco Era. The Village People were a pop group, a mixed bag of stereotypes — leatherman, Indian chief, cop—assembled by some marketing genius with the lowest common denominator in mind. They sang a little and moved their bodies in unison in what passed for dancing. Their songs, catchy and banal, suggestive too, were "gay" in this blood-curdling way. "There was someone for everyone," Kit recalled, although he didn't like disco himself and hated the Village People. He saw Mike's bicycle locked to the grating on Sam's landing, and Avery's big clunky Doc Martens laced over the railing, as though a drunken roadster had tossed them there on a spree. Kit liked these guys but they weren't very serious. He didn't see what Sam could have in common with them. For a minute he considered sneaking away, not even knocking, just slinking down the forty steps and getting the hell out of Minna Street. But conscience made him stay. He'd knock.

The things Sam had done and seen would make the earth stand still. If he could only remember them properly. Increasingly he had made the subject of his forgetting the subject of his fiction. He was writing a story about a vacation he had taken with his mother, not too long ago, in point of fact. He thought, it'll be amusing when the hero can't remember where the hotel is. Everything about his story amused him, except the wheeze in his throat when he rehearsed the sentences he'd make it out of.

Let's bring up a few of Sam's friends — Pierre, the nimble, black-eyed waif who got fucked in two French porn films; Mike, the quick-tongued Southern carrot-top; Avery, the tough nut with thin, sinister sideburns. Okay, they're at Sam's apartment and Kit's outside the door.

We'll bring them up to the foreground, like at a carnival, ducks in a shooting gallery we'll try to shoot down one by one.

"I've been watching a lot of *Jump Street* reruns," Mike confided. "I watch Holly Robinson 'acting.' She's tough and she's understanding, and that's it. I heard she's Angie Dickinson's retarded daughter."

"She's black!" Pierre said. "You can't have it both ways."

"I used to like to," Mike said, remembering a hundred back rooms in Memphis and Shreveport. "Isn't Angie's daughter black? Or who am I thinking of, Sam?"

"Jennifer Beals?"

"Just cause her name was Pepper on *Police Woman,* he thinks she's black."

"I never said that."

"I don't even know who you're talking about," said Sam. "Dickinson, Robinson, you're talking about poets."

The other three young men were silent for a minute, remembering Sam's admiration of Patti Smith. In varying degrees they appreciated the arts, and Avery was attending the Art Institute of San Francisco between shifts at the Gayety Burlesque. "Emily Dickinson," Mike remembered. He saw in his head this older woman with a bun, seated at a deal table writing scratchy lines on parchment. "But Robinson who?"

"I forget," Sam said. But that was part of it, his forgetting. He took pleasure in it now, after a year of anxiety attacks. Soon he'd forget his own name, or so he believed. His mother used to say he was a dreamy boy. "You'd forget your own name." Now that it was a literal possibility, he marveled at the coincidence, if such it was. Now he wondered if he'd forget how to write. "I've been making such strides lately — that would be a shame," he thought, with a thrill of despair. "Bob Dylan said Smokey Robinson was America's greatest poet. I know: 'Who's Bob Dylan?' "

Kit finally opened the door himself. "Sam?" There was so much racket he was holding his hands over his ears. Patti Smith — "Space Monkey," cranked up super loud. Sam faced him. Odd, the light in his eyes — shot with stars.

"Do you have any money, Kit?" Sam asked.

"Hello," Kit yelled.

Sam cracked a smile. "Hello yourself. Oh. Come on in, sit down." He called to the cats. "Look who's here, it's Uncle Kit!" Kit found himself calling out, "Where are those kit cats!" as first Blanche, then Stanley jumped into his arms. "You remember me?" he said to one. Then the other. They squirmed against his forearms and clawed their way to his shoulders, so that he stood there, in Sam's front room, a man covered in cat fur and loud meows. Sam turned down the volume on the CD. Sam's other friends left when they saw Kit — Kit, the man they hated for breaking Sam's heart. "See you, Sam." Slam — slam. He got the message. He was a nonperson in their world. He had committed all these crimes — getting his picture in the paper — deserting Sam when the diagnosis said HIV — leaving Sam for a rich boy. All these "crimes" and he was Klaus Barbie in the eyes of these tacky Village People "alternate" types.

"How's Danny?" Sam said brightly. "I saw how his father died."

"He's bearing up," Kit replied. "They weren't close or anything."

"Does he know you're here, handing out money like a mad thing?"

"He knows in general."

"And you've had a few drinks," Sam said. "I get weaker and weaker but in some ways I feel stronger. My senses are stronger. You've been around the corner, I bet, get your rocks off, Kit?"

"You're a good guesser."

"That man in that club is a slut," Sam said. "Get your dick sucked sort of thing."

"You look good," Kit said.

"I've been taking my vitamins," Sam said. "Ever miss me, Kit? Do I look like myself, or do I look sick?"

"You look good," Kit repeated. He glanced down the front of his pants, had they gotten spotted? No. Sam looked terrible, his face drawn and aged. His sinuous walk slowed down to the shuffle of an old man. He even had slippers on his feet, and socks under the slippers, where once he had prowled Haight Street barefooted, and Kit thought, bad circulation, he's cold all the time. How long had it been? Had it been at Christmas? "Call me if you need anything."

"I just need money," Sam said. "Oh, Kit! I'm writing the most wonderful story. I'm using a tape recorder and every time I think of another sentence I turn on the 'on' button and say the sentence. I'm getting better at writing, better at everything. These vitamins are so good. I owe everything to these great guys who make these vitamins, Kit. I'm going to live and I'm going to be great.

"Thanks for coming by and giving me money. It's always terrific to see you. I don't want you to feel guilty or anything. You're doing great work in ACT UP. I see you in the *Chronicle* all the time. You're so good-looking, no wonder the photographers always show your face.

"People think I'm on drugs or something. But I call 'em the way I see 'em. I'm just saying what you think. But sometimes, Kit, I say more than I think. I try to put my best sentences into my story, but I have these leftovers that don't go here and don't fit there."

*　　*　　*

His anxiety attacks manifested themselves in peculiar ways. It got to be bad when water tasted funny. He had special filters submerged in pitchers of tap water that drained out all the dirt, etc., supposed to leave the water tasting like a Swedish fjord. They worked, most of the time. But sometimes, when he felt stressed, he'd pour himself a glass of water and sip it, without thinking — and then the water tasted flat and sour, like old dishwater. Then he knew he was in for a bad night. He'd grab one of his monkeys and wedge himself into a corner of his bed, by the phone. When his mind cleared a little bit he would call one of the numbers programmed into his phone.

"Avery? It's Sam."

"Hi Sam — what's up?" Though it was easy to tell nothing was up for Sam. His voice was cracked in a dozen places, like old Staffordshire. Avery sighed and pulled out the footstool. "You okay?"

"Oh, sure," Sam said. "You know me."

"You're full of shit," Avery replied. On the other end of the phone, in another part of town, he "saw" Sam as if in a magic mirror. "Saw" him huddled in the sweaty sheets, naked, knees up, receiver held tight between his knees to free up his hands, which were pressed tight over his eyes to keep the knives out. "If you're having one of your things, why not say so? Don't make me guess, I'm not Nostradamus."

"Okay," said Sam after a pause. "I'm having one of my things."

"That's good," Avery enthused. "I mean — it's good you can admit it. See, if you hide things, inside, they shrivel up then explode like a raisin in the sun. Ever see *Dark Victory* with Bette Davis? She was repressed and uptight, ugly, frightened, a spinster in a world where women married at eighteen."

"*Now, Voyager,*" corrected Sam.

"Whatever. So you're on your way to getting better already." Avery had made Sam promise always to call him when he was having one of his "things," and regretted it about forty percent of the time, which wasn't a bad equation, not really. Working at the Gayety he regretted it about seventy percent of the time. It was a job which required a sturdy yet slim body, a sense of personal liberation about showing your dick in public, and a good sense of humor. So, he didn't have a good sense of humor, whose fault was that? He was an art student first and foremost, a stripper only second. And actually none of the other men he met backstage had any sense of humor either. The ticket takers did, as did one or two of the customers, some of the regulars who sat in Row A on Tuesdays and Wednesdays when the new acts were introduced. Some of those queens lived to laugh. They'd laugh at a guy's dick right in his face, if something about it struck them funny. Like say it was too big even. Never thinking that might be a sensitive subject for some in the entertainment business. Never stopping to think that a boy's costume wasn't always easy to think of and pull together. Or his whole routine either. Not on the shit wages of the Gayety management. Avery was still upset at the cavalier way some had laughed at him the time he'd come on stage by mistake. Not just entered at the wrong cue — if only. No, actually ejaculated. Just because he was high and forgot where he was for a minute. The tape was playing "Father Figure" by George Michael and I don't know, he kind of seized up because it was sexy. Next thing he knew Row A and half of Row B were hooting and throwing their handkerchiefs a mile upstage.

"Oh, I don't know how soon I'll be getting better," Sam said after a pause. "Except that I met this man. And I don't know."

Avery adjusted the volume on the CD. Madonna, *Deeper and Deeper.* "Who did you meet? You met a man?" God, how lame he sounded. It was just the kind of thing that was getting him in shit all the time at the theater. Someone asked him where he came up with the sideburns and he told them the truth, Luke Perry on *90210.* Now they called him "Overy," because Luke Perry was over. It made his blood boil every time he thought of it, these rough hot bubbles. Pierre and Mike were merciless when he told them about it. No sympathy whatsoever. "You let yourself in for it," said Pierre. "You should have told them Abe Lincoln rather than Luke Perry."

"I happen to think Luke Perry's way fierce," said Avery with dignity.

"But he's over," Mike pleaded. "Doesn't that mean anything to you?"

Only Sam kept his own counsel, just sat there at the kitchen table with a mug of coffee raised to his lips, his clear blue eyes watching Avery's gradual panic and fluster with a serene kind of emptiness. As though the spectacle gave him a queer relief. Well why not, Avery thought, smiling despite himself. Having the HIV virus was so awful that the tragedies of everyone else must seem like comedies. And indeed he had exaggerated his problems many times for Sam's benefit, encouraging him to laugh a little at the scrapes others got into. But who was this man? "He's just this guy I met through my support group," Sam said. "You know how in Europe they have different treatments, because they don't have the FDA?"

"Well, kind of, sure."

"This man Gary smuggles them in."

"Oh, does he?"

Avery had never known a smuggler before, and never thought very long about smuggling, except at the airport security checks, where one always does. But this sounded dangerous, seedy, and he had to work to keep his tone cool and like, almost interested. "Oh, does he?" sounded suitable. Like he didn't really care, except that if it was important to Sam, it was important to him. If Sam thought it was glamorous, or it would help save his life, then he'd feign interest, to the extent of pinching himself to keep awake through this long phone conversation. And in any case a new man on the horizon was just about his favorite topic of conversation, that and possible new costumes for his act.

Like just the other day this African American dude guy was

sitting on Haight Street with a tray in front of him, playing the shell game with some German tourists, and Avery, walking by, had this flash — of a deck of cards shuffling across his own body, on stage, under the lights — this deck with bright vivid colors, snapping from face card to face card, jack to ace, right down his body from his throat to his balls. Or something. And like, this apparition, this inspiration, was what had kept him going in the days since then. He kept refining it and trying to draw it on the pages of his Art Institute sketchbook. It was the first thing he thought about when he woke up, and the last thing at night, and he dreamed of those cards, but now how are you going to say to Sam, "Cool about your smuggling guy, Mister Man, but did I tell you about my blackjack outfit?"

It wouldn't revolutionize the world or cause a cure for AIDS but it would be very elaborate and colorful and sexy, and listen, don't we have to be sex positive now — isn't it the quality of life we're so worried about? "Can we talk about this guy some more?" he asked Sam hastily. "Can we talk about him at full length?"

Silence on the phone.

"Sam?"

"You mean in person."

"Yeah! I want to hear all about him, totally," Avery lied. "The thing is, I should get off the phone now; I'm helping Billy Boone install his show at Just Desserts."

"Fine," Sam said. "I wouldn't want to keep those cake eaters from the pleasures of fine art."

"Let 'em eat cake, right, dude?" Avery said quickly, having heard about the cake eaters from some old TV show about France. Or maybe from Pierre who was from France and never let you forget it, especially if you weren't dressed in Chanel or whatever.

"Right, dude. Well, thanks for calling."

"Any time," said Avery. "Heard from Kit lately?"

"He was just here, installing some shelves for me. Fascinating life I'm living."

"You miss him?"

"He won't go away," Sam said. "Thanks for calling, Avery."

"Sure." After hanging up he remembered Sam had called him. Like Sam really had it backwards, maybe the drugs . . . ? Later, plowing through the personal ads in the local free gay weekly, Avery circled one ad with a felt tip pen that almost obscured the number with a gluey pink. "Wanted." Well that's a good word, makes you feel like someone needs you. "Wanted: bad boys for adult video."

Kolin J. M. Ohi

From **A BACKWARD GLANCE**

Prologue

THURSDAY, JULY 31, 1952: CAMARILLO, CALIFORNIA

These few minutes give shape to my week. The straps on my arms and legs mark the boundaries of my body, the leather in my mouth reminds me that I'm alive. When the current comes, it's like meeting God; time disappears, and there is only light radiating from somewhere both inside and outside of me, as if I'm both fully alive and no longer exist. When I'm aware again, they're looking down at me curiously with what I think at first must be expressions of love. Maybe they don't know where we are either. Really, though, I think they're worried they might have killed me this time; it's the same expression my father used to get when he was looking into the engine of the car — a combination of hope that banging this piece of metal or tightening that loose screw might magically make the car run again, and dread that he might have broken it for good this time. After they realize that I'm still in one piece, their expressions change, and as they take me back to the ward they've already forgotten me.

I am, as the woman who admitted me here a month ago said, *not myself.* I haven't seen her since that day, but there was something comforting about her, about the idea that I'd come here to become myself again. Maybe it's a matter of tightening the screws, the loose ones at least. One of the doctors told me that it's like push-starting a car, and I think he's right, except that it's like being started at sixty miles an hour; there's a sudden grinding of gears, and an avalanche of images that pass like scenery, recognized moments outside of time — Sam turning around as he leaves for boot camp, a boy falling, shot in the stomach. These images are projected between me and the people bent over me when I wake up, as if the inside of my mind is visible — that is how they know they haven't yet cured me.

This, then, must be what it means to be beside myself. In this sense it's a lot like sex, the way these unmoored memories are inseparable yet separate from the rest of my life. It's funny that it was sex that brought me here, to the state hospital at Camarillo, where my doctors are helping me re-create that vertiginously distant perspective I thought only sex could bring. Here, they call it helping me.

MARCH 1942: LOS ANGELES, CALIFORNIA

Sam's father was arrested toward the end of January. Sam said that his parents were sitting at the breakfast table when the FBI came. Later, his father wrote that he and some other fishermen had spent the night at San Pedro Jail, that the next morning they had been put on a train. It was a train too old to use for the war effort, so the trip took days and days. The curtains were drawn for the entire trip, and when they stopped, it was between towns and under armed guard. They didn't know until they arrived that they had been headed for North Dakota.

My own memories of that time are a peculiar mixture of a general feeling of confusion and an exact picture of particular moments. Of course, I remember the day the Japanese bombed Pearl Harbor; it was almost time for Christmas vacation, and it was a Sunday. I was sitting in the kitchen eating breakfast when the announcer came on the radio announcing the attack — my mother stood with her back to me at the kitchen sink, and before I heard her say, "Oh," very quietly, I could see that she was stunned. More clearly, though, I remember that one morning early in January I saw our neighbor, Mr. Yamamoto, leaving his house between two white men. Like Sam's father, he was a fisherman, and I later learned that all fishermen were suspected of sabotage and of spying for the enemy. At the time, I couldn't see the pain and confusion in his face; I saw only the dignity, noticed only that he was standing straight, and I even imagined them coming to take me away, my own refusal to break under the kind of torture I imagined them inflicting. Real torture, I realize now, is much quieter than I thought as a romantic fifteen-year-old; the real torture has been accomplished long before they take a man away from the breakfast table or arrest him in a park. Real torture is inflicted by people with kind faces who are concerned about their victims, and I know now that I have no dignity in the face of this, that I would betray anything for them. *Success depends on the subject's desire to change.*

By the middle of March, I had turned sixteen, and my parents had been given three weeks to sell almost all of their possessions. We lived in a three-bedroom house near the store my parents owned in Long Beach, and it seemed that every day there was less room in the house for my sister Mari and me. The store remained immaculate, though it was getting emptier every day — white people had stopped coming sometime in late December, and even other Japanese were buying less. Still, every afternoon, I had to stand by the register, every evening before dinner I had to clean up, and my father looked over everything before he locked up at six, as if there were no reason that the rituals of our life should change at all.

One day, as my father was walking through the aisles of the store, I heard the bell on the door as it opened. John Hudson stood in the doorway, holding a covered dish and looking somewhere around my feet. We had been friends since we were little kids, but I hadn't seen him since before Christmas, when he had started avoiding me. He was about my height, but he was heavier, with light brown hair and faded green eyes, the hint of a mustache looking out of place on his boyish face.

"My mother wanted me to bring this to your mother," he said, indicating the dish with his eyes. "It's a casserole."

"I'll take it to her."

"I'll walk with you," he said, looking up at my father, who had come to the front of the store. I followed John out of the store and we walked side by side down the street without talking. Both of us ignored the dish in his hands — neither of us was old enough to know how to talk to cover our separate embarrassment at the mission his mother had sent him on. He followed me into the house and stood silently while I called to my mother.

"My mom wanted me to give this to you," John said when my mother appeared. He held the casserole out without looking at her.

My mother took the dish from him and put it on the kitchen counter. Even she, who had always talked a lot, seemed to be at a loss for words. She had always been bewildered by Mrs. Hudson's bizarrely well-meaning and inappropriate gestures, but this time she seemed too dazed to hide it. She looked around the kitchen at all the boxes, then back at John. Finally, she picked up a small box that said "tea set" on the side in her small, neat hand. "Here," she said. "Give this to your mother."

"You don't have to do that," John said.

"Don't worry," my mother said, laughing. "It won't fit in my handbag, so we'll have to get rid of it anyway. It belonged to my grandmother, so I'd like someone I like to have it."

John took it and thanked her, but my mother didn't answer — she just looked back and forth between John and me without seeing us, as if she were trying to remember something.

"Come look at my room," I said. John looked at me almost gratefully, then followed me out of the kitchen and down the hallway to my bedroom. My mother had thrown away everything except my schoolbooks and the clothes that fit me — even the walls were bare, and there were boxes from the kitchen stacked against the wall. I sat down on the bed, and he sat next to me, crossing one leg under the other.

"Looks bad, huh?" I said.

"A little," he admitted, then looked for a long time at the boxes against the wall.

"I'm leaving too," he said at last. "I enlisted."

"But you're not . . ."

"I lied," he said. "I'm going to tell my parents tonight. Bobby and Oliver already joined up."

"I wish I could go too," I said, and it was suddenly true, though joining the army was something that hadn't occurred to me before.

"Me too," he said, licking his finger and running it along the side of his shoe. The sole was coming loose on the side, and he worked his finger into the growing hole. "I should have come sooner."

I put my arm around him and squeezed his shoulder. Surprised, he looked at me blankly before he smiled and took my hand in his. He turned his head away from me, but I could see that he was looking at my hand, and I felt the scratch of his thumbnail tracing my fingernails. Suddenly, he threw his weight against me, and we both fell back on the bed. He rolled on top of me, then pinned my arms down with his. There were pale freckles along his cheekbones that I'd never noticed before, and the light caught the blond hair on his cheeks in a way that made his skin seem suddenly fragile. He let go of my arms and started to stand up, but I pulled him toward me and put my arms around him, feeling the line of his backbone and the flex of his muscles as he let himself relax on top of me. When he kissed me, his skin was rough and the stubble on his chin scratched against my face. My tongue found his and traced the back of his teeth, and then he pulled away from me and lay his head on my chest.

The sound of the floorboards in the hallway startled us, and as we were untangling and sitting up, my mother's shape appeared in the doorway. She didn't look surprised — her eyes met mine before she turned to leave.

"Can you stay for dinner, John?" she called from the hallway.

"No thanks," John said, looking at me. A blush spread up from his neck until his entire face was red. "My mom expects me."

"Okay," my mother yelled from the kitchen. "Thank her for me, and don't forget the box for her."

John squeezed my shoulder, picked up the box from the floor and stood up. In the doorway, he turned as if to say something, but then he disappeared. I heard him saying good-bye to my mother, and then I heard the front door shut. I lay there, listening to my mother in the kitchen and to my father's and sister's voices in the living room until my mother called me to dinner. After we ate, my mother took the lid off Mrs. Hudson's casserole and scraped it into the trash. Then she washed and dried the dish.

"Take this back to Mrs. Hudson and thank her," she told my sister, looking at me as she handed Mari the dish. There was no anger in the look she gave me, only a kind of distant, understanding, unforgiving sadness, and it was the only acknowledgment she ever gave of what she had seen.

The curtains on the train, like those on the train Sam's father took to North Dakota, were drawn most of the way to Manzanar, but there were no armed guards that I remember. Here, there are no guards, only nurses and locked doors, and I can look out the window of my room at a tree and a little edge of grass. The delicate octagons of the wire mesh on the inside of the window and the lines of the bars on the outside impose a pattern on the tree and the grass, making them seem two-dimensional, and as it starts to get dark outside, my own reflection appears slowly, suspended against the outside world, until the sunlight fades completely and I see only myself, lit by a single bulb and distorted by the glass and wire.

SEPTEMBER 1949: LOS ANGELES, CALIFORNIA

Looking back from far enough away, I can see that there was a strange kind of beauty about the place. Even then, there were times that I was dissociated from it enough to see it as it would look in a photograph, to follow the straight line of the identical barracks toward the mountains, to find beauty in its stark regularity. At the time, I thought Manzanar was most beautiful at its most bleak, when the light shone on everything straight from above, flatly, and there were no shadows, there was no contrast of any kind, only dirt or snow and straight lines. Still, the physical immediacy of the camp always made a distant vision impossible to sustain; up close, the cheap wood of the barracks was already weathering, and I can still taste the dust that covered everything as the wind blew it through the cracks of the buildings and under the doors. Now I am left only with this distant vision; it is the visceral sense of the time that I can't recapture. I remember lying in bed, listing the men I'd seen naked, and while I can still bring the pictures of these men to mind, I can't recapture the sense of longing and hopeless possibility they carried with them then. Desire is strongest when it works like an immediate memory, when bodies become topographical, untouchably everpresent, like the mountains that framed the camp. At the time, following the line of a man's spine down his back or the line of his neck as it disappeared into his shirt seemed a kind of sacred secret; each body I desired had a kind of photographic immediacy, uncomplicated by the desires and sorrows I now know each hides.

The problem, after all, is that nothing is unbearable; everything comes, inevitably, into perspective. When I remember Manzanar, I realize that it wasn't all that bad — I never had to worry about making myself dinner, and there was something comforting about the predictable order of my life at the time. I also realize that part of me likes where I am now, in Camarillo. Here, there is an order imposed on my life that I could never attain alone. Every detail has been thought through; there is no variation in the schedule, no color on the walls that might make us anxious. People are arranged like the barracks at Manzanar, in a long, unvarying straight line, and if there is no room for individual desires, neither is there room for individual sorrows.

The bar was unmarked, but everyone knew where it was — it had a kind of ostentatious anonymity about it, like a speakeasy during Prohibition. I suppose people walked by outside all night without knowing who was inside, but I can't remember a time when I didn't know where it was. Certainly, the police knew about it. It was plain on the inside, long and narrow, with cheap wooden tables and a bar, so it's hard to convey the sense of possibility that it held for me at the time. I went almost every Saturday night, and I was always nervous on the way there; looking at it from the outside, where the world seemed inescapable, meeting another man seemed both inevitable and impossible to imagine, the place itself almost unreal. Once inside, it was the outside world that seemed unreal, and if sex was anything but guaranteed, the possibility of it presented itself in the form of real men — men who, like me, liked men. Inside, there was the possibility of a separate world and, irrationally, I always felt safe, giddy with a childish sense of belonging.

Often, while I waited to see if my friend Chuck would come, I would sit at the bar, watching the negotiations between men out of the corner of my eye or in the mirror behind the bartender. I always arrived early in the evening, so I had time to watch the bar fill up, and at first I wondered if I looked odd, sitting at the bar and staring at people. Soon, though, I noticed something I've noticed at every bar like this one that I've been in since: men look a lot more than they talk, and stares that would seem intrusive in the rest of the world aren't meant to be rude. My own stares, then, were only part of the landscape.

"Seamen for sale," Chuck said, sitting down next to me and indicating a pair of sailors drinking at the other end of the bar. "You want to pool our resources on the smaller one?"

"Why buy the milk when you have the cow at home?"

"Is that a yes or a no?" he said.

"No," I said, "but you go ahead."

"Oh, I couldn't bear to leave you here alone."

I shrugged.

"So that's settled," Chuck said, signaling the bartender for a beer and pretending to pout. "Another night sitting at the bar until they kick us out."

"If you want to buy a social life, I won't stop you."

"You know," said Chuck, "the first Holy Virgin had to have Jesus before she got to be so self-righteous."

"The baby she had to bear was a lot smaller," I said.

"It's not that I want it," Chuck said. "It's just that it's for sale."

"I know," I said. "It's not that I don't; it's just that it's for sale."

Chuck sighed, took a long sip of his beer. "Have you ever been to Sacramento?"

"No," I said.

"I thought Los Angeles was hell, but at least you can drive to the ocean. Up there, it's hotter, and there's nothing but flat."

"Any boys?" I said.

"Not really," he said. "Everyone in the whole Central Valley is ugly."

"People everywhere are ugly," I said. "And just because they didn't buy your brushes doesn't mean they're ugly."

"It's not brushes," Chuck said, then looked over my shoulder. I followed his gaze to a man I'd never seen before, who stood at the entrance, framed by the door. "God. A man like that makes it worth it to just sit here looking."

Chuck was right — the man was beautiful, the kind of man whose face can't be remembered exactly. His eyes were green and his hair was light and straight, and I remember the shock of seeing his expressive eyes, the realization that the relation between a man's eye and the curve of his eyebrow could be perfected to the point that it was no longer merely beautiful, became abstract. He walked down to the other end of the bar, ordered a drink, and struck up a conversation with the sailors. I wondered if his beauty affected them as viscerally as it affected me, or if he would have to pay like everyone else. The man had an easy manner — he signaled the bartender and bought the other men drinks, and his smile seemed genuine as he talked to them.

"If you were going to change your mind," Chuck said, "it's too late."

"It's just as well," I said. "Now we get to talk to each other a little more."

"Sure," he said. "Seal the bond of friendship."

"It really does mean a lot to me to just sit here talking to you," I said.

"Aren't you the sweetest." He stood and walked toward the bathrooms at the back of the bar, turning to look at the sailors and the man as he passed them. The man smiled, turned back to the sailors and laughed at a joke one of them told. I'd seen a lot of men paying sailors to go to the alley next to the bar, but I'd never seen a deal look so civilized. It was as if they were making friends. Soon, though, they were standing, still laughing and smiling. The man threw a bill on the bar, and he and the shorter sailor walked out together. The taller one followed a few paces behind, but he didn't seem to be listening to their conversation, and I realized that he'd been quiet most of the night, that the conversation had been between the two who were leaving together. As he walked by, he gave me an indifferent look, then looked past his friends at the door and followed them outside into the night.

"Oh, to be those sailors," I said as Chuck sat down.

"I don't know," said Chuck. "That kind of man has always seemed a disappointment to me."

"We could follow them to find out," I said, and Chuck laughed. "Really—I want to go to the alley and see what's going on."

"Are you out of your mind?"

"I just want to see him again to see if he's really human."

"Lee," he said. "Some things a man's got to do alone."

"Like what?" I said. "A sword fight? Going to hunt the bear?"

"Give him some respect," Chuck said. "How would you feel if people took advantage of you that way? There are certain rules."

"Still," I said, standing up. "I'm going to go leer."

He didn't look up. "Send me a postcard."

As I walked out of the bar, I heard loud voices from the alley, and as I started toward them, the sailors turned the corner and walked toward me. The taller one didn't look at me, but the shorter one met my eyes without seeing me, as if he were thinking about something else. As he passed, he seemed for an instant to recognize me from the bar, but he looked away quickly. Later, I would think his look was one of remorse, but then it was too quick to communicate anything. I rounded the corner and saw the man from the bar lying on the ground, his head propped up by the wall of the building and his arm in the air, as if he'd fallen asleep hailing a taxi and had slid down the wall. Only when I got closer did I see that his arm was bent the wrong way at the shoulder and the elbow, that his beautiful face had been smashed in on one side, and that he was dead.

I reached down and stroked the cheek that wasn't bloodied, but my hand caught the tip of his nose, which had been broken and swam loosely under the skin of his face. My hand flew away reflexively, but I forced it back, then sat down next to him in the alley and pulled his head into my lap. I stroked his hair — his head had soft spots all over the back of it, like a baby's, and his hair was soft, except where it was matted and sticky with blood. Sitting there next to him, with his head in my lap and his eyes staring mindlessly into mine, it was as if he were my lover and I was soothing him after a nightmare. Even then, though, I realized that I was as far from understanding what had happened as I had been when Sam died, that even holding a man I had loved in my arms yielded nothing, revealed nothing, left this man's experience as unimaginable as it had been when he came into the bar.

Chuck appeared above us in the alley.

"I was holding him," I said. Underneath the smell of blood and sweat was the pungent and musky smell of the man's after-shave. I drew him closer and put my arm across his chest, which was still warm.

"What have you done?" Chuck said, backing away and staring at me and the man.

"I found him like this," I said, and I watched as Chuck saw what had happened.

"Jesus. We need to get out of here."

"Shouldn't we call someone?"

"Do you want to explain what was going on and what you were doing here?"

"No."

"Leave him. Someone will find him in the morning."

"Just let me stay here a while longer," I said, but Chuck grabbed my arm and made me stand up, then threw my arm over his shoulder and walked me toward the street where his car was parked. Without saying anything, he helped me into the car and drove me home. Neither of us spoke as he drove, helped me into my apartment, undressed me, and put me to bed.

"Chuck," I said as he turned to leave. He stopped in the doorway and looked back at me. "Don't leave me."

He sat down on the edge of my bed with his back to me, and I reached up and stroked the back of his head. He sighed and turned toward me, then leaned down and kissed me.

"Are you sure you want this?" He looked at me sadly, straight in the eyes.

"Yes." He turned away from me, took off his shirt, shoes, and pants, and slid into bed with me. He kissed me again, slowly at first but then more and more insistently, until gradually I felt feeling come back into my body, and I held him more tightly than I'd ever held the men I'd gone to bed with before. I kissed him back, and we made love quietly. Later, I would cry for Sam, whose death I had not seen or been able to imagine, for a man I didn't know who was beaten to death outside a bar, and for Chuck and me, stranded and uncomprehending in a world where things like this happened every night, but that night, I was strangely happy. Already, I could feel the moment beginning to crystallize: I was still young, the world outside was terrible but far away, and I could feel myself, already, beginning again to hope.

Karl Woelz

PORT KANSAS

IN THE EVENINGS, now, you can see fireflies, the shimmery green-gold globes of their bodies blinking and darting in the twilight-purpled air, magic tricks like the flashes of light in front of your eyes when you get up too quickly. They glow, here then there, dipping and sailing into the night always a few feet ahead of you. I like to walk at this time of day, beneath trees leafy and full with the sound of cicadas, the heat beginning to soften as the heaviness of bright air loses its weight and the sky bruises into violet, deepening until it becomes the rich, deep blue that is nighttime in summer.

When the evening breeze is weak, as it often is, and I know the air of the house will be close and still, wrapping around me like a child trying to avoid bedtime, I sit on the front porch and eat chilled cantaloupe. I hold the halved globe in one hand, its patterned skin surprisingly smooth against my palm, cutting and scooping the flesh with a spoon as I watch the young boys drive by in their newly washed cars, tanned forearms resting against indifferent metal, their music rolling up from the street, guitars and drums drifting over my head, the sounds losing shape and color as they float through the darkening sky. Sometimes I think about where they're headed, to bars or parties or the sagging, dirt-stained living-room sofas of friends; about the jauntiness of their bodies, of the expectations and possibilities of the flesh.

I'm making myself sound old, which I'm not, but you find yourself thinking like this when you sit on the front porch, eating fruit, waiting for the cool of nighttime to settle on your shoulders with the assurance that another day is over.

When Robert's home I don't sit on the front porch, eating fruit. We sit inside, reading or watching television or talking in that way people do when they've lived in each other's company for a long time. Or we work, each in our respective places; me in my study, Robert at the dining-room table. We are comfortable or mundane, depending on how you look at it. Depending on your perspective.

But Robert's not at home in the evenings much these days, traveling as he does, so I take my walks and listen to the humming in the trees. Eat my melon. Watch the boys drive by. Listen to their unfamiliar music. And I feel, more often than I like to, the substance of the air as it presses down on me, waiting.

I grew up on the Gulf Coast of Florida in a sleepy seaside town the tourists drove past, or occasionally through, by mistake, on their way to more exotic locales. I remember my childhood as shoeless, the soles of my feet, and those of my elder brothers, toughened by sand and rock and asphalt. We must have worn shoes to school and church and other such places, but I don't remember those times; only the hazy whiteness of days at the beach, the air a presence we moved through, and my lips traced always with the taste of salt.

*   *   *

Robert is never still. Even at rest, his body seems always to be moving; fingers drumming on a tabletop or thigh, leg swaying lazily back and forth in time to unheard music, head bobbing slightly with the intensity of thought. And when he moves — reaching for a pillow on the couch, walking to the refrigerator, climbing the stairs to bed — it's as if space makes way for him, all those atoms moving out of his path. And there he is, oblivious to the energy he creates, the air he displaces; comfortable wherever he finds himself.

The question, if there is only one — though I suspect that, really, it's a whole litter of questions crying blindly for the teat, groping for the sugary wetness that will make the sour feeling in the pit of the belly disappear — the one question, I guess, is *what am I doing here?* In both senses, large and small, though the latter is infinitely more horrifying. Is it God or Fate or your own ridiculous fumbling about, one long chain of half-assed choices that leads you to this point, this place, this wondering?

I don't know he's there until he knocks on the frame of the open door, saying my name, a question.

"Sorry," he says. "I didn't mean to surprise you. I thought you heard the outer door open."

"That's all right," I say, pointing to the chair beside the desk of my office mate. "Come in. Have a seat."

"I don't want to bother you. I can come back."

"No, not at all. That's fine," I say, swiveling my chair to face him. "Sit down. Do you have time?"

"Sure," he says, sitting, the legs of his shorts opening wide, allowing me a glimpse of his tanned upper thighs. "I just wanted to come by and tell you how much I liked the book."

"Even though you said it was rough going at first?"

He smiles. "Yeah. It's like I said in class," he says, raising his right leg up so that the foot rests on the edge of the seat, the shift of his body causing the white lining of his nylon shorts to slide into view against his left thigh with the excruciating heaviness of impossibility. I take all of this in in a split second, careful to keep my eyes on his face. "If I'd picked it up on my own I probably never would have gotten through it."

"You would have given up after the first thirty pages."

He smiles again. "Yeah, probably. But I'm glad you made us read it. I mean, I don't know." He looks down at his shoes. "It's pretty amazing."

"Faulkner often has that effect on people. That's how I felt when I first read it. When I was about your age."

He looks up at me with those yellow-brown eyes, like he does in class, every day, in the front row, just feet away from me with those lips that look softer than down pillows and the smile that plays always at the corner of his mouth.

"I'd like to do more," he says.

Am I imagining the subtle, barely perceptible shift of his hips forward? I look down, briefly, taking in again the fullness of that flimsy nylon lining.

"I'd like to read more. Can you recommend something?"

I smile. "Sure," I say, turning away from him to reach for the books, sentinel spines at attention, lined up neatly on my desk. "Try this one," I say, handing it to him.

"Oh," he says, surprised. "Thank you." He holds the book low between his thighs, having to know that we are both looking there, at the yellow-edged pages as he flips through it, at fingers and paper and crotch. "I didn't mean for you to give me your own copy. I could've gone to the library."

I smile again. "Books are to be shared. Just try to ignore my scribbling in the margins."

He smiles, too, eyes sparkling. "It'll be cool to see what you were thinking when you were reading."

"Don't believe everything you read," I say. He laughs. "I've changed my mind about things a couple hundred times since then. You're probably better off ignoring me."

"Thanks again," he says, returning his right foot to the floor. "I'll let you know what I think after I'm done."

"Great," I say. "We can get together and talk about it. See if you're still a fan after *two* novels. Just don't get behind in your reading for class."

He smiles. "I won't. Promise."

I'm standing in the kitchen, slicing bell peppers for our salad, when he gets home.

"How was class today?" he asks.

"Fine," I say, smelling the trace of his cologne before I feel him behind me. He wraps his arms around my waist, pulling me against him, and kisses the back of my neck.

"They had a heated argument about Margot Macomber's guilt. You smell nice."

"Thank you," he mumbles into my neck. "You're on Hemingway already?"

"Started yesterday. How was your meeting?"

"Boring," he says, removing the knife from my hand, placing it on the cutting board, and turning me around to face him. He puts his left hand on the back of my neck and pulls my face to his, kissing me, opening my mouth with his tongue.

"You taste good," he says, opening his eyes to look into mine.

"Cantaloupe," I say, pulling my head back slightly so that I don't go cross-eyed.

"I missed you," he says, fingers rustling through the hair at the base of my neck.

"You were only gone three days."

"I missed you all the same." He leans in again and my mouth opens, feeling him inside me. He leans his weight against me, the tongue more insistent now, and I know that dinner will be late.

Afterward, I lie on sheets damp with our sweat, listening to the water of the shower as it sweeps over his body, glancing off tile and plastic before splashing on the floor of the tub in quick, slick thuds. The lettuce will be wilted, lifeless. I want to stay here, sleep. The thought of standing in the kitchen makes me leaden; I can feel my back sinking into the mattress, my spine expanding like one of those werewolf horror movies, splitting through skin, all ivory and blood and gristle and ear-splitting cracks until I am nothing but a sticky, ghoulish hunk of bone.

Robert moved here because he's afraid. Because he believes in the possibility of escape. That's what he's paid for, after all. Finding escape routes. Saving the sinking ship. Bring Robert in when the hurricane winds are howling, when the bow can't be seen. He'll roll up his sleeves. He'll put on his glasses — those so-smart frames that make his nose look even sharper, bring out the hardness of his jaw — and he'll sit down with miles and miles of printouts, and he'll look and look and look again until he finds an answer. And all the while the little pigs he works for are standing discreetly behind him, wringing their hands, listening to the huffing and the puffing outside, softly chanting "Robert, Robert, Robert" under their breath, waiting for him to put down his pen and take off his glasses and tell them what they want to hear.

And he does, always, which is why he's in such demand. And then the little pigs sigh with relief and pat each other on the back and look at Robert as if he's turned the water into wine, which he has, and they cut him a nice big check while some other husband or mother or best friend or daughter is flung out into the weightless, heaving darkness of the firmament.

Downsizing. It sounds like some kind of overly vigorous exercise regimen. Obese women in shapeless, flowered-print housedresses, necklines drenched in sweat, squatting and lunging and stretching to a relentless disco beat; a perverse, fast-forward motion that melts the flesh from their bones. A wasting syndrome, of sorts. *Trimming the fat,* Robert likes to say. But what happens to all that skin?

When it's done — when the fat's been trimmed — Robert comes home and takes me out to dinner and we talk about repainting the kitchen or switching dry cleaners or where we might "get away" to some weekend when our schedules will allow it. And when we come together later, in bed, I look over his shoulder, through the window, out at the night sky, and I see the constellations of men and women that Robert's pen lets go, their bright, silent pain twinkling in that cold, soulless black.

As Robert sees things, there's always a way out. Which is why we're here in the middle of the middle of America. We left the past, the City, because it had become too much. Too much pressing down — terror, grief, regret — and Robert's three personal little pigs chanting "Go, go, go" as the huffing and the puffing grew louder at the door, throaty and relentless; one more breath all it would take to send the bricks hurtling out into space.

Robert put on his glasses and uncapped his pen and made up a list. And another. And another after that. Columns of the dead, of facts, of figures. This is why we must go — first person plural — *this is why.* With the passage of time two become one, intertwined, I becoming we becoming I again. Speaking as we, which is I. *We must go.* But *this I* didn't want to go. Did not. There was too much to do, to be done, to help. I didn't want to go, to leave, to escape — because there is no escaping, a fact of which Robert, and not all that deep down, is more than aware — but I did. He didn't say *If you love me . . .* Dot. Dot. Dot. He didn't have to. First person plural. I left. And for that I am guilty; can and should and must be held accountable.

I don't know if they're sunflowers or just enormous, mutant daisies. I suspect the former, considering geography and all, but I know nothing of plant life. Do they sprout just anywhere? The bush, growing wild in the alley behind the house, is enormous — obscene, almost — its battalion of yellow-crowned crimson-faced flowers either flapping whorishly in the breeze or standing imperiously at attention, stiff and bold beneath the flat blue sky.

Because he grew up here, I ask the boy, Thomas, about sunflowers when he returns to my office.

"Yeah, they grow wild. But if you want to see really big ones you have to go out of town. Out Fifty-nine or down Seventy a ways."

And what about Faulkner, I ask, bringing us back to the reason for his visit.

He smiles, shakes his head. "This one's pretty rough going. I mean, I like it — or I think I kind of do — if that makes any sense. But sometimes you just want to throw it down and say enough. You know?"

"Yes," I say, nodding. Smiling. Encouraging.

"I like the whole idea of people telling the same story over and over again. Or trying to. Trying to understand what the truth of it all is by piecing together these overlapping fragments of the story they know — am I making sense?"

"I think you're describing the experience of the novel perfectly."

At this he unleashes an enormous smile. "I mean, *that's* really fascinating. All these people trying to explain the truth of this story, but their perspectives keep getting in the way so that there never really *is* any kind of truth — not with a capital T. Just all these *versions* of it."

*   *   *

The shoeless days of my childhood. So many shades of blue. Skin like cinnamon. Hair bleached to flax by the sun. Lips dusted with salt. We were adventurers, my brothers and I, always scrambling over dunes and sifting through sand, searching for treasure. Under our beds, in discarded shoe boxes, we stored our finds: collections of sand dollars, metal bottle tops, forgotten sunglasses, lost bracelets and rings.

It was a clock radio — abandoned, broken, probably flung from a car window in disgust — that caught my brother's attention. Sun bouncing off cracked plastic. He was crouched over it when the car with the Pennsylvania license plates swerved to miss a possum, sliding for no more than a second or two onto the sandy shoulder, the noise only a high smack — the snapping of his neck, no doubt — nothing out of the ordinary. And then the screech of brakes, making me turn around, seeing first the orange-yellow plate below the bug-splattered grille, KEYSTONE STATE in small navy capitals, before thinking *That's where he was,* looking past the marlin-blue tail of the car to the motionless heap lying in the weed-choked sand, a cloud of dust unveiling the familiar cutoffs, caramel skin, a smear of red where there should have been yellow hair.

After my brother's death we moved away, up north, far from the coast, to a large blank state which could accommodate our mother's despair.

I watch the fireflies float through the twilight air as I walk, listening to the sound of my heels on the dull red brick of the sidewalk. The trees, heavy and drooping, hum around me. It's like a movie, this place. Credits should be rolling. *A Night in the Heartland.* Teenage couples whisper on front porches while June bugs beat against dim yellow lights above screen doors. Inside, mothers clear tables and wash dishes while children play in front of droning televisions.

Downstairs, beneath ground, fathers sharpen knives and oil guns in the hushed cool of basements. Alien spaceships hover over the fields, taking prisoners in blinding shafts of light, whisking them away to prod and poke and probe. Pod people peel their skin in the privacy of dimly lit bathrooms. The walking dead rap at windows, hungry for warm flesh. Lovers abandon one another.

Young women in pairs power-walk purposefully, ponytails bouncing, skulls braided with headphones, each in her own world. Shirtless boys jog past me, the front of their shorts dark with sweat, their breathing harsh and tight. Dogs sniff at patches of grass, owners lagging far behind, the ends of their cigarettes glowing orange in the darkening sky.

Violet hour. Twilight man. Where you'll find me. What I've become.

A postcard comes from the City: *Martin died a week Tuesday. Tasteful service at Riverside M — flowers out the ass. Jerry's back in St. V's — lymphoma gone mad. I've taken the infernal Lucrezia in so he won't worry — and of course she's in heat, so I've got the vapors 24/7. Fucking pets! Still at the clinic. Everyone sends regards. Jane says WRITE! You missed Fab party at the Saint — it travels now, don'tcha know? (ho's on wheels! says Peter. Bitter, bitter man.) Fell in love thrice before the first Madonna remix. Something in the water these days . . . And the Heartland? Beware the Great Pumpkin! Not much else here. All the same. Neighborhood desolate without you. Or just me? Miss morning kaffee klatsch. Love —*

Martin gone. A man who could dance all night, lost in the communion of souls, the music of the spheres. Another figure for Robert's columns.

Thomas offers me a ride home. It's too hot to walk, he says. *Century days,* the weatherman calls them.

"Summer in Kansas," he says, shaking his head, hand and foot moving thoughtlessly in concert as he downshifts. "It'll probably snow tomorrow. You never know around here."

"It's hot, yes," I say, looking out the window as we descend the first hill, gliding away from campus.

"Where did you move here from?" he asks.

"New York."

"City?"

"Yes."

"Wow, that must be great."

"Living there or leaving?"

He laughs. "Definitely *living*. This must be a big change of pace for you."

"I'm adjusting."

"I have a cousin who lives out there, and I keep meaning to go visit, but it never seems to happen."

"You should go. You'd like it, I'm sure."

"Oh, totally. There must be so much to do there."

"Twenty-four hours a day."

"You must find it — here, I mean — awfully . . ."

He's looking over at me, a hint of red in his cheeks. "Awfully?" I prod.

He shrugs, offering me a sheepish smile. *"Stifling,* I would think."

I return the smile, then look straight ahead through the windshield. "That's one way of putting it."

He downshifts again, the knuckles of his right hand grazing my left knee.

When he pulls up in front of the house I thank him for the ride, ask him if he wants to come in for a soda or a beer. And when he says yes I see it all spread out in front of me: Fingers touching briefly as I hand him the bottle; the color, barely perceptible, coming to his face; a shifting beneath the fabric of those shorts. Holding his eye for a moment too long before brushing past him into the living room. Close on the couch, showing him the books on the coffee table, fingers meeting again. The eyes. The sound of his swallow. Leaning over, so slowly, seeing the movement of his cock, his desire palpable. My lips brushing against his cheek, and then mouth, the weight of him sinking into the couch, the thud of his heart, the palm of my hand against his bicep. Eyes closed as a new world lurches on its axis.

"You don't live here alone, do you?" he asks, brushing hair from his dampened forehead.

"No," I reply, the taste of him still warm on my tongue. "I don't."

"So what does that mean?"

"Mean?" I ask, running my hand along his tanned thigh, its muscles at rest, slack. The skin, traced with golden hair, is moist, hot.

He doesn't say anything. There are too many things he might be thinking. My fingertips glide slowly back and forth over tanned flesh. His cock begins to stir, an answer of sorts.

"Think of it," I say as his hips roll toward me, "as an overlapping narrative. One among several competing versions of the truth."

Robert holds me in the night. Constant. Anchor. House of brick.

In the dream, I move slowly, inching out from beneath the weight of his arm to the edge of the mattress. I keep my eyes on the neon green numbers of the clock. Minutes pass. I listen to the wavelike motion of his breathing. In the dark, I move from bedroom to bathroom to kitchen, quietly collecting clothes, keys, wallet, shoes. The car is parked in the driveway rather than the garage. On the floor of the backseat is a bundle of newspapers and a can of lighter fluid.

I go out Fifty-nine, passing only a few trucks as I speed out of town. It takes about thirty minutes, as Thomas said it would, until I see the field on my left. The stalks stand silvered in the moonlight, the crowns atop them bowed as if with weariness, swaying lazily in the steady breeze from the south. Everything is blue-gray, all color drained under the reflected light of the moon.

After spreading most of the dampened newspaper in a jagged line at the far end of the field, I make my way through the plants that tower above me. They are thicker, rougher than I imagined, a forest of hairy giants that may once have been ordered rows, but are now a tangled mass of rustling limbs that brush across my face and scrape against the diminished bundle I carry under one arm. Once past what feels like the center of the field, I make a small clearing for myself and sit down. I set the remaining papers and the almost empty can of lighter fluid in front of me. The wind has picked up, rustling the stalks around me so that I can't hear the sound, if there is to be such, of crackling paper.

There's nothing to see yet. I sit, watching the swaying wall of flowers in front of me, searching for flickers of light. The smell of earth is strong and bitter, the dankness of dirt and bugs and stalks heavy in my nostrils. I breathe through my mouth. I can feel the soil, cold and damp against the seat of my jeans. Minutes pass. I see Robert, adrift in the ocean of our bed, asleep on the bright aqua sheets I pulled from the linen closet after Thomas slipped back into his shorts and stepped out into a world upon which the sun shone differently, tilted at a new angle.

It's while I'm looking up at the hazy white ring encircling the moon that a flash of color catches the corner of my eye. I turn my head toward it and see, there through the breathing wall of stalks, tongues of flame licking their way toward me across the field. It caught, I think, relieved, my heart catching for just a moment before it starts to pump faster.

Since the wind is not that strong, the flames move steadily but not quickly, crackling like heavy-booted feet on dry leaves. I look again to the moon, its blank white face now partly obscured by a thick black cloud edging slowly across the sky. Stars look down silently from millions of miles away.

Here I sit in the heart of a field, black of night, in the middle of the middle of America, waiting.

I close my eyes, see sun and sand and three little boys scrambling over dunes to the sea, so far away now. The streets of the City emptied of too many hearts once treasured. Faces. Bodies. The melon-green glow of fireflies at twilight.

The crackling is louder now. Flames sweep up stalks, coloring the night green and yellow and orange. Swirls of gray smoke lift heavenward. The air grows warmer as the wall of dancing flowers before me succumbs to the heat, glowing fast on its path toward me.

Robert's gone, away on business. I sit on the porch, in shorts and a T-shirt, looking up at constellations whose names I do not know. Points of light, of reference, so far away that the very idea of distance becomes unthinkable. A breeze, soft as a child's breathing in sleep, tousles hair against my forehead. I think of others, for there must be others like me, scattered across the Republic, looking heavenward, a silent brotherhood, each connected to each beneath this canopy of unknown stars, listening for the music of the spheres. Each alone, waiting.

Night in the heartland. What I've become. Where you'll find me.

D. Travers Scott

TRUNCATED OFFRAMP

THE BOY'S COCK rose from his crotch into the shower spray like a fleshy forearm laced with thick veins, a junkie arm fix-searching — only terminating in a blood-engorged stump where the open hand should be.

He leaned against the partition, thrusting waist into water, closing thick-lashed eyes. Water collected in blond bush, ran down his dick and fell from knobby head in a dribbling rope.

The man showering across from him punched his soap dispenser five times, filling his palm with banana-scented liquid. The thumping of the plunger echoed among the blue tiles, marring the near-empty showers' hushed rainfall.

Kid works, Jim thought. Always up to kick it. He lathered up his shaft with fruity slime.

He glanced at his own crotch and saw distinct camps of warring contrasts: dark abdominal plains surrendering to a moat of white lather, from which arose triumphantly the brown cock. Only its dark skin was a Trojan horse. Jim stroked his fire and the foreskin pulled back to reveal light hues hiding inside as the purpley-pink cockhead emerged.

Jim faced the boy, hot splatters against his back. The steaming drops swept away sweat's secreted poisons. Joules of gorgeous force exerted to draw out fatback and Black Rabbit Porter in a saline sheen washed away.

The boy turned to Jim, pulled his dick, jaw slack. He circled his thumb and index finger around the base of his shaft — sort of an OK handshape — and squeezed while pushing his balls back. It made his dick look bigger.

Fierce joint, Jim thought. And since he's deaf he never gets in your face with that chatty shit at your locker. Dig it.

Jim pinched his right tit, pulled earthy brown flesh out from his heart. He lowered his eyelids and jaw like Joey Dempsey: *Advocate Men,* vol. 3, no. 2, Nov. 86, p. 76.

The boy's face contorted into an "oh, yeah" grimace as he dispensed white globs onto ceramic squares. His eyes eased open. He grinned sheepishly and kicked come with the side of his foot as if soccer dribbling. The globs sloshed into their gushing water goal at the shower's back wall, whisked out of sight by a babbling brook's ballad into their rusty iron-grate gaol.

He grabbed his silvery trunks and punched off the water. Offering Jim a tentative smile, he flicked two extended fingers away from underneath his right eye.

Jim peered around the partition. The kid headed toward the lockers, trunks in a Safeway produce bag. No one in the dry sauna except a couple of anxious young Asian guys. He sighed, stuck his head under the flow.

He decided against getting off. Save his spunk for the final catch. He switched to cold and rinsed, dick wilting. He leaned against the partition, killing seconds on his waterproof watch till the kid was probably gone.

Jim chucked his gym bag into the old Buick Regal. The workout cast him in relaxed confidence, outweighing the frustration of his incomplete deaf-kid cruise. The evening air tingled residual alcohol on his cheeks. He cocked his ear and followed a ruckus of cheers and grinding noises.

SKATE EXPO, read the banner hung from postmodern faux-relic columns across the brick plaza. Pioneer Courthouse Square was the heart of Portland and Jim loved its packs of punks, street kids and shirtless hacky-sackers. The cruising cockhound inside him regularly found excellent rubbernecking. The frustrated architect, however, always inserted irked notes re. the Square's design: chopped-up multiple stair landings, disintegrating columns, segmented waterfall — nothing solid, continuous or steady. The wide, elliptical center was shattered by overlapping brickwork designs. Even the smooth plane of each brickface was marred by donor names.

Anyhow, he thought, the name's fucked. Ought to be Pioneer Courthouse *Plaza* or *Circle*. Sure enough ain't square.

Joey Dempsey muzzled Mike Brady as Jim situated himself atop the central stairway. He felt saliva in his mouth. He surveyed the rollerbladers and skateboarders going aerial on the big central ramp. Cops leaned against bug-eyed ALIEN WORKSHOP signs. Dirty rat-children hung. Circles of skatekids tested equipment, some decked in helmets and pads.

Clueless and carefree, Jim mused. Zooming on hormones and emotions. Wicked highs and nightmare lows. Shit, so luscious and so alone. If only it wasn't such a risky trip — I could give one such groovy loving. The touches, the words, the stories no one ever told me.

At the foot of the steps he noticed a lithe mixed-race kid with droopy eyelids and wild dreads, bouncing honey-brown cords. He was trying out some new skateboard: a duo of wheeled boards, each just under a foot or so square, connected by some sort of metal axle in such a way that they moved and twisted independently. The svelte dude zigged and zagged like an iceskating sidewinder, lots of hips and waist twisting opposite his sinewy trunk. He wore nothing but green suede tennis shoes and enormous corduroy cutoffs, well hung below plaid boxers. Jim visualized a downward spiral of tight, dark curls. He swayed and undulated, skin and nipples shimmering in sunset, ridges of wiry ribs and abdominals.

The boy hopped off the board. He scanned the crowd on the steps. He scowled intently at Jim. Jim sprang to attention and leaned back to advertise his basket. Work.

The boy squinted. He pushed the board with his foot toward another ratty guy, who slid him a regular board in return. The dreadlocked boy smiled and kicked his board up into his hands. He tossed Jim another glance and pushed through the crowd to the double doors beneath the waterfall.

Jim's heart jumped. The public restrooms were in there: underneath Starbucks, adjoining the Tri-Met office.

The boy paused in the doorway, holding open the glass door with his foot. He looked over his shoulder. Jim stood up. The boy walked inside. Jim followed, lips flattened firmly together in a smile.

Jim leaned back from the urinal. He shook off the final drops again. The boy's stream tapered. Jim thought fast.

"Gnarly board, cuz."

The boy pulled up his waistband. He shot a wad of spit to chase down his draining piss. He locked eyes with Jim.

"Jesus," he muttered and grabbed his board.

*   *   *

Jesús nodded his head as the glass door swung closed behind him.

"Parole!" he shouted.

He hopped on his board and wove through the crowd toward the curving ramp's end, his friend racing along above and beside him, dirty blond bangs flying behind as he steadily curved down lower and closer. Jesús flashed on crashing right into Parole, his brown shoulder crushing into his friend's freckled cheek.

Parole whipped past him, dismounted and ran back over. Jesús swung out wide at the lip and turned around, hopping off his board and kickflipping it into his hands. "Qué pasa? Fuck you go?" Jesús asked.

"I done saw Spit over there'bouts, spare-changing, so's I went on over to go badger him about Andrea. Course he was such complete M'sieu la Toast it was for shit. You'd done gone once I got back here."

"Pissing." He rolled his eyes. "Fiesta del Troll."

"Ugh. You go on and send him over to Spit?"

"Spit at him."

They laughed.

"Forgot Spanish for come-guzzler."

"Can't say's I believe that. Ask one of your sisters, then."

Jesús nodded. "One of those three'd know."

The boys looked past each other to scan the crowd, thinning as the sun set. Mothers and sisters appeared, dragging plastic bags behind them as they collected the day's litter and refuse.

"Vamoose?"

"Yeah now. We going on to Burnside?" Parole asked.

"Take you somewhere else."

"*What* somewhere else, now? Some other park?"

Jesús nodded, biting his lip. "Chill park. No, fucked but chill." He grinned mischievously. "Trust me, cherito."

Parole's face warmed. "Go on, amigo. M'sieu le Surprise."

*   *   *

At the apex of the bridge, Jesús and Parole hopped off their boards with rolled eyes to let a tandem-cycling couple pass.

"So how'd you find that snakeboard?"

"Sucks. Guy did these nifty spins, jumps. I tried. Easier than ollying 'cause your feet're attached. But that's it. They got teams, videos, all that shit, but it seems like a kids' toy."

"Vraiment? Well, seeing as how I can't rightly turn a proper olly in the first place, it's no grand fuck pour moi. You see now, I got on all into skating real big-time back down in middle school, but then the fellas I skated with all got themselves in some spot of trouble and scat to New Iberia. I just went on gave it up till about before I met you. Feel now like some grande flake trying to go about learning all this shit again. Complete Monsieur la Loser."

"Don't worry. I quit four years, nada. Started again five months ago. Took forever to get used to thin boards. Used to fatties. Comes back. Don't be so sorry on yourself!"

Parole flushed red and looked down at the water below him to hide his stupid grin.

"Stop *talking*. Bust up in front of everyone, that's skating. Just skate."

"The best thing, though, you know what?" Parole said, looking up at Jesús. "It's when I get myself up in the air-abouts, even for just now like a tiny little second. But then I get all worrying about coming down. I'm thinking thinking thinking so much it gets all like every little thing's so fast yet so slow."

"One day you just do it; you'll see."

"Think so, you know?"

"Def." Jesús' gaze shot out upriver. "Mira! Lower deck on the Steel Bridge's down."

Jesús leaned against the Burnside Bridge's spoke-pattern metal rail and pointed at the Steel: wide rectangles crossing the river with two heavy vertical lifts spiring upward midway.

"Only telescoping vertical lift in the world."

"What now?"

"See how there's the upper deck that cars, MAX and shit go on? Below's lower deck for trains. Usually that big chunk's missing from the bottom for boats. Steel trusses slide into the upper deck like a telescope. Can keep it raised for boats without raising the upper deck and stopping cars and MAX. Never been duplicated. Fucker's built in 1912."

Jesús pointed as boxcars crept across the river, suspended on the Steel Bridge's lower deck.

"Up most all time. Hardly ever get to see it lowered."

"M'sieu le Bridgemeister in the house!" Parole smirked.

"Gonna take you higher, vraiment, sir." Jesús smiled. "Did Portland Bridges for Northwest History. Tiemann creamed; M'sieu le Trainhead."

"You know the gig, bien sûr. Work him."

Jesús laughed once, darkly. "Can't help it. Memorize all this shit then can't get it out my head. Mira." He turned north, nodded upriver, and inhaled. "St. John's. Too far outside town to see. Portland's solo suspension. Rad. Two-tone cable steel suspension, steel deck half-through truss design, viva-Gothic piers."

Jesús pointed three bridges up to the lean and sterile decks of the Fremont, rising from industrial sectors into the air well before approaching the riverbank. "Fremont. America's longest tied-arch orthotropic bridge. No piers in the water? Muy cool. Design lets it carry its own weight. Engineering trick Europe thought up after World War Two. Steel was scarce." Jesús shifted his finger, gaze. "Broadway."

The boys scanned the Broadway Bridge: chunky, like a hasty Erector Set project, stuffed atop the river on squat brick piers. Small girder-arches stood independent, connected, blended, stretched: nothing regular or patterned. "Más grande drawbridge in town. Double-leaf Rall bascule, steel through truss design. All the birds in it? Shit mixes with rain, turns acidic, eats the steel.

"Steel Bridge. Already told you that."

Parole nodded. "Two-in-one-action, c'est . . . c'est . . . c'est it ain't so. You MC Bridge thang, amigo." Parole shoved Jesús' shoulder playfully. "Ami," he said, voice lowering. "A-mi." His hand pressed against Jesús.

Jesús shoved his hand off, shaking his head.

"Amy!" Parole teased. "Amy Mary Sister Louise Girl, ma chérie."

Jesús rolled his eyes, looked down at his feet. "Cut the fag shit," he grumbled.

Parole crossed his arms, closed his lips. "C'est bon," he announced. "Continue the lesson architectural, my bridge-man." He scuffed his foot like a tap dancer.

"Here we rest: Burnside," Parole said. "Right?"

Jesús looked back up, smiling. "Mucho scandal when they built this," he offered.

Parole nodded. "Tell it. Testify, crucify, dites-moi. What all you be seeing roundabouts." He cocked his head back, waiting, anticipating.

Jesús looked westward past Parole's shoulder. The White Stag Sportswear sign, a gigantic neon deer encased in an outline of the state of Oregon, poised midleap above Parole's head. Jesús turned south. "Morrison." The bridge exuded pragmatism: a no-nonsense drawbridge with wide, heavy river piers. "Bor-ing! Hawthorne."

The boy's eyes focused further.

The Hawthorne echoed the Broadway's girder humps, but with two rising vertical lifts like the Steel. "Hawthorne's got all these freak accidents: kamikaze steamers, spans lowering too soon, Jeep driving off into the water for no reason. One night two Rose Fest Princesses walking down the middle fell into the river. They were okay but vacuums how it happened."

Parole laughed.

Jesús squinted. "Marquam." The Marquam lumbered up from two entranceway spaghetti-bowls. Like a deformed fetus whose DNA suddenly decided to stop growth on that left arm, its unfinished exit ramps to nowhere ended dramatically midair.

"No one cared when they opened it. No ribbon-cutting, no fanfare, nada."

Jesús pointed. "See the Ross Island?"

At the river's bend, the Ross Island Bridge's steel deck soared over its namesake rookeries. Crisscross support girders varied the line, complementing thick piers and thin arch. Two twenty-four-inch mains crawled up from subterranean East Portland and cut through the air, suspended from the bridge's roadway. "Carries water," Jesús whispered. Knowing the bridge delivered sustenance to Westside residents gave it personality, Jesús felt. It seemed maternal — or was it paternal? fraternal? — Whatever, it was like the Ross Island cared for you.

He shook his head, licked his lips. He looked at the cement under his feet, trying not to see the river flowing underneath. The close proximity of so many different ways of accomplishing the same simple goal dizzied him. The air cramped thick with competition. All these bridges, then all seventeen in the metro area, each yearning and stretching and aiming to please in so many different ways. The crowded family, their visual cacophony screaming for attention like combative siblings — why was so much variation necessary? Shouldn't utilitarian objects be simpler somehow, like words? More of a common denominator based on what works best? Why so much difference?

Parole bounced his board's wheels loudly against the concrete. "Hey, M'sieu le Nod, snap out! You okay? School's out for summer." He eyed Jesús. "You got Le Grand Surprise to lay on me?"

"Yeah, C'mon. Vamoose, pronto. Gotta get there on time to skate." He nodded sheepishly and hopped on his board.

"Show me show me show me . . ." Parole sang, following after him. He knew Jesús couldn't hear him over their boards, but he sang to him anyway. "Show me how you do it . . ."

*   *   *

"Zacharias was, like, one of the biggest nobs there was."

The bleach-blond twenty-four-year-old man peered at the crowd of skaters over his Bible. His baggy T-shirt proclaimed sk8 CLUB MINISTRY.

"This here now is the grande fuck," Parole whispered under his breath. "We going to be skating anytime hereabouts?"

"After he's done."

Parole gazed around at the dozens of teenagers squatting uncomfortably on the cement floor. They giggled, tossed paper wads back and forth. Only a few listened. Many looked longingly at the wooden quarter-pipe ramps in the church warehouse's basement. They loomed silent and neglected for a half hour till the man got the kids' souls, or at least some inroads to them.

"And so everyone who touched the ark of the covenant got totally toasted!"

Parole glared at Jesús.

Jesús smiled, nodded and raised his palm. "Chill."

Jesús and Parole crashed out in the wooden chairs on the ramps' periphery, catching their breath.

"Preacherman's fucked totalement, yes sir, but this here is a good bit of a change from under-Burnside."

"Très bueno, yeah?"

"You see now that young man's three-sixty there'bouts? Man-oh-how one does manage that? I'm not the book."

"Hard to explain with words: You shove it. When it gets almost horizontal, you flip it out like a kickflip. You rotate your front foot and your back foot scoops behind you to spin the board. Hard part's staying above it. After you got the flip down you work on getting the rotation all three-sixty."

"Bien sûr, but then I get myself in the grande bust."

"Cut that shit! Once I was just trying to olly over this manhole.

Didn't see this car of jocks coming. Landed on their windshield. Bust del mejor bust."

They laughed.

Parole frowned. "You know, I find it here'bouts in my dreams, you know? Yourself and me all-out doing these tricks of fatness. I'm in my dreams and we've got a whole park just now for ourselves, this park of radness, vraiment, ramps and everything. We're going about wearing nothing-on now but our boxers! No to the pads, no to the shoes, no to the socks. Full run-on verts we're doing in boxers seulement! And these way-over-the-top airs, planting hands, lien-to-tails my friend, ollies of fakie, rock and rolls, grinds and the lovely fifty-fifties."

Jesús grinned. "Come on. Show you why we came here."

He led him out into the hall and stairwell, down a dusty landing into a subbasement with a dirt floor, wood beams and pilings, and the roar of skaters overhead. Parole surveyed the underground.

"Cool, sure enough. Here'bouts we're underground, under-water swimming, swimming like underneath all those bridges-of-which-you-love."

Parole turned to his friend, eyes narrowed and smiling.

"Good place for the quick fuck fuck fuck."

"Huh-huh," Jesús laughed. He rolled his eyes impatiently and pushed his hand against Parole's chest.

Parole grabbed his wrist and pulled him close. They kissed, Jesús' neck and shoulder muscles going limp. Their lips hurt, flattened between teeth as they crammed faces together. Parole gasped, stretched open his mouth. He wanted to eat Jesús whole, feel his body living inside him.

Jesús pushed him away, shaking his head. "Later. Fuck, just come over here. Listen."

Jesús stretched up and pressed his face against the wood. The splinters pressed across his face, an array of pinpricks poised against his skin.

Parole pressed his face up across from Jesús, holding similarly steady against the splintery grain.

"Hear it?" Jesús whispered.

Jesus' breath warmed Parole's face. He retasted the mild mouth-rank. He closed his eyes and smiled partially.

"Yes sir now," he whispered.

The ramps upstairs in the basement transmitted the noise of the skaters into the wood floor. Grinding 608zz Black Russian ball bearings, their rapid spherical journeys of surface contact, amplified out through 40mm wheels. The vibrations traveled through trucks and out along boards' noses and lips, wood and slick alike radiating vibrations. They pushed through rubber soles of Etnies' Screws, Airwalks' Blue Suedes, Vans' Old Skools and Authentics. Porous acrylic-weave sweat socks offered a flimsy barrier. Like determined pathogens passing through cellular membranes, the tattoo of sound entered a skater's body. The buzz rippled skull, jostled hammer-anvilstirrup, kept time on eardrum, made waves in eustachian fluid and broke down finally in the nautilus of the cochlea. Cilia searched the waves for their unique nerve message to identify, searching to give the brain a simple yes/no to the question "What about my stimulus?" Their biological binary language, now a cackling current, bolted up to the brain to be composed into the cacophony the skaters perceived.

Minus minor filtration, the same story transmitted downward to Jesús and Parole.

"Shit now," Parole whispered. "They're skating right across your M'sieu le Brain it sounds like."

Jesús removed his face from the ceiling and nodded. The sound of the skaters still carried through the air around them, aerograms on dust and gas.

"Intense." He hunched down on the dirt floor, wedging himself into the corner crawlspace. "You can feel it against the wall, too. Aquí."

Parole slid his ass backwards to the wall.

"Feel it?"

"Not for real much, amigo."

"Get in close." Jesús scooted over a few inches. "Beam or something carries it."

Parole wiped dust under his nose, felt saliva thick and acidic in his mouth. He turned away from his friend and spit into the dark.

"Yeah, okay."

Shoulder to shoulder, they leaned back against the wall and absorbed its message. The soundtrack whispered about them in the dusty air.

"Ma cher, hear it now!" Parole said and pushed himself back flat against the wall. His shorts dragged against the dirt floor, waistband sliding down toward his bent knees. His leg pressed up against Jesús'. Their hairs touched and tangled, tactile shouts up into Parole's head.

Parole kept talking in a steady, dreamy meter. "I mean now, you listen and there's like a music to the skating. You are Major Vacuum when you're doing it, but you get away enough here'bouts and you do rightly notice it. There's this stop/start rhythm. Now, it's not no drum action but, ma cher you know, it's the bass. And you got your grinding and whacks and jumps and then the breaks when it's up-in-the-air time."

Parole continued, hands conducting in the air before him. "And there'bouts you got all these-here skaters going on at once, now and it's like the Major Band, an orchestra now yes? It's everyone going off on their own trip but they all together are the Song-Makers. These skinny high notes there-up on the pipe, then some noisy old-school board roars on by and it's all deep, and someone else is all bouncing around doing tricks in the corners pop-pop-pop, these high notes, all staccato."

Parole caught his breath. Jesús nodded knowingly. He sighed, leaning back into Parole's side. Parole lowered his hands, resting a palm inside Jesús' bare thigh. Parole closed his eyes. He'd run out of words.

Their spines and fingertips vibrated.

Jesús' head rolled to the side, resting in the crook of Parole's neck. He breathed in slowly, smelling his friend's sweat.

"It is the So Chill you know now, how you can hear them go up in the air," Parole murmured. "BrrrrrraaaaAAAAAH — up! — *Brack!* That pause, that break when you go on up in the air it is The Kick-ass. Ma cher, do I just love that. There'bout's the whole reason I skate. It's all fast and noisy and your heart's Mr. Pounding, your head's all about buzzing and you're moving and thinking and shaking and everything all at once. Then you leave up off the ground. You break through this here crack to where you're up midair, in another place. Whereabouts? That there's the moment where everything's silent and perfect, for the Tiny of Seconds."

Jesús nodded.

"You know you're that, too, don't you now? You're Mr. Midair to me."

"Yeah. Know all that shit."

Above their heads the roar continued, noises sounding the same but with different meanings, homonyms and homophones in a thunderstorm of ghosts:

> *jangling wallet-chains / rattling tambourines / rain*
> *skate-shoe stomping / flamenco footstomps / thunder*
> *grinding wheels / border-crossing boxcars / tornadoes' roar*
> *unlubed ball bearings' squeak / disco's* LET'S ALL CHANT
> *"ooh-wa ooh-wa!" / shrieking winds*
> *gasps of exertion to kickflip and olly / latenight breaths of*
> *Mardi Gras concertinas / kiss of wind*

The sounds rang in their ears. Grunts of queer skaters fucked by their gym-toned elders, bent over steel bridge trusses, sprinkles of sweaty rain mixing with birdshit, acidic white drops splattering across stripped backs and whipping away skin, screams falling on deafened ears. Together, the boys listened.

William Sterling Walker

INTRICACIES OF DEPARTURE

I'M STANDING AT Eighty-first Street and Broadway listening to this piece of music in my head when my eye catches a book going into a pocket of a peacoat behind the window in Shakespeare & Company. I look up at his face — it's a beautiful face, a vision — and suddenly I stop wondering where Sunday will take me.

Then he winks at me and disappears from the window, out of frame, off camera.

I'm wondering how he's going to get through the antitheft device at the entrance. I wait at the doors of the shop. He's milling about the stacks and displays in front of the sales counter, buying time. His jacket is draped over his arm. The only way out is through that electronic turnstile; he'll never get away with it. Then I see the blue playing card in his hand which means he must have something checked. I walk into the store and stand before the turnstile. I pick a name for him.

"Nathan," I call out. "Why don't you hand me your jacket while you get your bag?"

He doesn't look up immediately, but I know he's heard me. There's a crowd by the sales counter, and constant traffic into and out of the store. No one is paying us any mind. His head tilts to the side like a parrot's. He glances up at me and grins. Then he moves toward me and hands me his jacket way over the turnstile. I stretch out for it. We must look conspicuous, but the alarm doesn't sound. I go outside, trying to be casual, and wait under the awning. It's colder now; the bite in the air cuts through me. The sun falls behind buildings as he joins me.

"Thanks," he says looking both ways, up and down Broadway. "Good thing you're so damn tall."

I hand him his coat. "You didn't have it all figured out, did you?"

"Nope."

He pulls on the coat, wraps his scarf around his neck and slings the book bag over his shoulder. My legs are rattling. We start walking.

"I'm not a klepto," he says. "I just need to come clean with that." He lights a cigarette and blows a long stream of smoke. "But once I started this, I couldn't stop. I had to go through with it." He has an accent.

"What book did you take?" I ask.

He pulls the book out of his pocket and hands it to me: André Gide's *The Counterfeiters.* He stops, drops his cigarette to the sidewalk, and grinds it out with his boot. Then he tells me he has never taken anything in his life, and I believe him. I don't know why. I look at him, and I think of a myriad of questions, but all I ask is if he comes from the South.

"New Orleans isn't really the South."

"What's your name?"

"Nathan," he says.

Maybe it's a lucky guess. Probably not. I don't believe in lucky guesses. On second thought, the guy's a thief, maybe he's a liar. Now I'm a thief for helping him. Am I a liar? I think this as we continue down Broadway. We're both shivering. We have no idea where we're going. We've circled the block four or five times, I realize; we haven't gone through a crosswalk since we left Shakespeare & Company.

We wind up in this dive called Pier 72, though it's nowhere near the piers. Over coffee, cheesecake, cigarettes, he tells me about what he left behind in New Orleans: the afternoon light, his favorite café in the French Quarter, coffee with chicory. He says he misses coffee and chicory the most. I tell him I've never had it, and he tries to describe its taste, muses on chicory's bitter delicacy. I listen to the lilt in his voice, the music of his accent. I glance at his reflection in the window, transparent over the rubble of ice and snow on the sidewalk. A cloud of smoke wraps around him. The snow falls through him.

"I took the train to get up here," he says. "I love trains. You have time on the train, time to think about where you've been instead of where you're going."

"That seems true enough to me. How long have you been here?" I ask.

"I've lost track," he says. "Not long, two weeks, maybe. I don't even know what day it is." He laughs and turns away to the window. We can't look at each other for very long. "Isn't it funny how when you like someone, you can hardly say a word to them?" he asks.

"I wouldn't call it funny."

"I guess not," he says. "I don't know. If I'm not into someone, I end up telling them my life story, for some reason. Or at least a version of it." He takes another cigarette from my pack on the table, rolling the cigarette between his thumb and forefinger before he lights it. This seems to be a way of absenting himself from me.

"It's like you have this premonition of how the whole thing will end up. Maybe that's why you don't say anything," he says to the window.

"You? Or me?" I ask.

"Me. You. Yes, you. You don't say much either, do you?"

"I never know what to say."

"We could talk about movies or books," he says.

"Perhaps we shouldn't talk about books."

He laughs. We talk about movies. He loves silent movies, Buster Keaton movies, loves their rawness, the grainy quality of the picture, the wordlessness. He asks if I've ever noticed how riding the subway is like living in a silent movie. "No one talks to each other on the subway, do they?"

"Words sort of collect in your head when you ride the subway," I say.

"You see a face and you know," he says, "you just know there's something passing between you in the silence. But then he gets off before your stop, or gets lost in the crowd."

"People bob up into your life all the time," I tell him. "Then they're gone. You try and accept it and move on. Or get waylaid." As soon as I say this, I wonder why I did. But then I tell him, "You can't connect with the world."

Until six months ago, Nathan Morrow — my other Nathan — kept his medications in wineglasses on the kitchen countertop. The assorted Crayola-colored pills and capsules had innocuous names, as if some chemist had culled them with kindergarten randomness from a bowl of alphabet soup. I suspect Nathan might have done better with something holistic. But I got tired of feeding him newspaper clippings, arguing with him about alternative treatments, and I left the glasses alone. Still, I can't stop thinking about them. Nathan had a glass for each day of the week. This is Monday, and the glass is empty. The seven glasses are all here, clean and in a row. All of them are empty.

My landlord sits with a half-full cup of coffee, rolling the rent check around his middle finger, lecturing me. "Those yuppies are all managers. No convictions. Bottom-line boys. No accountability. Just cut their losses."

"I know what you mean," I say.

"You do?"

"I'm not a yuppie."

"But you dress like one," he says.

"I don't dress like this all the time," I tell him. "Occasionally, I wear a smart little Donna Karan number and —"

"Ah. Don't tell me shit like that. You guys are all alike." I've known this man almost a decade, but only today does he seem really old to me. As he slides his chair away from the table to leave, the glasses on the counter catch his eye again. They catch everyone's eye.

"I was just kidding," I tell him, laughing it off.

"Yeah, yeah," he says under his breath. "The wife had a nephew that was one of Those."

"One of what?"

"You know," he grunts. "The kind that like to dress in women's clothes. Came from good people, but he fell in with that Warhol crowd. Then once, when we were going to the clinic for her chemo, we saw him in Port Authority. He didn't even recognize us, family. Doris tried to talk to him, but he just started growling at her, and I had to pull her away."

He folds the rent check into a small square and sticks it in his shirt pocket. He clears his throat. "What the hell happened?" he asks, not expecting any answer.

In the city, you get the same what-is-the-world-coming-to-now that I got from the folks in the provinces, where I grew up. You still have to shut out, ignore what you see on the streets, out of necessity. You become a New Yorker by a process of petrification. The inorganic subsumes the organic. It's gradual, and natives hardly notice how calcified they get. You wind up entombed by your own body, cracking under pressure, like sidewalks from the snow or heat.

After the old man leaves, I pass a boy sleeping on the sidewalk at ten in the morning. A cardboard sign tents over his head: AIDS BLOOD TRANSFUSION NEED 18 MORE DOLLARS TO GET HOME TO KENTUCKY. No cup, no change. A torn, green army coat covers him. Is the sign fact or fiction? We want to believe people. We want people to believe us too. At least I do. Years ago, I used to give money to a panhandler who worked the block between two haunts of mine off the strip in Galveston. One Sunday I saw her waiting for the bus, done up with a veil on her head like some deaconess of a Baptist church, a pair of white pumps, and a bright dress the color of bird eggs. Now, what were the chances of me seeing her dressed that way instead of in the rags she wore on the corner by the Rawhide Tavern?

I guess it doesn't matter.

I like the thief. He stole a copy of *The Counterfeiters*. I like his sense of irony. He had absolute faith, in me, if for only a flash. And he didn't get caught. The fearless of the world: someone will always look after them.

The wanting only seems to come over me now in waves. Nathan is sprawled across my bed, smoking a joint. I sit in a chair under the window. Steam wheezes through the pipes; the radiators are working overtime, so I have the window cracked open for air. Wind whistles through the opening. We are in darkness with the blinds drawn. Blue light from the street comes through the slats, and stripes the wall.

"I'm in the middle of the only fucking city in the whole world," he says.

It amazes him. I can hear it in the way his voice catches. I don't have to see his face.

"Listen to it," he says.

I close my eyes and concentrate. Taxi horns blow short, blow long minor chords of flatulence. Sirens, major sirens, cacophony. Sirens, the sough of the city. Angry city. Six alarms, count them. Support units. Maybe seven. Maybe nine. Engines of the streets exhausting themselves. I open my eyes, and the walls seem to waffle from the sound. I feel like I've been dropped into a well.

"Today, this man on the subway," Nathan says to the darkness, "was giving his spiel. He was preaching to us, saying shit like, 'Try and remember what it was like to be hungry.' "

Nathan has the oratory part down pat.

"Then he shoves a McDonald's cup in my face. I tell him I *know* what it's like to be hungry. He walks past me and yells in the subway, 'If I was a dog, would you give me a can of Alpo?' This woman sitting across from me — you could tell she had scads of money — she just wrinkled her nose. But this other woman —" Nathan pauses to suck on the joint. It glows in his face, then subsides. "— this other woman was so convinced by the speech, she's shaking as she empties out her pockets of loose change. It was like in those televangelist shows. I couldn't believe her. I thought she was going to hyperventilate."

"She must have been a tourist," I say.

He sucks on the joint and exhales. Then he tells me about the man he's been seeing every day playing the violin in the Columbus Circle station.

"Do you tip him?" I ask.

"Today, I gave him the Gide book."

"Nathan, why did you come here?"

"Even a retreat is an advance."

"No. I mean, now — tonight."

He ignores my question. I guess I shouldn't have asked. Now I don't want to know. Being stoned seems to amplify the stillness.

Then he reaches on the floor for the ashtray, his arm's shadow arches over the wall behind my bed. It's meant to be a dramatic gesture, and reminds me of how he reached to give me his coat Sunday. He rubs the roach out but smoke lingers.

"Someone told me to read the Gide, an older friend from high school. Said I would need it one day to live by. He told me on my eighteenth birthday. Said I should read *The City and the Pillar,* too, but I couldn't fit both books in my pocket."

He laughs. I smile at the wisdom of his anonymous friend.

"I had gone to Shakespeare for a job Saturday. I swear it," he says. "I go up to the kid watching the book bags — you saw him, the gangly one — and I tell him I want a job. I say it just like that, 'I want a job.' It throws him off. He says I need to go to the information desk to see *Her.* So I walk with my bag over my shoulder and *She* says to me, 'Stop. You need to check the bag.' And I say I want a job. Again like that. And she says to wait right here and points to the floor.

"I stood there fifteen minutes. The woman forgot me. I could have filled up my bag with books and run out of the store. What could she have done? So I walk back to the counter and give the gangly kid my bag, and he hands me the Ace of Fucking Spades. No use in going to see the woman now, because I'm doomed, but I do it. I go and see her, and I wait. I don't want to wait, but of course I need a job. I give her my spiel, and she says that she wants to hire me but first I have to fill out this application. Then she thrusts a form in my hand and says in this really patronizing tone, 'Be sure you read the back portion first, before you fill the rest out on the front.'

"Fine? Not fine. Basically it says, 'Sure we'll hire you, but you have to get fucked for five dollars and five cents an hour.' How is someone supposed to live in goddamn Gotham City on that?"

"That's when you decided to take a book?" I ask.

"No. I didn't decide to do anything then," he says. "But Sunday, before I met you, I knew I would do something. I went back there.

I didn't plan it, but I knew I'd do something. The Gide was Sunday. Today was this one."

He reaches for his coat lying on the rug. I watch the shadow of his arm arch on the wall. Then he flips a book at me. It seems to come out of nowhere, landing in my lap. I hold it to the light in the window. It's *The Selected Works of Rainer Maria Rilke*. I look up and strain to make him out in the darkness. I don't want to think how he smuggled the Rilke out of the store. But I wonder if he intends to bleed Shakespeare & Company dry, book by book.

"Rilke says we carry our desire and death around like a seed inside our bodies," he tells me.

I crack open the book in the middle and read the first thing I see.

I have my dead, and I would let them go, and be stunned to see them so comfortable, so soon at home in Death, so calm, so different from their reputation. You, you alone turn back; you brush against me, you linger, knock about, that the sound may give you away . . .

"A gift," he explains. "For yesterday. Hope you haven't read it yet. Only thing handy."

Oh, don't take from me what I am slowly learning. I look at him long enough to see him, to have seen him. Then I close my eyes. *Don't take from me what I'm slowly learning.*

Thursday evening over dinner, Nathan tells me that a temporary agency sent him to work for a very old securities firm down on Broad Street, which needed someone to inventory their files for storage. He had to sort through files and ledgers in a cellar, some over a century old. Grunt work he calls it. The firm apparently didn't believe in throwing anything out, and the cellar was very dusty and disorganized — but warm.

"Do you know what the irony of it is?" Nathan asks.

"What?"

"That there's a lot of steady work as a temporary."

"Really now?"

"It's postmodern economics. 'Temporary' is a euphemism. What it means is that the company doesn't have to pay for your health insurance."

"And this is your own discovery?"

"I made it today." He reaches down into his book bag under the table. "I brought you another gift."

He hands me a large, old ledger.

"Open it," he says.

It's from before World War I. The ink is brown, and the entries are in a florid script that is almost illegible.

"You must return this," I tell him.

"They'll never miss it. Look how old it is. Do you think they'll go back and look for it in an IRS audit?"

He has a point.

"What will I do with it, Nathan?"

"I don't know. Look at it, put it on the coffee table."

"But you stole it."

"I prefer purloined. The Purloined Ledger."

I laugh. I can't help it. I'm beginning to amass a library. He starts to tell me how he snuck the book out of the cellar.

"They left you alone down there?" I ask.

"I have a sincere face," he says.

After we leave the Chinese restaurant, we trudge across Amsterdam Avenue again. I have the ledger and he has his book bag slung over his shoulder like a rabbit hunter. He also has his white takeout carton. The streets on the West Side are littered with slabs of ice and snow, like chunks of gypsum.

"I'm going to grow my hair long and get an earring. What do you think?" Nathan asks. He's wearing a baseball cap, ski parka, jeans, hiking boots.

"I'm not sure. I like you the way you are now, but if you want to, then go ahead. Who am I to say?"

"I feel like I need a change. But I'm afraid to spend the little money I have on clothes. I did buy this new Yankees hat."

He tells me how his roommate borrowed his favorite baseball cap and didn't return it. "Says he lost it."

"I guess you're not really in a position to complain."

"Yeah, seeing's how I'm quite the urban nomad these days, and everything I left home with I carried in this book sack."

Nathan's been crashing at the apartment of old acquaintances from New Orleans, on a hide-a-bed sofa in the living room, and when the sliver of light goes out from under the bedroom door, and their animal noises die out, Nathan lies there sinking in the middle of the tortured mattress, wondering what in the fuck he's gotten himself into. Then he beats off. He says that there isn't anything remotely sexual about it and that he doesn't get any satisfaction from it. It's more medicinal, a sleep aid. He lies there with spunk on his chest thinking about New Orleans. Thinking about home is unavoidable.

"Thought you were pretty resigned to being here," I say.

"I thought it was what I wanted before I got here. I don't know. I spent a good portion of my adolescence believing nothing was ever going to happen to me," he says. "No. That's not true. I grew up never imagining anything significant happening to me. Now I'm here and I can't decide if I'm regretting it or thankful."

"Yesterday, I thought about going home," he says. "I mean I actually imagined myself on the southbound *Crescent,* staring at the countryside. But then it all started to dissolve into other thoughts, and I decided I wasn't all that homesick."

"But the most significant thing I've done is leave," he says. "Guess I've mastered the intricacies of departure now. Trains make for great exits."

We cross Broadway and head for the subway station at Lincoln Center. There are old men in front of Tower Records with milk crates and planks set up to display coffee-table books, all unbelievably half-priced. We browse. They're beautiful, thick, expensive art books: Monet's water lilies, Mapplethorpe's women, treasures of the Hermitage. They're probably all hot, or have fallen off the truck, so to speak, and I think, This is why you can only get five dollars and five cents an hour for a job in a bookstore, Nathan. But I don't say anything.

We pass the frozen fountain at Lincoln Center as snow begins to fall. We seem to have the whole plaza to ourselves. It's very cold, in the teens, and we walk to the station at a brisk pace. He grabs my hand and holds it, until a couple appears in the stairwell of the station. He's cautious about that sort of thing.

On the subway, a shriveled old man in cutoff shorts and tank top limps toward us. He has a genuine prosthesis. He pleads for something to eat. Nathan's face tightens. He looks at me, then hands the man his white container of leftovers. The old man snatches it and gets off the train at Times Square.

"I knew there was something about that shrimp and garlic sauce," Nathan says.

"I hope he eats it," I say.

The gentleman across the car from us, who had been watching stone-faced, asks if the takeout was tomorrow's lunch.

"It was."

"I could smell it," he says.

"I had this intimation about that carton when we left the restaurant," Nathan whispers to me.

"Yes, but you would have gotten to my house and stuck it in the fridge and left it there, and I'd have ended up throwing it out."

"Giving things to the homeless only encourages them to remain on the streets," the gentleman says.

"Fuck you," Nathan says to the man, who gets up and walks to the other end of the car.

"That was unnecessary," I whisper.

"I couldn't help it," Nathan says loudly. "I keep thinking of something my mother told me about my grandfather once driving around town looking for an open grocery that would sell him a can of dog food on a Sunday, back in the fifties when Louisiana still had blue laws. He wanted to feed this stray hound, you see. My mother said he hated to see animals neglected, but he'd only give it one can. He didn't have the heart to call the pound, because he knew they'd put the pitiful thing to sleep, and his daughters wouldn't understand. That's probably what happened anyway, because it ended up disappearing. But when it came around that Sunday, Grandpa only fed it one can. My mother watched the dog lap up the food in an old hubcap, and she asked him why didn't he give it some more, and he said to her, 'Now, sugar, that dog wouldn't know when to stop eating. He'd eat and eat till he gorged himself to death.' "

I finger him until he writhes with whatever he's feeling. Before I enter him, this pinhole opens inside of me, and, as through a camera obscura, I glimpse everything upside down and inverted. I think I've become him.

Then the expression on his face when I'm inside of him, when he comes, is a kid's with something fragile in his hands, who suddenly, inexplicably lets it go.

"Why do you look crestfallen?" I whisper.

He closes his eyes, shakes his head. Then he climbs out of bed. He goes to the window, finds a pack of cigarettes, wrings one from the pack on the sill and sits by the radiator.

He's told me he's never had a lover, but now I know. He's a widower. It comes to me in the simplest of gestures: The way he palms his cigarette, the way he furrows his hair behind his earlobe. The way he stares out the window. I see beneath his sedentary vigil, anger densifying on some focal point of concentration beyond the glass and whirling snow.

"You know what desire is?" he asks.

"What?"

"It's that throbbing numbness you feel after you've been truly reamed, after someone pulls out of you," he says over his shoulder.

I want to vomit.

He leaves me alone in the bedroom, and stands in the hall. He sees the wineglasses on the kitchen counter, and I imagine him counting them; I imagine him knowing. I close my eyes. Steam courses through the pipes. The apartment is breathing in the silence. I hear him pad into the bathroom. Then he comes back to bed wearing boxers.

"I thought I gave you what you wanted," I say.

He stands at the bed with his head bowed. I didn't want to fuck him, but I did. Now I want to blame him. I was giving him what he wanted. I didn't feel anything between my legs, just the rhythm, the motion of our bodies rocking.

He lies down next to me, and I put my arm around his waist. "You're a fine piece of work," I whisper.

"You'll either hate me or not." He shudders against me.

"Which one should I feel?" I ask.

"I don't know."

After he has gone to wherever he goes, I sit on the sofa with the ledger on the coffee table and all the other books he's swiped the past week, and I think about mailing them back to their respective owners. It would be the ethical thing to do. And I consider doing it, but these books are souvenirs, and the owners, not missing them now, will never realize they've been taken away. Perhaps in some distant inventory, some far-off settling of accounts, the books will turn up missing, but what are the chances? I know I'm rationalizing. I know this, but I lie down in the dark thinking that every time he leaves, I never know if I will see him again. It's the nature of the city. It's that part of the city I hate. The snow whizzes by the window. The sky is leaden. I live in an insular, little world. I think I need these books as proof that he exists.

*   *   *

Grief isn't something that lessens with time passing. This is a lie so many old folks have sputtered out. They believe uttering these words makes grief dissipate. But they're dead wrong about it. Sometimes the coming of grief isn't as obvious as in a sad movie. Sometimes it can be the way two shadows follow, drift, merge over pavement; the unexpected sweetness of wood burning; the riff of an old song, long thought buried in the silt of everydayness.

I go to the bodega on the corner for cigarettes and the *Village Voice*. Snow sweeps across Bleecker Street in great swaths. Streetlamps disclose its gauze of motion. It still amazes me how snow muffles sound. The street has the silence of a museum. Nathan Morrow is gone. But in this silence I hear his music, or rather my own rendering of it, over and over in my head. I can't concentrate on anything else but his music and the sound of my own breathing.

I asked him once to copy the music out for me so that I might learn it. He put me off, said he couldn't transcribe it. He had a wonderful ear but hardly any theory. But I think he liked the fact that no one else could play it. It was not meant for me.

He did ask me what I thought of it, but I couldn't tell him. I might've described what I heard as a series of moments drifted through, a succession of rooms, all suggesting some emotion, but what? Tell him I never knew how much desire could sound like despair?

Walking home in the snow, watching it fall, I think of the years we were together. We never said how we felt about anything. We played out desire on the body; it was never spoken of, never written out. I remember how frail he was, on the bench at the piano, a ghost in white pajamas, his feet hardly touching the floor, a wineglass filled with ice water on a plate next to him, slender fingers floating over the keys. It's what I picture when I think of his struggle to remember, as he slipped into dementia. It enclosed him. It encloses me. The rhapsody had become an interior for him, as it is for me now. I remember every note he played. But he left no map for me to find my way out of it.

Russell Leong

PHOENIX EYES

AT THE SAME Buddhist temple downtown where my friend P. and I used to go whenever he visited L.A., I prepared to don the gray robes of a layman. There was no chance of my becoming a monk, but I wanted to hear the five precepts for myself.

A dozen people would take the vows today. Each of us would be asked the same questions by the monk. I was the last to step before the altar. Now the monk was repeating to me: "Do not kill sentient beings. Do not steal. Do not lie. Do not drink alcohol. Do not have improper sexual relations." At the fifth precept, I balked. The monk looked me in the eye and said, "You must answer me, yes or no." My days of pleasure and sensation, it seemed, would cease. I was past forty. Yet sweat was flowing down my back. I squinted in the haze of the burning punk sticks and yellow candles.

*   *   *

Twenty years ago, I graduated from Washington State College with a double major in theater arts and business communications. Ba and Ma had high hopes of me, of a wife and children soon, and a stucco duplex where they could live with us in their old age. When I told them I would never marry, they threatened to disown me. From then on, I did not show my face at family banquets, at baby parties, or even at funerals. It was as if I, the offending branch, had been pruned from the family tree. I was hurt, then angry. But I also felt free to pursue my life as I saw fit. As always, Older Sister supported me after I explained to her why I wanted to live in Asia.

"If I'm going to make it as a theater designer in America," I said, "my training in Asia ought to open a few doors. Look at black artists in Paris. They make it there first, before they come back here." I promised to keep in touch. I promised to send money for the folks, if I had any to spare.

But besides my artistic ambitions, and unbeknownst to my family, I was leaving the U.S. because I had fallen for an airline steward based in Taipei. We had met the summer before on a Tokyo–Taipei flight — I had been spending July studying Mandarin. He was my first Asian lover; at that time in the States, Asian men going together was considered "incestuous." Even if we were attracted to men of our own race, we didn't move on it, fearing we'd be ridiculed.

Every other month, the steward had spent a weekend with me in Seattle. When I finally graduated, I worked all summer to save for a ticket and then in the autumn moved to Taipei to join him. His tenth-floor condominium was on Chunghua Road, near the hotel district. The teakwood furnishings were a far cry from the wooden crates that had surrounded me growing up in back of a grocery store in Seattle's International District by the tracks.

Besides sex, he wanted me to serve him — draw the bathwater, polish his shoes, massage his brow with green eucalyptus oil, teach his friends dirty jokes in English. Even with my help, he took half an hour to tie a silk ascot around his neck; I took one minute to throw on a T-shirt and Levi's. He drank at odd hours and chewed candied ginger and Wrigley's gum to cover his breath. Where was love, I asked myself. It was hell. After six months, it all ended one night after I'd eyeballed the singer at the Hilton Skylounge. The steward and I got into a brawl in the parking lot. He kicked me out the next day.

That year — 1972 — Nixon, Kissinger, and Winston Lord broke twenty years of Cold War policy toward China, and I was stranded on a hot, dusty street in Taipei, with a hundred dollars U.S. in my pocket, a duffel full of clothes, and an art-and-business degree to my name. I sat at a fruit stand, drinking a concoction of condensed sweet milk, crushed ice, and mango, trying to decide what to do with my life. Taiwan was a small island near the equator shored up by coral reefs, U.S. dollars, and cheap labor. In all fairness, the Portuguese were right when they named it *Formosa,* beautiful island. Between the hills and the sea, though, shanties hugged the dirt, poor relations to the mountains of condos and mansions above them. Certainly I did not want to be overwhelmed by lack of money, by lack of love, or by too many English students, which is what usually happened to foreigners forced to earn their keep.

I found a cheap room in a prewar Japanese-style boarding house. A notice posted on the inside of my door read, in Chinese, "Do not use over 30 watts, no loud music, clean the toilet after you're done." The absentee landlady, a widow, would rifle through our rooms while we were at work, unscrewing bulbs with too high a wattage and unplugging radios and television sets. But the boarders, mainly office workers, tolerated the "widow's house," because of its convenience to bus lines and the low rent. Jerry-built townhouses edged up to either side of the wooden structure. This colonial relic had been beautiful in its day, but it was only a matter of time before it would be demolished.

*   *   *

Before I ran completely out of money and out of luck, I ran into P. at the National Palace Museum. I was taking notes and sketching Tang dynasty terra-cotta burial figurines. I noticed how the wide sleeves and low bodices — fashions influenced by the foreign traders who plied the Silk Route — accentuated the body. These styles seemed to reveal, rather than hide, the body's robustness. Absorbed in my observations, I was startled when a man standing next to me suddenly began speaking in perfect, high-pitched English: "You're an ABC on a summer visit?"

"Me? Yeah, like you said, I'm an American-born. Here to learn what I can. How did you know I spoke English?"

He looked me up and down, smiling and pointing to a stocky, half-naked clay figure tethering a yellow-glazed horse.

"Persian or Turkish, not Chinese," I said.

"Imported labor," he said. "Exotic, like you. You'd have been a good model for a stable boy."

I blushed, realizing that no local boy would have dared enter the museum dressed as barely as I was — in cutoffs, tank top, and plastic sandals. I retorted: "And you are a Tang prince waiting to mount the horse?"

It was P. who brought me out — to the *hung kung syan,* the international call line. The circuit was made up of high-priced young men and women who made themselves available in Taipei, Hong Kong, Manila, Bangkok. As the tiger economies began to flourish in the seventies, so did the demands of (mostly) Western businessmen for after-work entertainment. Our clients were German or American, with a few English, Dutch, or Spanish — and even a few Asian businessmen — thrown in. On our part, we could be of any nationality, Taiwanese, Thai, Chinese, Vietnamese, and of any gender: man, woman, or pre- or post-op transsexual.

We hung out in the same cafés and shopped the same boutiques. After our clients spent over $100 on food or clothing, we'd get a five percent kickback — and a New Year bonus in an embossed red envelope. As I saw it, food is food to the belly, and cloth is cloth to the back. Most of us ordered vegetarian dishes for ourselves, but for clients, we selected the richer braised meats and fancier seafoods that they preferred.

The boutiques were staffed by the same slender, clear-skinned young men or women. The clothes, as everyone knew, might have been labeled BLUETTE MODE-PARIS, but they were knit in a local factory that made "imports." No matter, the salesperson would try the clothes on for the buyer in the private dressing room. My well-built buddy, Wan, would wear nothing under his trousers. A certain Ivy League professor, known for his translations of Sung poetry, loved, whenever he was in Taipei, to stop at the boutique and have Wan undress and dress for him.

As P. taught me, the main thing was not what you did in bed, or even how good you looked; the key to referrals and comebacks was skill and charm in "talking, walking, welcoming, and leaving." You had to make your client feel intimately involved; you had to make him long for your presence after he'd left. After all, P. said, if they could afford you, they could afford someone even younger or better-looking. But not necessarily smarter or more personable. A street hustler or bar girl didn't need education or social graces, but an escort or companion did.

That meant you had to know at least two languages and the common cordialities in Japanese, Chinese, and English. Read the newspaper every day. Know your food. Hold your liquor. Don't order the most expensive entrée or wine, but something appropriate to the season, to the country you were in. "Take a lesson from me," P. said facetiously. "In Kyoto, don't order Hunan pork. Admire the view from between the shoji, and accidentally brush your hand on your client's thigh without looking directly at him." Bringing his hand to my face, P. suddenly traced my lips with his fingers. "Save this part for me."

Last, but not least: Keep it simple, but as good as you could afford. No white shoes or polyester shirts. Not too much jewelry or luggage. When business was slow, P. said, I might consort with horny American sinologists from prestigious Ivy League schools who'd come to Taipei to hone their classical Chinese. They were suitable for conversation and culture, as they loved to pontificate about their studies, but not for their allure or their dollars. They were the orientalist tightwads of the Orient, he joked. They didn't know much about fashion, food, or how to spend money, but, as P. said, you could always learn a bit more about Sung *tzu* from them. "Which might come in handy with your next client: Watching the moon from the hotel balcony, you could recite a stanza or two."

P. didn't need the money like we did, but he did what we did anyway, for pocket change and for fun, he said. Sometimes, after double-dating with clients, or having drunk too much of our favorite cognac, P. and I would fall asleep on the same bed, feeling safer in each other's arms.

One morning, as we woke up together, he had a sudden desire, he said, to visit the lotuses that would now be at the peak of their bloom. I asked him why today, because I knew that he had a valued client flying in.

"Then I'll just cancel him. He can wait until tomorrow." He dressed, tossed me a Diet Coke and a banana, left a message for his client, and rang for a taxi. We were on our way to the Lin Family Gardens, just south of the city, a classic eighteenth-century Fukienese family compound. We passed through endless corridors, dank rooms, and carved door lintels, to the lotus pond in the back. There seemed to be no tourists anywhere. From the depths of mud and dark water, hundreds of white lotuses had pushed themselves up to reach the sun. Upon seeing these, he began to tremble. I put my arm around his shoulder. His grandmother, who had raised him, he told me, had always looked forward to the beginning of summer and the blooming of lotuses in the small rock pool in back of their family house. As the third wife of her husband, and being from a country background, she had the lowest status in the large household. Her room was the smallest, her clothes the most meager, because she could not produce a male heir. Yet she had raised P. as her own son, picking his hair for lice, bandaging his scrapes when he would fall. Each year, during the two or three weeks that lotuses were in full bloom, she would, just before dusk, pour clean water onto the bulb of each pale flower. At dawn, she would use a tiny spoon to collect the water that remained on the flowers. This precious liquid, mixed with morning dew, would make the purest water for tea, enough for a single cup, which she would sip with him.

The red taxi whisked me to the peaks of Yangminshan estates, to where the sour smog of the city basin gave way to the scent of pine and jasmine. The doorman smiled and opened the black-lacquered double doors, flanked by two sago palms.

Making my way to the outdoor bar, I spied Tan Thien, the thin, effeminate scion of the Tan Tan ice cream family, which had branches all over the island and was establishing plants in Singapore. Then there was Jerry, a muscular Taiwanese, kept by a restaurant owner in Osaka. And Marie, a French-Algerian student who had found it more exciting not to study Chinese — we'd had a brief affair. One night when we were making love, I went on and on about the Jun vases I had seen that afternoon at the Palace Museum. She told me that I opened my mouth at all the wrong times, instead of putting my lips where they belonged — quietly, between her legs. She swore at me in French, and I at her in Cantonese, and we parted. After me, she drifted to pretty-boy types who usually borrowed money from her and never paid her back.

About then, I think, she started going out with older businessmen, again through P.'s referrals.

I kissed her lightly on the shoulder. "Marie, *Nijen meili.* You look wonderful." And she did, in her simple black cotton shift and pearl earrings, her upswept chestnut hair.

"So do you, Terence. But you're as dark as a peasant. Your phoenix eyes give you away, though."

"Eh?"

"Longing and lust. That's what I see in them."

I kissed her again, and moved on.

I moved among Otto's usual crowd of slender Asians in their twenties, and important antiques — a gilt Burmese Buddha, ox-blood porcelain vases filled with orchids, and Ming country furniture.

Otto was a Swiss cookware manufacturer, and a regular at the Hilton Skylounge. Because of his bent for Asians, he kept villas in Jakarta, Chiang Mai, and Taipei, along with his family home in Geneva. He preferred, he said, the sensual aspect of darker Malays, but tempered with common sense, "at least one quarter of Chinese blood."

I pressed the gold pinky ring chiseled with my Chinese surname tightly against my palm. We were all accessories. Whether we were from the country or the city, whether pure-blooded Chinese or mixed with Japanese genes during the colonial occupation. Or Malay. It didn't matter. We were beads on a string. A rosary of flesh. We gave up our youth to those who desired youth. There was some room for variation, for beauty was in the eye of the beholder. I myself was called *feng-yen* or "phoenix eyes" because of the way the outer folds of my eyes appeared to curve like the tail of the proverbial phoenix. Such eyes were considered seductive in a woman, but a deviation in a man.

It was at one of Otto's get-togethers that I ran into Ping-li again. He was a well-known modern dancer who once asked me to design a stage set for him that would give him the illusion of height and weight — he was well under five-four. I ended up creating a series of painted silk banners that moved up and down on invisible nylon strings. During the last act, the banners slowly lowered behind him, effectively shutting out the rest of the troupe, so Ping-li appeared much taller. The editor of *London Dance Magazine,* who was making his annual Asian junket, saw the performance at the Sun Yat-Sen Memorial Hall and was impressed not only with the dancers and the stage set, but with the designer, me! We had ended up at a Taiwanese restaurant eating garlicky sautéed squid, boiled peanuts, and noodles, drowning it all with beer and getting thoroughly drunk. I was in no mood to talk design with the balding British editor, because I had been smitten with the dark long-haired waiter. I gave the editor my card and insisted my friends take him with them.

After slipping the manager a few bills, I asked my waiter to spend the night with me. Even though I'd moved out of the "widow's house" to my own fifth-floor studio, I never brought people home. P. was the only one who would visit and sometimes stay the night. So I drank coffee until the last customers and the manager left around three, and the steel door clanked down over the entrance. I helped sweep the floor and refill the condiment jars — pepper sauce, soy, and oil. In the airless basement dining area, the waiter set the air conditioner higher and put on a tape of Dionne Warwick. We pulled a table out from between two red vinyl banquettes, then pushed the upholstered seats together. We lay on the slick vinyl, sweating and breathing hard, undoing each other's shirts. In the darkness, I fumbled for the glass jar on the table that now blocked the aisle. Pouring the liquid onto the palm of my hand, I sniffed it: sesame oil. I began to massage his shoulders and the small of his back, steadily working the oil and sweat between his legs.

The barking of dogs on the streets awakened us. Bleary-eyed, he stumbled to the kitchen and fried an egg over leftover rice. We ate and drank last night's cold tea in silence. His damp hair fell in a mop over his forehead. I brushed it away from his eyes. We smelled of sesame, stale cologne, and sweat. He smiled and shrugged his bare shoulders. Could I introduce him to customers, he asked me, as he had to pay for his brother's tuition at a private English-language school. He wanted to know if I had any American "friends" studying in the colleges who needed companionship. I pulled a fifty-dollar bill from my wallet. "My pleasure."

"No," he said. "Brother, you are Chinese. We look the same. Swear the same. Fuck the same. *Yi chuong tung meng* — though we sleep in different beds, we have the same dreams!" I hugged him, and promised to bring American friends to his café in the future.

That's where my dual career began: in Taipei, then on to Hong Kong and Osaka. Twice a year, P. and I flew to Hong Kong to set up private parties and modeling shows for jaded wives of rich businessmen. A family limo would meet us at Kai Tak airport. When their husbands were on trips to the U.S. or Japan to meet their mistresses, we would set up parties for these *tai-tais*, who paid well for good-looking men. Struggling (but handsome) students and out-of-season soccer players were my specialty. Women, we found, went for the strong thighs and tanned calves of the players, limbs that performed more diligently than the listless ones of their pale husbands.

One thing led to another. Shopping for fabrics one day in the Landmark Mall with a Mrs. Chi, we were introduced to her Tuesday-night mah-jongg partner, an art dealer from Shanghai. His gallery, Contempo, showed modernist Chinese artists from the twenties and thirties, now very collectible. He would take the time to educate younger collectors, including me, about painting styles that derived from Qi Baishi's minimalist renderings of fruits, flowers, and vegetables.

The following day he drove the four of us to the Chinese University of Hong Kong to see paintings by the eight eccentric

Qing masters of the Yangzhou region. They were, he explained, the eighteenth-century precursors to the art of the New China. Yangzhou was near the tributaries of the Yanzi River and the East China Sea, a cosmopolitan metropolis based on the salt and fish industries. I was impressed by his erudition. At the same time that he could appreciate esoteric old masters, however, his sensual tastes ran to young, unschooled hairdressers and bartenders with thick hair and bright eyes. Through him, my appreciation of Chinese modernist painting — and of men — improved.

Men were no problem, but I couldn't spend money on this caliber of paintings. Twice a year, I sent some money home to Ba and Ma, care of my sister. My own studio in Taipei was as spare as a stage, with books, a bed and desk, and track lighting. I needed spaces to exercise, to create, and to escape. Out of odd pieces of stone and lava I had assembled a rock garden on the balcony and potted some bamboo to hide the high-rise apartment across the way. I was three years on the Taipei–Hong Kong–Osaka circuit before I got to do anything bigger in London, Canada, or New York. P. and I used to match our clientele in the same Asian cities so that we could rendezvous later and compare notes. In the meantime, I was the only Chinese American male on the *hung kung syan.* Despite my eyes, I never considered myself exotic or different. But I used my English and my art background to advantage with my clients — mainly men, but an occasional woman. I always sent flowers to the women after I left them, usually a spray of pink orchids, and a subtle-patterned tie to the men. In Bangkok, on a trip with a Chiu Chow businessman, I had picked up three dozen silk ties at discount. My callbacks and referrals were no worse, and probably as good, as those of men who were much better-looking. I had strong features, and never hid the irregularity of my slightly rough skin with makeup, like the others who tried to smooth over their imperfections. I smiled or complimented a person, however, only when I really meant it. I guess even my jaded clients could appreciate that.

*   *   *

Evenings, I would drink with middle-aged Chinese or Japanese businessmen: average length of marriage, eight years; one wife, maybe a mistress, two children. The Japanese were fastidious about their skin and bodily cleanliness, bathing before and after sex, so I preferred them. Then again, Chinese from Hong Kong or Singapore enjoyed talking, and eating, before and after the act.

After dinner I would go to the Club Fuling, a bar for Japanese and foreign businessmen near the Majestic Hotel, in the Shilin district. Unlike other clubs, the Fuling had no neon sign, just an engraved bronze plate with the club's address. Membership was by referral. New members — and that included locals as well as foreigners — could only join through an introduction. No street trade. Even we — companions, escorts, or entertainers — had to pay a nominal fee.

Entering the inner courtyard, I would pass through a Japanese garden with its plantings of red-leafed nandina and wisteria. Two entrances led to different parts of the club. The left door, sheathed in verdigris copper, led to a western-style bar with leather and chrome chairs and glass tables. The right entrance, sheathed in rosewood, led to Japanese tatami rooms, and was considerably more expensive due to the imported foods served. I usually worked the western-style side. No food, just local salted peanuts and dried cuttlefish.

The club's waiters were at least five feet ten inches tall. Some were of aboriginal origin from the Hualin mountain area; others were ethnic Chinese from Seoul or mestizos from Manila. The club catered to Japanese and Asian men over forty years of age. Being a shorter generation due to the war, the patrons were fascinated with younger and taller Asian men. The waiters turned heads and opened wallets. They were dressed elegantly, in white linen shirts, black slacks, and black patent-leather shoes. They slicked their short hair back behind the ears. They would never go home with clients, otherwise they would be fired. Each had been selected and trained by the Fuling's rich owner, a local trader who had made his first fortune exporting refrigerators.

Daytimes, I would read, go to museums to research, or go shopping. I recall that one day, as soon as I entered the neighborhood around Lung Shan Market Street, my shoes started kicking up dust. Lung Shan was in the older, western side of the city near the river, for locals, not fixed up for tourists. The air was raucous with the voices of straw-hatted peddlers selling everything from watches to perfumes to human-shaped ginseng roots laid out on blankets on the street.

The leveling of some pre–World War II housing blocks had turned the sky yellowish gray with dust. Shoeshine boys prodded me until I gave in. One examined the leather of my shoes and said the leather must be expensive. "We do not have this here." I turned to him and nodded my head, mumbling that a friend had sent them from Hong Kong. I tipped him a dollar for polishing them.

In the middle of the sidewalk, people with shopping bags were pressing around something or someone that I could not yet see. I walked toward the crowd. Edging my way to the side I saw a man sitting on the ground, with a short haircut. His eyes did not look up. It was a young man no older than I, pale-skinned, with the leanness of a soldier. His straight shoulders ended abruptly at the armpit. It was warm, and he wore no shirt. His gray pants were rolled up to his knees.

He was painting. I looked at the crayfish emerging as his toes deftly controlled the bamboo brush. A bowl of water and a wooden box full of brushes and pots of paint were at his knee. Passersby tossed coins into a tin cup.

I squatted down so as to be the same height. A voice in the crowd shouted: "How much?"

He said, "Seventy-five dollars."

"Too much," the voice said.

He calmly answered, "I don't lower my price, but neither do I raise my price for anyone." With his feet he pushed two pebbles to each corner of the painting to hold it down. Squatting, he repositioned himself to prepare another sheet of white. This time he bent over, inserting the brush into his mouth, between his teeth. As he bent down, I could see the inverted triangle of his shoulders and back tapering to his bare waist. Someone kicked the stone on the corner of the unsold crayfish painting. He lifted his eyes for a second and looked at me without expression. I lowered my gaze. The green carapace of a grasshopper emerged. Coins continued to drop into the can. The crowd thinned out, and then thickened again with the newly curious. His tongue flickered pink for a second, to moisten his lips. He had gleaming white teeth, except one that was badly chipped. His forehead and chest were lightly glazed with sweat, and a line formed on his brow as he continued to paint in the humid afternoon.

Had he been maimed? Or had he been born without arms? His pupils were the gray of an agate. As I examined the crayfish painting, I wondered if he washed his face in a plastic basin at home. Or if his sister or wife or mother did that for him. How did he bathe or cook or make love. Despite his lack of arms, he seemed to have something that I lacked.

The *pock-pock-pock* of a monsoon shower took us by surprise. Quickly, he used his feet to roll up his paintings, before the rain could spoil them. From the crowd, a younger man, perhaps a friend, helped him scoop up the rest of his materials. He rose from his haunches. He was taller than I expected. The shower was now a torrent, and the painter and his friend turned into a muddy alley off the main street. Without thinking, I hurried after them, sloshing my way through uneven, potholed streets. The rain pummeled down; I sought shelter under a doorway. When the rain stopped, as quickly as it had begun, they were nowhere to be seen. Soaked, lost, and breathless, I flagged a cab to take me home.

*   *   *

That evening, I went back to the Club Fuling, where the headwaiter
introduced me to a number of visiting Japanese businessmen. We
had a few drinks, before I settled on Tanabe-*san*. He had a wife and
children, he said. Every year he would go back to Osaka to impreg-
nate her, to "keep her busy." I laughed, only because I had heard
the same line several times before. He said that I reminded him of
a well-known *Kyogen* actor — with the same square face, ruddy
complexion, and red lips. We spoke in halting English, with a bit
of Chinese and Japanese slang thrown in. I would write down the
characters in *kanji* for him on a paper napkin. As I did so, he
gripped my wrist in his hand.

His blunt fingers were strong. He asked if I had ever been
bound. I said no, that I didn't do that. He laughed. He put my
hand over his wrist and told me to squeeze as hard as I could. I
did. He said, "Too weak. You've never lifted a shovel or a hoe! We
must use other things." I asked "what things," and he pressed his
glass of bourbon to my lips. He had his ways. I looked toward the
bar. The bartender squinted at me, out of the corner of one eye. It
was the "Okay — he's clean and solvent" signal.

We taxied back to his hotel. He turned on the bathwater, I
turned on the television, ordered two Remys from room service,
and stripped down to my jockeys. I had emptied both glasses before
he emerged from the dressing room in a blue-and-white cotton
robe. Flustered, I began to run my hands over the covering that
concealed his body.

With a click, he opened his leather valise. It was full of thick
white cotton cords, organized by length. He had me tie his wrists
and arms back, pinioned to the sides of his body. Between the
bands of white, his blue-and-red tattoos glowed: dragons and ser-
pents attempting to escape from their prison of bound flesh. I
placed my lips on the head of the red serpent that encircled his

chest. Then I drew back until I could bend my knees and place the soles of my feet on his belly.

I worked my toes downward, foraging in a triangle of dark hair until I managed to insert his cock between my feet. With my soles, I kneaded until it became engorged, the bluish veins pulsing beneath the skin. I did not touch him with my arms or hands. Flexing my calves and thighs, I pressed my feet together until finally he could not contain himself. At that moment, in my mind, I could see the painter whom I had lost in the rain.

At fifteen, I remembered, I had read Thomas Mann's *Death in Venice*. I had seen that perfect beauty could kill, as the pursuit of it had killed Aschenbach and quite a few of my friends. Death, like beauty, could arise slowly, through frustration, liquor, or disease, or strike quickly, through anger, accidents, or suicide. I had decided I could live better with imperfection, as long as I could live with myself.

In time, as my theater and design work materialized and I began to earn more from those efforts than I did from "other" work, I told myself that I would leave Asia for good. I was happy that I had been able to put a hefty down payment on a stucco duplex for my parents, who were, at last, able to tolerate me, in their way.

From L.A., where I had settled, I flew to Seattle for my father's seventieth birthday banquet. I had not been seen at a family banquet for twenty years, though I had seen Ba, Ma, and Sis briefly, on and off.

That afternoon, Ba put on his Brooks Brothers navy suit, bought in San Francisco; Ma donned her best jade rings and pendant. Sister was in charge. She had arranged the menu and tables at the Hong Kong Low, bought the 24-karat "long life" gold peaches from the jewelers, and made sure that a play area for infants and children adjoined the main room. During the dinner, members of the Hop Sing Association praised Ba's contributions to building a high school in the Pearl River district that he was from in Guangdong; the International Settlement Civic Association of Seattle gave him a plaque; and Sister, on behalf of the two of us, talked about his virtues as a father to his daughter, the pediatrician, and to his son, the designer. I had no words to say, but led the toasts after the speeches.

Accompanying my parents from table to table, I felt the heat and sweat seep from my body. I could see questions in people's smiling faces: Where are his wife and children? Why isn't he married yet? Does he make money? What exactly does he do for a living? I was imagining things, I told myself — these kith and kin of Cantonese farmers and small businessmen didn't really care that much about me to begin with. If I had stayed in Seattle and lived their lives, I would be asking the same questions. I was glad when we reached the last table to toast. We lifted our shots of brandy, just as I had at my own farewell meal at the Club Fuling. There, the members of my adopted family — P., Marie, Wan, Tan Thien, Otto, Ping-li, and all those others whom my blood family would never meet — used me as an excuse to toast each other, the future, and the next man they would meet. I suddenly felt orphaned with my memories. At the same time I felt moved to see Ba and Ma in public, flushed and beaming, until the last guest had shaken their hands.

Sis and I drove them back to their apartment, where I picked up my bags.

"Bye-bye, Ba, Ma," I said. "Have a good trip. Sis and I have already reserved the hotel in Vancouver and boat tour."

Without ceremony, Ba suddenly thrust a large package wrapped in recycled green Christmas paper and twine, into my arms. Ma told me to open it. It was a red Pendleton blanket, a Pacific Northwest specialty. He grunted. "For you — king-size — big enough for two, heh?" Ma said: "See the label here — all virgin wool. Not a cheap one. We get it closeout." I could only nod my head. My eyes were wet. I had not realized how much I had missed them all. Sis touched the material but didn't say anything. It was late, so I bowed to the three of them. And I left for my hotel.

After his mother died, P. also moved to the West Coast, to San Francisco. Wherever he moved, his family would buy him apartment houses to manage.

The last time I saw P., three months ago, I noted that his features had aged well. In his late forties, he could still pass for thirty-five. He attributed his glossy black hair, pale smooth skin, and flexibility to his Southern Yunnan ancestry. I always thought that it was due to his vegetarian diet and yoga. He had no outward symptoms of the disease. At the time, he was drinking bitter melon *fugua* juice daily, a native drink favored by Beijing researchers studying immune-building drugs at Johns Hopkins.

A card I got from him, postmarked San Francisco, read, in Chinese:

Dear Terence
When my feet leave this earth the calendar will turn
    a new leaf, with a new birthday on a new month
Light incense for me, wherever you are.

P.

I called immediately, but his line was already disconnected.

Three days later, I read about his death in the Chinese paper, but the family and the police did not disclose details. The family whisked the body back to Taipei. No funeral services were held in the States. His family had apparently not been willing to admit at all that the myth of Asian invulnerability is simply a myth. They were not alone in their desire not to see or hear about AIDS. In Asian families, even in the nineties, you just disappear. Your family, if you have one, rents a small room for you. They feed you lunch and dinner. They leave the white Chinese deli boxes pushed up — discreetly or not — against the door. Rice, fish, vegetables. That's all. Asian families do not want to have anything to do with what the American welfare system can offer the afflicted: Supplemental Security Income, food stamps, Medicare, hospice care. They simply cannot call AIDS by its proper name: any other name would do — cancer, tuberculosis, leukemia. Better handle it yourself, keep it within the family. Out of earshot.

Perhaps our lives are marked, as our bodies are destined to be beautiful or maimed, before we are ever born. But neither prayer nor desire have worked to bring back anyone I have loved. Only now can I say his name, because now it doesn't matter.

Peter Hsieh, beloved grandson of the general Hsieh Hung, who fought so valiantly during the Resistance. Now there's nothing more to fight against, or resist.

Even though I've tested negative for the virus myself, I'm afraid of simple moves: Today I won't open the door and walk across the street, not even for a six-pack of beer or aspirin. I don't trust cars, pedestrians, clerks, janitors, nurses, bank tellers . . . not even children, anymore. Nothing to do with the L.A. riots, carjackings, or fear of being robbed. It's something else entirely.

I thought I was prepared to accept the news of his death, but I wasn't. Rereading his card, I began to tremble from the fear and beauty of his words. "A new birthday in a new month." Being nominally Buddhist, he believed in rebirth, and in good or bad karma begetting similar karma.

Enveloped by spiraling smoke, the monk had been waiting for me to answer. His clean-shaven pate was beaded with sweat, but his black eyes were steady and cool. I had repeated "yes" four times to the precepts — not lying, not stealing, not drinking, not killing.

And, finally, "yes" to the last, not having improper sexual relations. If these vows would change things, or if it was too late to change my life now, I did not know. *Dok. Dok. Dok. Dok. Dok.* As he began to strike his mallet on the wooden fish-drum, others in the room picked up the chant, *Nam mo ah ye da fo . . .*

I could sense his presence nearby. He was not the one whom my eyes had sought and loved, or the one who had already lived and died. He was another — the one still waiting to be born.

Scott Thomas

MAINFRAME

THE E-MAIL GREETING Dale O'Keefe received from his employer, the Guarantee Insurance Corporation, on the morning of his forty-fifth birthday triggered a familiar and disturbing tension. The greeting, a morale builder that had been well received by most employees, was, O'Keefe knew, nothing more than a clock ticking away, a series of binary ticks that day after day, week after week activated additional ticks, producing messages expressing management's good wishes for birthdays, anniversaries, holidays. He knew this because he had grudgingly created and installed the program. Momentarily, he toyed with the idea of removing his name and birth date from it, but the thought seemed to exacerbate whatever was building inside him. He deleted the message from e-mail.

O'Keefe received one other birthday greeting that day, from Lena Cohen, a receptionist he had met on his first day with the

Guarantee; she had then been middle-aged, younger, in fact, than he was now. The woman's card, humorous, even slightly suggestive, was delivered midmorning on the mail cart, a canted tank that wheezed up and down corridors and would, on occasion, lose contact with its invisible track, run into an obstacle, a wall or desk, and buffet it until a maintenance man could be found to drag it away, like a horse that had died in harness. O'Keefe read Lena Cohen's card twice before carefully slipping it back into its envelope and dropping it into his briefcase. Later, at home, it would go in a drawer with other cards, a lifetime of cards he never looked at.

Dale O'Keefe lived alone in the house in which he had grown up, a stout, brick bungalow on a street of stout, brick bungalows. After his mother died, he had toyed with the idea of selling it and moving into an apartment on the lakefront; but the year after his mother's death had been difficult, and making such a major change would, he decided, only make things worse. At first, he believed he missed his mother, that he mourned her, but eventually, he concluded that it was not his mother he missed, but the routine of life with her. So, he set about creating a new routine: he took his meals, breakfast and supper, at a neighborhood restaurant, where he became a fixture, one of those men whom waitresses call hon and automatically bring coffee; he hired a woman to come in twice a week to clean, do his laundry, iron his shirts; he went to bed at the same time, got up at the same time, and evacuated his bowels at the same time; he carefully regulated the amount of alcohol he drank; he paid his bills promptly on the first of the month, saved a certain percentage of each paycheck, and gave money to the church he no longer attended. On Friday nights, he went out; that is, he had dinner at a downtown restaurant instead of a neighborhood restaurant. In a surprisingly short time after instituting this regime, his depression lifted.

In the process of deciding that it was not his mother but the routine of life with her that O'Keefe missed, he acknowledged to himself that they had, in fact, said almost nothing to each other in years. They had exchanged "good mornings" and "good nights," discussed the weather. She would remind him that he needed new dress shirts, a new pair of shoes. He would ask if she had remembered to pay the real estate taxes, if she wanted a ride to the cemetery on Sunday. They existed in a well-constructed frame, each looking after the other, without actually intruding on the other. The last real conversation he could remember having with her was in the spring after he had graduated from college. "I'll ask Father William," she had said. "He'll speak to somebody, and you'll go from there."

"That's crazy. What good is talking to a priest going to do? I think I'd do better in New York or maybe Los Angeles."

"What's the point of doing that? Here, at least, you can live for free. There, I gotta send you money till you get on your feet. Look, Father William knows everyone. This is what a parish priest is good for."

"But why would he help me? I don't need his help."

"Because you're a good boy, the son of a poor widow."

"That's demeaning."

"You are a good boy, and I am a widow. Listen, he calls somebody up downtown, somebody in some big office, who likes rubbing elbows with the archbishop . . . Father William has dinner with the archbishop every week . . . and he says, 'Dale O'Keefe is a good boy. Just graduated, with honors no less. He stayed home with his mother, a widow woman in my parish. Good parish family.' See. And the guy in the big downtown office says, 'Sure, I'll see the kid. Send him down.' That's the way things work. I'll call right now."

And that's the way it worked. She called, and things were set into motion. A week later Dale, in the gray suit she had bought him for graduation, went downtown to the Guarantee Insurance Corporation and was given a job. And because he had graduated summa cum laude in math, he was put in the computer department, which was new and which nobody knew much about, except that the machines had to be sealed off, kept cool and perfectly clean.

On the evening of his forty-fifth birthday, Dale O'Keefe stepped out of the elevator to the sound of his name echoing through the cavernous marble lobby of the Guarantee. Annoyed and hoping to silence the voice, he hurried across the lobby to the desk in the center and set his briefcase on the heavy counter that encircled Lena Cohen. "Thank you for the card," he said. "It was nice of you to remember."

"Because you're one of the nice ones," she said and stood, stretched across the counter, and squeezed his arm, which was as high as she could reach. "Lean down and let me give you a birthday kiss." Slowly, he leaned over the counter. "There," she said. "Oh, dear. Lipstick. Stay right there." She pulled a tissue out of a box under the counter and wiped his cheek. "All better now." She was a very short woman, who had managed to maintain into her seventh decade the rather remarkable figure of her youth. She was cute as only cunningly made miniatures are cute, and she understood this as only a person who has been admired since childhood understands the wellsprings of praise.

"You look nice. As always," he said.

"Thank you," she said loud enough to set off another echo across the lobby. The single aspect of her person over which Lena Cohen had never learned to exercise absolute control was her voice, which was, O'Keefe believed, all the more irritating for emanating from such a package; she was a goldfinch with the call of a crow. "I keep myself up because . . . listen, all they need is an excuse to replace me, and I'm not about to give 'em one. I've been here so long, I know where all the bodies are buried, but then so must you, up there in the tower inside that main thing."

"Mainframe."

"Well, I'm glad it's you up there in the mainframe, and me down here. But, you were bright to get into computers when you did. It's where the future is. Listen, what do you know about this acquisition thing?"

"I don't know any more than anyone else," he said and picked up his briefcase. "Thanks again for the card."

"So, you going out, birthday boy?"

"Yes," he said, realizing that's what he was going to do.

"You got a date?" Date reverberated across the lobby.

"With buddies," he said and looked at his watch. "Gosh, I'm late. Lena, you take care getting home. And thanks. For the card."

"Have fun," she called after him. "You're not young for very long."

The wind seemed to inhale, sucking him out of the revolving door and onto the sidewalk. Christ, I hate winter, he thought. What did I like about this when I was a kid? He pulled up the collar on his coat, lowered his head, and began walking. That familiar and disturbing tension that had come upon him with the e-mail message was the first such reoccurrence he had experienced in nearly four years, and it scared him. He had so carefully stuck to the routine, believing that this alone had saved him from what he thought of as the chaos that had enveloped him following his mother's death. I should go home, he thought.

Dale O'Keefe became fully conscious after graduating from high school that his mother did not want him to leave home. "Look, you decide," she had said. "I can just afford to send you away to the university downstate. It's a state school and cheaper. Or I can send you to the Jesuits, which is better, but only if you live at home so we won't have to pay room and board."

"Why is Loyola better?"

"Private is always better." He went to Loyola.

Over time, Dale became aware that she almost never crossed

him, never argued with him; did nothing that would upset him, that would drive him away. She ignored the handful of times he came home drunk while in college, ignored the handful of times he stayed out most of the night in the years after college. She didn't seem to care whether he dated or did not date. When she once reminded him that he needed to make a confession before Easter and he replied that he wasn't going with her to church any longer, she had said, "It's a phase. You'll come back someday." But she never mentioned it again. He came to believe that she did not care what he did as long as he stayed with her. But he was never able to fathom exactly why. He knew that she loved him, but at the same time she did not seem particularly to enjoy his company. She was not a fearful woman and not a weak woman. She was not sick and did not harbor illusions of being sick.

When Agnes O'Keefe had received the telephone call from the plant manager informing her that her husband had fallen over dead, she was sad, but not devastated. For a while, she worried about money — until she found that the house was paid for and her husband had left a surprising amount in various savings and loans. With the life insurance and social security, she could easily live and raise the fourteen-year-old Dale without having to go to work.

The devastation came later. Six weeks after she had buried Matt O'Keefe she began wanting a man, which led to a long assessment of her situation. She was only forty-two years old, but she was a woman over forty, a woman with a son. Most men do not want to raise another man's son. She owned her own house and had a tidy sum of money out at five percent. But the men who would come for the money would be the mean and greedy, the ne'er-do-wells. She was strong and hardworking, but she had no intention of becoming some widower's unpaid housekeeper. Nor was she interested in assuming responsibility for an old man. She was not unaware that women went to bars to pick up men, but she knew herself to be a plain woman. Even if she were able to get over her distaste for the idea of picking up strangers, she doubted that a stranger would notice her. She was stuck. And that was that.

Agnes Lowry had not dated Matt O'Keefe. He knew of her through mutual friends, through church. One night, he simply called on her and, after some fumbling conversation, proposed. He told her about his job, his savings and insurance, and reminded her that both his parents were now dead. "Can you buy me a house?" she asked him.

"What kind of a house?" he asked.

"A brick bungalow, in a nice neighborhood. Not here. On the North Side. Maybe out northwest someplace."

"Yes," he said. "I can buy you a house like that. It would be a lot closer to the plant anyway." So Agnes Lowry married Matt O'Keefe. She was twenty-eight and a virgin. He was forty-eight and knew nothing of women except the whores of the Levée, who considered speed a manly virtue. After the first month of marriage, neither Agnes nor Matt deluded themselves about the success of that side of their marriage. He reached across the bed for her less and less, and after she became pregnant, not at all. It did not bother her, and if it bothered him, she was unaware of it. She hadn't married for love; she had married to avoid being an old maid, to avoid having to care for her aging parents. Matt was considerably better tempered than her father and was happy, not mean, when he came home from the tavern on a Saturday afternoon. And he was generous. When she tried to return what was left of the money he had given her for household expenses, he told her to keep it. "Well, then, I'll save it," she replied.

"Buy yourself a dress or something," he said smoking a cigar after dinner at the kitchen table. "We're all right. You don't need to scrimp over every little thing. I save, from my pay envelope, every week. And during the war, I made good wages and lived with my old lady, so I saved most of that in war bonds. If you want to save, save up for something nice to wear to church." Agnes had never known generosity, and she was touched by her husband's and by his reference to their finances.

When Matt returned to Agnes's bed, six weeks after Dale was born, his touch was different. He didn't seem particularly interested in climbing on top of her, but instead stroked and kissed her face, her neck, arms, and breasts. She touched him and held him in her arms. It was several minutes before she realized that he, in the process of sucking at her breast, was taking milk, and when it came to her what was happening, she gasped and pushed him away. He sat upright on his knees. In the streetlight through the window, she saw the extent of his excitement as well as the look on his face, so when he struck her, it was no surprise. She had grown up being slapped around by a man who bullied his wife and children, and automatically she reverted to passivity. "All right, Matt," she said. "Just don't ever hit me again." She lay back down against the pillows and attempted to relax. Without making a sound he lowered his head to her chest. When she fully comprehended the excitement that this aroused in him, actually felt it coursing through the body against her own, something began within her. It excited her that his excitement came from her, from what she gave him. And for the first time, she wanted a man inside her. When finally he entered her, she began to shudder and then to buck. When he came deep within her, she for the first time in her life lost control over herself and, for the first time, understood.

In the morning, when she began nursing the baby, felt the lips suckling at her breast, she again began to shudder, and she clamped two fingers around her nipple and pulled it from the baby's mouth. Across the kitchen table, Matt O'Keefe sat watching her. "Don't take it away from the kid," he said laughing, "or there won't be any for his old man."

"Just you shut up," she barked, and the baby gave out a cry. But after a moment she relaxed and released the nipple to the son. Eventually, she raised her head and looked across the table to her husband. When she read the gratitude in his eyes, she smiled in spite of herself. The child nursed until he was nearly two years old. Matt O'Keefe never hit his wife again.

"So, you need a trim?" asked Caesar as he snapped the smock over Dale O'Keefe in the barber chair. "Is it me? Or is it you turned upside down? Your regular is Fridays, right?"

"I just felt like coming in. For a shave. Can you give me a shave?"

"Of course I give you a shave. The best in the city. You've never had one of my shaves before?"

"No. I've never had anybody's shave before."

"So you're in for a treat. Relax."

"Maybe that's why I came in. For a treat."

The barber, a short man of about O'Keefe's age, ran both hands down O'Keefe's cheeks, under his chin, and around his neck. "Relax," he said. "So, is this a special day or something?"

"Not really," O'Keefe said, after a moment.

"First we lather you up." And the man set to work. "In Sicily, where I learned barbering, I give lots of shaves. But here, not so many. Everybody is too busy. No time."

O'Keefe closed his eyes and listened to the barber fussing at the counter behind the chair. When O'Keefe felt Caesar's hands rubbing soap into his beard, he audibly exhaled. The act seemed to him strangely intimate, far more intimate than the process of getting one's hair cut; and while it seemed strange, it also felt natural, as if the ease of the barber's touch was rubbing away at O'Keefe's self-consciousness. "Did your customers in Sicily come in for a shave every day?" he asked.

"No, no. Once a week. A rich man — every three days, maybe. When you get a good shave, a perfect shave, you don't need it every day. You'll see."

O'Keefe listened to sounds in the shop, the buzz of conversation between the barbers and their customers in the chairs, the twittering of the manicurist's patter, the buff and snap of towels on shoe leather, the swish of Caesar's razor across the leather strop. "Now," said Caesar, and with two fingers he stretched the skin of O'Keefe's upper lip, "we begin." O'Keefe felt the blade of the razor. Caesar worked methodically, stretching and scraping a single square inch of skin at a time. The barber's fingers were strong and vigorous, and he wielded the razor forcefully. "Never," Caesar said as he worked, "shave up, against the grain. Do you feel pain?"

"No."

"That is why. I do not understand how Americans shave, against the grain. They like pain, I think. And electric razors. Why would you put a machine to the face? Americans are crazy for the machines. When you shave yourself, do you use a machine?"

"No," O'Keefe lied.

"Good. And always a clean blade. Every day, a clean blade."

"Do you use a straight razor every day?" O'Keefe asked.

"Of course. Just like I'm doing for you. I even shave down my chest some. Too much hair. If I don't, the hair comes out over the top of the collar. You know?" Caesar said. He set the razor down on the counter, picked up a towel and wiped soap from his hands. "Now I go in the back for the towels."

O'Keefe again closed his eyes and tuned in to the conversation of the man in the next chair. "So he claims he's been framed and wants me to get him out of it, and I say, 'Listen, don't lie to me. Nobody framed you. If you didn't do it yourself, then you let it happen, out of inertia.' I told the bastard there's no such thing as a frame. See, people get themselves into trouble — out of greed, lust, or whatever; mostly from stupidity or just plain laziness. Nothing just happens. You know what I mean?"

"That's right," said the barber.

"Now we do the balm," said Caesar out of nowhere, and he slapped the palms of his hands across O'Keefe's cheeks. The sting of the alcohol and the force of the attack quickly retreated into a not unpleasant, lingering tingle. "It's good, no? Refreshing. And now the towel." He pulled a towel out of the bucket on the floor, twirled it with a flourish ending in a twist of steaming white terry cloth, and draped it around O'Keefe's face. "There. Good? Not too hot."

"It's fine," O'Keefe said.

"It should be too hot, but not too hot. You know? Say when it begins to cool, and we'll do one more."

O'Keefe again tuned in to the conversation at the next chair. "You got him out of trouble?" asked the barber.

"Oh, sure. 'Course he lost the suit, and the other side was awarded everything he had, but they won't get anything."

"How's that?" asked the barber.

"We delayed the suit long enough for the wife to divorce him and take everything. So there's nothing left for the plaintiff. The fucker's in bankruptcy now."

"The idea, I take it, is that the wife's supposed to remarry him when everything settles down," the barber said.

"Well, that's the idea, but I've got a funny feeling about her."

"You ready for another towel," Caesar said, whipping the first from O'Keefe's face.

Under the second towel, O'Keefe dozed, drifting from daydream to half sleep until he was lying in his bed, which in the summers of his childhood was always moved into the dormer of the second-floor room that was his. Through the dormer window and an identical window in the next house, ten feet away, he watched the neighbor boy, a young man four years older than he. Light from a half-opened closet sliced across the bed and the young man's naked body, browned and hard-edged on the white sheets. The size of the penis and the mass of black hair at the base of it mesmerized Dale, who lay absolutely still, afraid to move or even breathe for fear the young man would discover that he was being watched. Only when the young man increased the speed and intensity of his motion did Dale allow his hand to creep under the elastic waist of his pajamas and around himself. He felt a hand grip his shoulder and yanked his hand from under his pajamas.

"You fall asleep, Mr. O'Keefe," said Caesar, his hand on O'Keefe's shoulder.

"Sorry there. Am I finished?"

"No, no," said the barber. "Now we begin again. I lather you one more time."

Because Agnes O'Keefe had been seventy years old when she died, an autopsy was not deemed necessary. When Dale O'Keefe found her, sitting at the kitchen table, her hands around an apple, he knew she was dead and called the family doctor. On the death certificate, the doctor filled in as the cause of death congestive heart failure. Had an autopsy been performed, Dr. Day would have been surprised to discover that while Agnes O'Keefe did, in fact, die of heart failure, her liver was rather seriously compromised from drink. The information would also have surprised Dale O'Keefe, who had never in his life seen his mother take a drink.

On the night that Agnes O'Keefe came to the conclusion that her chances of having another man in her bed were hopeless, at least on any terms that were palatable to her, she carried the bottle of Irish whiskey that her husband had always kept on a pantry shelf and a cut crystal tumbler, part of a wedding gift, to her bed. She drank until she fell asleep. The next morning she washed the tumbler and placed it and the bottle in the nightstand next to her bed. On the following night, she again drank herself to sleep. The morning after she finished the bottle she took a bus to another neighborhood and with some trepidation went into a liquor store and bought a bottle of Scotch whiskey. When she finished that bottle, she went to another liquor store and bought bourbon. In the end, she settled on Scotch, but continued to rotate liquor stores. The only change that the fourteen-year-old Dale O'Keefe discerned in his mother was that she had begun reading, checking out novels from the local branch of the library. He had never known her to read anything but a newspaper. "Oh, when I can't sleep at night, I read," she told him, which was true enough. And she began to enjoy the books, which became as integral to her nights as her tumbler of Scotch. While this was not, she decided, an ideal situation, it did seem to work; if her hunger for another human being could not be sated, it could be deadened.

It was when her son went away for the first time, to church camp the second summer after his father had died, that Agnes O'Keefe came to believe that she could not trust herself. In the middle of the week that he was gone, she decided that there was really no reason why she should put off her first drink until ten o'clock at night; and by ten o'clock, two large drinks under her belt, she had convinced herself there was really no reason why she shouldn't go out to a bar.

The man she met and took home was, she knew, married. This was better, she told herself, because a married man would be less likely to have a disease. The man did not make love to her as Matt O'Keefe had learned to make love to her. He used her, hard, as she assumed a whore was used, and she got through it by urging him on. "Yes," she whispered in his ear, "go faster." And, finally, when she knew he was through, she rolled out from under him and got out of bed. "You need to get out," she said. "My husband . . ."

"I thought you said . . ."

"I lied. Just get out." When she was alone, she bathed herself, stripped and remade the bed, and made herself a drink. Immediately, she was sick. "Oh, Jesus, God," she said, her head over the toilet. "I'll never . . ." In the night, she woke with her cheek against the cold tile of the bathroom floor. When she lifted her head, she was sick again, but unable to bring anything up.

Agnes O'Keefe had no knowledge of the more subtle effects of alcohol. The combination of depression, remorse, and self-loathing she felt the following day was, she believed, a manifestation of guilt. In the afternoon, she dragged herself to a church where she was not known and confessed the entire episode, which did not make her feel better. Only later did she find relief, halfway through her first tumbler of Scotch. If Dale had been home, she reasoned, none of it would ever have happened. He needed her, couldn't do without her.

During the following school year, when he asked if he could spend the night with a friend, she suggested that instead he ask the friend over to stay with him. "I'll go to bed early," she told him. "You two can sit up and watch those horror movies on the TV. It'll be more fun that way 'cause you'll be alone." The following spring she bought him a tent, which he came home to find pitched in the backyard. "It's called an umbrella tent," she said, her head through the tent flaps. "Because of the frame. See how the pole opens out, just like an umbrella. You can have your friends over to camp out."

"How'd you get it set up already?" Dale asked, standing inside the tent.

"When Spalding's delivered, I got the delivery man to set it up. But he left instructions, so you'll know how to take it down and build it back up . . ."

"Pitch it."

"Pitch it . . . on your own. You like it?"

"Sure, I guess," said Dale. In the tent's gloom he could still see his mother's face. "I mean sure, it's neat."

At dinner on the night of his forty-fifth birthday, Dale O'Keefe, breaking the primary tenet of his routine, ordered a second drink and then a third and left the restaurant pleasantly drunk. Assaulted by the unbearably cold wind, he hailed a cab. "Vermont and Franklin," he said, settling into the seat. While denying it to himself throughout the day, O'Keefe had known that this would be where he ended up. Eventually, the driver turned under the El and began weaving around the ancient, riveted beams of the iron frame from which showers of sparks mysteriously rained over the cars and pavement. When the cab pulled up to the corner, O'Keefe handed the driver a five-dollar bill and said, "Keep the change." He stood at the corner, waiting for the cab to disappear before walking away.

Inside the door, O'Keefe stood before the high counter. The ancient storefront, long and narrow, was brightly lighted, hot, and smelled of disinfectant. Behind the counter, a bullet-headed man with long, cascading bags under his eyes mumbled, "Dollar admittance."

O'Keefe responded softly, "Twenty dollars' worth of quarters. Please."

"What?" the man said.

"Twenty dollars' worth of quarters," O'Keefe said louder. When he reached up to drop the twenty-dollar bill on the counter, a dog, unseen behind the counter, growled darkly.

"Shut up," the man barked and dropped the rolls of coins on the counter. O'Keefe slid the rolls off the counter, turned, and walked hurriedly toward the rear, past men standing, leafing through magazines. At the back, two men before racks of video boxes turned and stared as O'Keefe walked past and into the dark.

On either side of a long corridor, above rows of doors with numbers, tiny red lights blinked off and on to the dull mechanical clank of dropping coins. Cries and moans, grunts, panting, and curses poured like smoke from under the doors. O'Keefe stopped and carefully leaned against a space between doors. He would wait. He hated waiting, hated the tension across his forehead, and the fear that someone would demand to know why he didn't take one of the empty booths, which were all on the side against which he stood. The weight of the rolls of coins in his pocket made his coat hang awkwardly, and he reached into the pocket and lifted the hard rolls into his hand. The warm paper wrappers felt good against his palm, and he thought of the damage the rolls might effect if smashed, like brass knuckles, across a nose. A man came into the corridor and stood next to him. The man lit a cigarette, and in the flash of the match their eyes met, then disconnected. The man took a long drag, audibly exhaled, dropped the cigarette to the floor, and walked out. In the center of the row of doors, a light went out. O'Keefe listened for coins to drop. When he heard nothing, he pulled at the door, knowing it would be locked. A second man came into the corridor and stood against the wall. O'Keefe remained before the door. "Drop coins or get out of the booths," a disembodied voice spewed from out of the dark. O'Keefe heard someone stand up, chair legs scrape against the floor. The door opened in a rush, and a huge man, tugging at his coat, burst out. O'Keefe immediately stepped up and into the booth.

A video screen, heavily framed in metal, cast blue light through the closet-size space, which was five degrees warmer than the corridor. It smelled of sweat and funk and cigarette smoke. Cigarette butts and wads of Kleenex littered the floor. In one corner, a rubber lay like a giant slug flattened by the tires of a truck. Fearing the awful voice demanding that the machine be fed, O'Keefe opened a roll and began dropping quarters. The light went up as the screen came alive. He placed the rolls of coins on the top of the machine, draped his coat over the back of the chair, and sat down. He then began clicking a button on the metal frame, switching up through channels: through white couples, black couples, mixed couples; through groups — threes and fours and fives; through gang rapes and Nazi brutes menacing inmates of prison camps; through flagellation and toe suckers and dildos and tattoos; through the grotesque — midgets and giants, the fat and bestial; through women on women and men on men and men on men before the watching eyes of women; through the ugly, the beautiful, the black and white and Puerto Rican. Finally, he spread his legs, opened his trousers, and waited.

To his left, a finger inched through one of two holes drilled through the wall at different heights and tapped insistently. O'Keefe bent forward and stared through the circle — an old man with his pants and shorts around his ankles as if he were on a toilet. Beyond, through the hole on the other side of the old man, O'Keefe could see an arm pumping slowly. He turned to the holes drilled on the other side of his booth. Hands, young, with clean, manicured nails, cupped the unzipped but closed fly of dress trousers. Bringing his eye to the hole, O'Keefe looked up. Above a white shirt and a silk tie thrown over a shoulder, a face, strangely beautiful in the blue, flickering light, stared straight ahead at the video. Muscles across the jaw clenched and unclenched, then the face turned, momentarily, and O'Keefe looked into pale, frightened eyes. The face instantly turned back to the machine. Looking straight through the hole, O'Keefe saw through the next hole a cock standing and, through the hole beyond, another. When he straightened up in his chair, he realized he was very hard. He felt those eyes staring at him, and he lifted his hand from his own fly. A long, narrow finger flicked across the hole, dropped and rested, motionless. O'Keefe again bent forward. The eyes retreated. After a moment, the clean, long fingers folded back the trousers and released a long, hard cock. When O'Keefe tentatively placed a finger on the frame of the hole, the body stood. O'Keefe watched, in amazement, as the head and the shaft came through to him. The person beyond pressed himself flat against the wall until all of it, framed by tufts of honey-colored hair and by the outlining halo of wood, stood before O'Keefe. To O'Keefe it was something completely disembodied and yet the essence of this man, who O'Keefe would never know, never speak to, and certainly never touch except in the most anonymous, yet intimate, of ways. When O'Keefe gently placed a hand around it and closed his fingers, he felt the slightest of tremors move through the man and pass across the palm of his hand. A trigger very deep within him went off, and O'Keefe lowered his head and took into his mouth all he would ever know of this person hidden beyond a wall.

If O'Keefe had been sober, if he had not received the phony e-mail birthday greeting or the single birthday card, he might not have done this, taken this man within himself. He came to this place — not often, but he came — when things built up, when things at the Guarantee got under his skin. But it was not his habit to take, or even to give. He watched and, strangely, felt connected to the others watching in their own dark booths. He felt no more pity for them than he did for himself, but assumed that they, like himself, preferred this. He did not understand why he found pleasure alone and was not particularly interested in why. He had been with men and with women, had found pleasure with both. But when it was over, he wanted to be disengaged, to be away. Once, he had waited for something else to happen, but O'Keefe never met another human being that he wanted sufficiently to dislodge whatever it was that kept him alone. Finally, at some point, he simply accepted that this was the way he was and the way he would be.

When the man beyond the wall began to come, O'Keefe felt on his tongue the first gout coursing up the shaft. And when it shot into his throat and he had swallowed it, O'Keefe knew a contentment that was absolute yet haunting, as if he had somehow known it all before. He sucked greedily and took all he could get until the man, in pain, pulled himself from O'Keefe's mouth. He watched the man slowly sit down and lower his head toward the hole. "Please," the man whispered. "Give it to me now." And because O'Keefe felt gratitude to this man, he stood and presented himself. Almost immediately, he began to come. Beyond the known sensation of orgasm, he experienced intense pleasure in the man's undisguised relish at what O'Keefe could give.

When it was over and the man had whispered to him through the hole, and O'Keefe had leaned forward and whispered in return, he sat, motionless, listening to the man stand, zip his trousers, put on his coat, and leave.

In the cold outside, under the El, O'Keefe suddenly understood what had passed between them, and he felt as if he had been struck hard with a fist. Standing stock still, tears welling in his eyes, he saw the frame, so carefully constructed, shatter, and he cried out in terror.

John R. Keene

MY SON, MY HEART, MY LIFE

SANDALWOOD, Jaime whispers to himself, recalling the vendor who had sold Tony and him the three little vials of this scented oil and the five foil packets of incense. He had a makeshift stall outside the bus terminal in Dudley Square. Wearing an embroidered red and black tarboosh and an immaculately white T-shirt, on which had been silk-screened in exquisite calligraphics the simple phrase LIFE IS THE FINEST ART, he was probably in his early twenties — and *handsome,* Jaime thought now — though hard living had so weathered his face and hands, his gestures, that he looked much older. Beside Tony, however, the vendor had appeared almost a boy. His thin, dark fingertips, sallowed by the oils, the incense, cigarettes, perhaps even the plate of curried goat that sat at the edge of the display table, fanned slowly over the array of offerings, patchouli, lavender, musk, Rose of Sharon, anise, something called "Love," something else called "Power," which Jaime had not noticed before. Which one *you* like? *Sandalwood,* Tony had snapped out without deliberation: it was the only scent he had ever worn.

— What*ever* you do, baby, don't forget your algebra notebook! — Jaime's mother's call rings from the kitchen, where she is preparing breakfast for his two younger sisters, Tatiana and Tasha. Having awakened early as always with his older sister, Teresita, Jaime has already wolfed down a banana and a piece of white bread with strawberry jelly for breakfast, before his mother and the girls rise, to stay out of their way. Sometimes he will drink a cup of coffee and chat with Teresita — whose position at the nearby springs manufacturing plant occasions *her* early mornings — but not this morning. He has spent the entire time since he woke, ate, and showered in reading over his poem — *his poem!* — which his teacher and classmates, everyone, including perhaps even his mother, will all be talking about for weeks to come, and checking his equations. After proofing his Spanish against the dictionary, he struggled over a seemingly unsolvable *"xy,"* and came up with the only answer that allowed the equation to work: this, he tells himself, calls for a celebration, a *game.*

— Sí, Mami, I promised you I wasn't gonna forget it again. — That stupid notebook, Jaime grumbles, why can't he forget it altogether! He sits up on his bed, which he has just prepared to his mother's former specifications (since Tony's death, she no longer has to scold him every morning, he now makes it instinctively), and opens the palm-size, amber-colored vial, one of the few personal effects of Tony's that neither his mother nor Tony's girlfriend has hoarded as her own. As he had observed Tony do every morning for the last few years, he places his index finger over the opening, upends it, then daubs the sweet, masculine fragrance under both ears; again, then lightly across his collarbone; one last time, a straight line from the point where his Adam's apple has begun to appear to the soft point of his chin.

This fragrance, Jaime realizes, almost smiling now, almost tear-ing as it takes root and blossoms in the loam of his consciousness, still lingers upon the surface of everything in the apartment: this matted wool comforter on which he sits; on the top and corners of the particleboard dresser that he and Tony had shared; upon even the mildewed plastic antislip stars plastering the bottom of the bathtub in which they had stood huddled together when they were younger, all redolent as though permanently coated. Today, for good luck's sake, it will trail him as well, throughout the morning, on the way to school, as he stands before his class and reads his poem.

Done, he shakes his head as Tony would, wipes his eyes — no one had seen him cry at or after the funeral and will not now — then hides the vial under the stack of underpants in the top drawer of the dresser that has become his alone. As he stands before the open drawer — how they had fought over where their clothes would go! how he, Jaime, had *always* lost and wished that he could claim the entire thing as his own! — he feels like a blackboard from which everything has been erased, on which anything can be written. Tony. Alone, he drops onto the bed, tries to think of the day before him, the bus ride, school . . . his poem. His poem, which Tony would have read with approval, maybe even awe, as he had done with the other poems, the drawings, the stories Jaime would write, sometimes off the top of his head. . . .

Silent now, he can hear beneath the floorboards his uncle Narciso, rearranging the merchandise on the shelves of the bodega he and his aunt Marisol own and operate. Above him, their apartment slumbers. Jaime is glad to have been occupied and to not have had to help out this morning. Often his mother will send him downstairs after she has awakened the girls and begun to get them ready and before his bus arrives, to seek something to do, to help his uncle and aunt out, as if she owes them something for living here, especially since his father left, as if his sacrifice is her part of the bargain. Sometimes he aids in moving pieces of meat around the cold locker and shelving newly arrived canned and boxed goods when his uncle asks him to. Undoubtedly there will be some bubble-gum box to be refilled, some soup cans to be shifted around or transformed into a stable pyramid, some moldy bread to be turned over so that the nearby loaves will mask it. This morning, however, her mind has latched completely on to that notebook.

Outside this room, music, laughter, the cacophony of glass against metal, voices, the television against the hour's stillness.

Tony, Jaime reminds himself, had never helped out in the store. He had gone simply from mornings and afternoons before the television and Nintendo games to the streets and a crew of similarly minded boys and couriering, which meant that Uncle Narciso and Aunt Marisol never wanted him around; his presence, at least in their eyes, and that of his boys, his *chicos,* usually spelled trouble. It was an out to which Jaime had no recourse: *Send Jaime down to help me out,* Uncle Narciso was always saying, *so I can make a man out of him, keep him out of trouble.* Jaime's mother only too eagerly assented.

Hoisting his backpack onto the bed, Jaime pulls out his Spanish poem to read once more, which jogs his memory: they had had to wait until nearly the end of the school year to write poems, and why? Because of the "turdles," as he and Vinh, his classmate and best and only friend, have often laughed to themselves at lunch, though neither would dare call the mass of their classmates, even the girls, this nickname face to face. Despite the fact that they have occasionally had to write a paragraph, or even a short essay, they are mainly doing multiple-choice quizzes, nothing more advanced, more creative, even though this class is supposedly accelerated. As usual Mrs. Donovan has given them nine regular words and a bonus word, and this time, unlike before, she has allowed them to create *a poem* of at least one hundred words from these. *Too simple,* Vinh had cracked under his breath, against the general groans of the class; Jaime had nodded, though he disagreed. As the lines now sing inside his head, he is sure this poem will merit an A, as will Vinh's, which he has not yet seen. Most of the other kids, even those whose first language is Spanish, will end up with B's or C's, whether they hand in homework or not, since Mrs. Donovan is unwilling to embarrass anyone, even the most "slow-dropping" of the turdles, with anything lower. They had to wait almost the entire year, Jaime sighs, but now he will show them.

The words read, in this order: *hijo* (son), *parar* (to stop), *pedir* (to ask for), *cada* (each), *corazón* (heart), *broma* (joke), *hallar* (to come across), *sangre* (blood), *anochecer* (nightfall), and the bonus word *fugaz* (brief).

Such words! Vinh had said after fourth period that Mrs. Donovan had torn up a Spanish dictionary and picked the entries one by one out of a hat, but Jaime is convinced that she pulls some of them out of whatever she has been reading at home, some novel, some book of poetry, because there are always strange or unusual words, like *fugaz,* that are nowhere to be found in their Spanish book. He has never heard anyone, not his mother, nor Uncle Narciso nor Aunt Marisol, nor any of the Spanish speakers in the neighborhood or at church, nor even his grandmother, uncles, aunts, or cousins in Puerto Rico, ever use this bonus word *fugaz* even once in conversation — he and his sisters speak only English regularly, as did Tony — which for him is the giveaway. *This* word, he thinks, she has selected just for me.

As a result, he wrote (with the translation beneath it):

> *Cada día al anochecer*
> *voy esa cama y pienso*
> *sobre mi hermano muerto,*
> *Antonio José Barrett.*
> *Fue mi hermano solo*
> *y tuvo quince años y medio.*
> *Yo halle la sangre y su cuerpo*
> *que estaba acostado*
> *sobre la acera como un G.I. Joe.*
> *Durante el funeral mi Mami preguntó*

al Dios, "¿Por qué, God, por qué
mi hijo, mi corazón, mi vida, mi Tony
por qué my baby ahora?" Mi tío
Narciso dijo toda la iglesia,
"¿O Dios, mi amigos, quando la muerte
va parar?" Nadie le respondió.
Desde entonce hay una cosa que yo sé:
en mi barrio vivir es muy fugaz
y el futuro estará una broma grande.

Every day at nighttime
I see that bed and I think
about my dead brother,
Antonio José Barrett.
He was my only brother
and was fifteen and a half years old.
I found the blood and his body
lying on the sidewalk like a G.I. Joe.
During the funeral my mother asked
God, "How come, God, how come
my son, my heart, my life, my Tony
why my baby now?" My uncle
Narciso said to the whole church,
"Oh God, my friends, when
is the dying going to end?"
No one answered him.
Since then there is one thing I know:
in my neighborhood living is too brief
and the future is a great big joke.

One hundred and eleven words he counts, and he has used the past tense correctly every time; he has verified this twice this morning against his Spanish book. No misspellings that he can spot, and even some words they have not yet learned, but which he has gathered from regular conversations or his own reading: Mrs. Donovan will *have to* give him an A! When he recites it, she will comment on the rhymes in Spanish, on the flow, on the *feeling:* in her eyes there is *nothing* he can do wrong.

What else is there for today? For social studies he has his notes for his presentation on a country in West Africa. He has elected to report on Senegal, where he imagines his father's (and mother's, maybe) ancestors came from, instead of Cape Verde, his other option. Jaime shuffles his note cards in order: there are seven. He makes sure they are all there, then stores them in his backpack on top of his Spanish notebook. He has no homework (when do they ever have homework?) for any of his other classes, except algebra. He glances again at the figures cleanly printed in that notebook and on the loose-leaf, and on which he spent two hours last night, and at least one this morning.

His sisters are clamoring in the kitchen, he can hear; his mother never tells them to shut up anymore, or even slaps Tasha when she talks back as she had always done before. Jaime never talked back in the first place, though she would still sometimes slap him for whatever reason (because he would not clean his room, because he sulked all through dinner, because he was switching and batting his eyes, because he reminded her too much of *that black man who had left her*), but now she is always asking him what he is doing before she gets home, how he is progressing in school, what he is *feeling*. My son. He always lies and tells her nothing beyond the barest outline of what happens to him each day, because he is convinced she would not understand anyway, or care; she has never understood a thing about him before in the previous thirteen and a half years of his life, nor cared, and she understood even less about Tony, whose name was always on her lips, though no longer. *Tony.* My heart. Nor about any of his sisters, except Tatiana, the *true* baby, who seems to gain her care and concern, though how long will *this* last, Jaime wonders, how long? My life.

Why is it so quiet downstairs? He descends the stairwell quietly and crosses the narrow hallway, through the double-hinged door, into the store. Quiet, empty. His uncle Narciso has obviously gone into the storeroom down in the cellar, or perhaps out into the small cold locker in back, and Aunt Marisol has not yet come down. The shade on the front door is still drawn, and the triple-bolts have not been unlocked, nor the gratings raised and furled.

Jaime leans back against the wall of candy racks behind the cash register and brushes curly, raven bangs back from his forehead. In the mirror of Plexiglas surrounding the register area before him, he chances upon his reflection: the spit and image of his father — the eyes two new black backgammon chits; the nose the face's anchor, an inverted mahogany cross; the lips as pale and swollen as two undercooked link sausages — whose actual face he has not seen in two years, he finds himself *almost* handsome, though not like Tony, who more resembled their mother, and was thin, lean, wiry. He, Jaime, is still too plump, *muy gordo.* Though no one calls him Porcelito anymore, since he has lost some weight over the last few months, his first cousin Niño, who had been a year ahead of him at school until he flunked out and was placed in Catholic school, has not stopped calling him Gordón every chance he can. At least he no longer has to hear that nickname at school, or Niño's other gem, Chunky and Chinky, for when he and Vinh were together. Being *gordo,* however, he has never been expected to be cool or popular or have a girlfriend or have *juice.* Those expectations fell upon Tony, who satisfied them amply, which allowed Jaime thus to be the inverse, his reverse: the "smart," "quiet," "artistic" one, the little chub who spends all his hours in his room, drawing, reading, writing, devising imaginary scenarios and games by and for himself. . . .

Since Tony's death, however, not even Niño or his mother calls him those *other* names, those names that had lacerated Jaime in their truth and viciousness, that had left him in tears when not driving him to fights he could not win, though no one, not even his mother, had ever dared utter them in Tony's presence. That

Tony would never tolerate, Jaime remembers, nor had he ever called Jaime those names, not even while playing, though he must have known. . . . Now, since Tony failed to father a little boy, he, Jaime, has become his mother's *only* son, the only *man* in her life . . . the thought sometimes makes him shudder, as now.

Mi hijo, mi corazón, mi vida.

Still by himself, he empties into his mouth an already opened box of Lemon-Heads which was sitting under the register and probably belonged to Aunt Marisol, who is always munching on something sweet. At his feet he notices about six chewing-gum wrappers, which means that Aunt Marisol, or Lisa, a woman neighbor who fills in at night, worked the closing shift: Uncle Narciso would never tolerate trash lying anywhere on this floor, so he has not yet been back behind here. Jaime gathers them up and, as he is tossing them in the wastebasket, notices the Browning Hi-Power 9mm semiautomatic, clipless, poking out from the lower shelf. Who left this thing out? Catching no light, the barrel does not flash as it normally would; Jaime's thoughts recoil from the cold metal. He has held this handgun before, and had held Tony's many times; with his toe he pushes it back onto the shelf so that it is no longer visible.

Before his uncle returns, he pulls the shade to peep out the front door. A small throng of people is collecting at the bus stop several feet down from the front of the store. This group of about seven people, all of them neighbors, mostly work downtown or in Cambridge, and there is a woman Jaime recognizes as one of the teacher's aides in the special education program now housed at the back of his school. Hardly anyone is milling around, as usual, so frozen are they to their spots, even at this time of year. Within seconds the bus, already half-full, screeches up. These commuters, as is customary, are pushing and shoving each other out of the way to board. Jaime's mother always says that the Orientals push hardest because they have to claim seats first or they will never be able to muscle their way into one, that Portuguese will give up their seats if you look tired enough because they are a sad people, that the Irish usually smell like whiskey or beer so you will want to give them your seat, that the West Indians do not care how tired you look if you do not look West Indian, and that black men never give up their seats for an older woman, unless it's their mother. But Jaime knows these kernels of maternal wisdom do not hold; he was once knocked out of his seat by another Puerto Rican, and Tony always gave up his seat for an older or pregnant woman, if she was black or Puerto Rican or Cape Verdean. Truth is, everyone, as Jaime knows, can be rude, mercenary, self-interested.

— Ai, Negrito, ¿qué tal? — Jaime feels the thick, spatulate fingers softly digging into his shoulders, the protuberant stomach pressing against the slope of his shoulder blades. It is his uncle Narciso. He tenses. His uncle's breath, warm and somewhat stale, wets the hairs on the back of his neck, as his hand slips like a scarf around Jaime's neck bone.

— Nada, Tío. — Jaime turns around to face his uncle's sloe eyes, a virtual mirror image of his mother, in male form. Narciso is of medium height — Jaime has never been able to guess heights on sight, but his uncle is taller than Tony, who was five-eight — and, like Jaime's mother, slender, except for the belly. Jaime comes nearly to his uncle's forehead. He backs away, to prevent Narciso's mustache from scouring *his* forehead like a small hairbrush.

— You didn't come down this morning. Tío was waiting on you. — His uncle grins, exposing a row of teeth like kernels of Indian corn.

— I was working on my algebra. I'm *failing*, you know. — Jaime stops against the counter. — I told you that, Tío. — He knows his uncle is not listening, as usual.

— Tío was *waiting* on you. I had a lot for you to do this morning, didn't your mother let you know? — He approaches Jaime, both his hands squirming beneath his bloody apron like two small, trapped birds.

— I was just checking to make sure the bus was on schedule.

— Jaime rolls his eyes, darting out of his uncle's path, toward an aisle. — I'm gonna be late if I don't hurry up, Tío.

— You don't got any time left to help Tío this morning! I was *waiting* on you. — Jaime cants his head around the corner to read the clock: he has only about fifteen or twenty minutes before his bus arrives. His uncle sweeps a lock off Jaime's forehead, reaches down, and tightly embraces him. Like always, he is mouthing something onto Jaime's earlobe, his neck, but Jaime has long since stopped paying any attention; he just goes slack and waits for his uncle to let go. In the back of the room, beyond the door to both the apartments and the cold locker, he can now hear someone, probably his aunt Marisol, scuffling toward the storeroom in the cellar. Abruptly his uncle releases him, picks up the cash box at his feet, and slips behind the door that forms a clear, though somewhat rickety, protective partition around the register.

— I'll help out tomorrow morning, Tío, I promise — Jaime yells out, before bounding out of the store and upstairs so as not to be late. When he reaches the top of the stairs, he hears his mother saying:

— And I told Mr. Morris to call me if you was skipping class or not doing you homework, Jaime, because I don't want you failing math again. — Had she heard him come upstairs or had she just automatically launched into this? he asks himself. His mother, splendid in her nurse's aide's whites, emerges from her bedroom, and now stands before him in the narrow strait of hallway between the rooms. She is frowning, blankly.

— Did you *hear* me?

— Yeah, Mami, I heard you. I'm not gonna skip algebra any more, and I *did* my homework, just like Mr. Morris wants. Do you want to *see* it? Do you want to see my *poem?* — As though by default she shakes her head no; she seldom looks at any of his homework, though she will sometimes check to make sure that he has at least packed the notebook in with the rest of his school materials, and she never looks at his other things, his other notebooks, full of his writings and drawings, which he now keeps hidden behind his bed in a small bag that had belonged to Tony. Most of these he has shown to no one except Vinh, who draws pictures of his own, keeps similar notebooks. Vinh's consist mostly of action figures like the X-Men or the Fantastic Four, which he copies from the comic books he collects (Jaime collected them, too, at one point but stopped when his mother got laid off the last time), but he always changes all the eyes and hair so that they become Vietnamese and usually much more muscular than they appeared originally. Jaime's, all drawn from his storehouse of memories and fantasy, usually consist of people he has seen on the bus or on the street or in the bodega, or at Downtown Crossing or in Central Square when he slips there on Saturdays or sometimes after school, and occasionally he even draws pictures of Tony, and rarely his father, though never other members of his family. Other renderings, completely from his imagination and of a different, vivid, and more explicit nature, he reveals to no one. So much no one knows about him, he realizes, now that Tony is gone.

As they stand there wordlessly, Jaime places one hand on his hip and licks the palm of his free hand, flips back his bangs coquettishly, bats his eyes: this once provoked a reproach from his mother, but no longer. She stands before him, saying nothing, bemused as if she were looking upon someone she had never seen before in her life, when his youngest sister, Tatiana, just barely five, materializes, her jumper misbuttoned and her socks mismatched, her ponytails uncoiling from beneath her barrettes. She drops in loud sobs to the floor at his mother's feet. Jaime flees into his bedroom.

A glance at the Teenage Mutant Ninja Turtle clock — had he really been *so* into them? — alerts him that he has only about five minutes to spare. He checks his backpack to ensure everything is there, including that stupid algebra notebook. He even makes sure that he has the loose-leaf of arithmetic work tucked into the front inside cover of the notebook; Mr. Morris likes to receive the homework this way, so that he can verify the answers in the notebook by the preparatory work on the loose-leaf. Only for such a white turdle, Jaime notes, does everything have to be so complicated. On top of this, Mr. Morris is always pushing Jaime to do better, cornering him after class, stopping him in the hallways, calling his mother *at home! — He could easily be an A student, Ms. Barrett —* but all those variables and commutative laws tend to drive Jaime to distraction; he likes Spanish and language arts and social studies much better, since they afford him the freedom to order things — words, worlds, his life — to his satisfaction. Still, he has to admit that there is no reason he should *fail* algebra, because if he does, it will probably spell the death of his chances of getting into the Latin Academy, where he, with Vinh, has vowed to be, come ninth grade.

Below the clock's green-diode glimmer, Jaime gathers up the change off the small desk he had shared with Tony, and funnels it into his pockets. Maybe he will buy a pack of doughnuts from Uncle Narciso to eat on the way, or maybe he will save the coins for a tonic after school. *Tony.* It is so quiet these mornings, and evenings, too, now that Tony is no longer around, and yet Jaime no longer has to keep quiet when he wakes for fear of awaking Tony, who would be lightly snoring by now after having come in just around dawn from a long night out, probably dealing. This last year and a half Jaime would occasionally find a few dollar bills, mostly ones but occasionally a five or ten, lying in his house shoes when, still half-asleep, he climbed out of bed to go to the bathroom in the morning, and he did not even have to look across the room to realize these signified Tony was home and installed under the covers. Jaime had been saving these small gifts, which totaled about fifty-six dollars after a few withdrawals, and now keeps them tied up in a sock in the back of his drawer, for a future emergency. He has told no one about this, not even Vinh.

As though it were a talisman, he fingers his sock-bank, restashing it carefully, then slips on a green plastic wristband that he had won at the West Indian Festival last summer, before zipping up his backpack and heading downstairs.

His mother had said nothing about his yellow T-shirt, his baggy red shorts, or his matching red hightop sneakers when she saw him earlier. Teresita would surely say he looked like a clown, but she has left for work already. No one would even notice the wristband, he bets, or what the colors together represent. His keys: he pats the three of them, which hang from an extra-long shoelace beneath his shirt down into his briefs.

— Mami, I'm going. — Where is she?

— Jaime? In the kitchen. — He pokes his head in the doorway.

— You be good and be careful, okay?

— I will. — She has Tasha in one hand and Tatiana in the other. The two girls are dressed like twins, even though Tasha is three years older. His mother is obviously on her way out as well.

— Jaime, you got your algebra notebook? — He nods yes, tapping his backpack where he thinks it is tucked away — *because I just want you to do well, to not end up like your brother, to get out of all of this* — then gives her a quick kiss on the cheek.

As he runs down the stairs, he can hear the *I love you* trailing his steps.

Through the bodega, where his aunt Marisol is now planted behind the register, chewing on a stick of gum, past his uncle Narciso, who is lifting the last of the outside grates and larks out a good-bye in Spanish and English, onto the already hot, uneven, tar-gummed pavement: the bus has not yet arrived. Jaime crosses the street to his bus stop.

Only one other person is waiting for this bus: a young man, Corey Fuentes, who had dated Jaime's sister Teresita. As Jaime looks up and smiles, Corey sneers in reply, then lights up his Newport. Corey is out of work, has been for about a year, Jaime has heard, but this morning he is wearing alligator loafers, nice pressed gray slacks, an ironed white shirt, and holds what appears to be a brand-new clip-on tie in his free hand, which leads Jaime to suppose that he is going in for a job interview (very unlikely), traveling somewhere to meet his parole officer or some new criminal associate (more likely but still unlikely), or heading downtown to make a court date (most likely). Jaime does not dare inquire.

The spring heat has not yet fired the streets, and a breeze, almost gauzy in texture, carries pieces of trash and some seedlings toward the horizon. The other bodega, owned by the Cape Verdeans, stands behind and catercorner from them, somewhat dilapidated on the outside, with its warped grates, yellowed newspapered curtains, and its faded beer signs, unopened. To their right across the street in the distance, down near the wrought-iron fence that garters the Social Services building, a corpulent straw-haired white man, whom Jaime recognizes as Father Peter O'Hanlon, is chatting with a woman employee, unknown. So what if Fr. Pete was removed as assistant pastor of St. Stephen Protomartyr's for spending so much time with the gangs? Tony, Jaime remembers him saying, is not a lost cause. He will surely be in the bodega gossiping with Aunt Marisol and sipping a Coke, laced with rum, in about twenty minutes.

— Where *is* that fucking bus? — Corey hisses, checking his wrist graced not by a watch, but by an ornate gold bracelet.

He leans backbreakingly against the bus-stop sign pole. He is staring off into the distance, envisioning what? Jaime wonders. What sort of plea bargain his attorney will arrange? Whether his new girlfriend will show up to escort him back home, on his own recognizance? What the penalty will be for "uttering checks and credit cards" for the third time within one calendar year? Jaime is familiar with quite a few of the court careers of other people, such as Tony, and Teresita's current boyfriend, Eric, and her ex-boyfriend Andray, so that it is not too difficult for him to figure out what this "small-time booster," as Tony had labeled him, might be facing.

As he ponders Corey's fate, his eyes trace an invisible line from the slicked, raven crown of hair to the full, pink lips to the satiny brown neck bone, which a white undershirt almost completely conceals from view. He has dreamt about Corey before. Jaime's eyes linger on that downward slope and the cloven pectorals below, imagining them supple beneath his grasping fingers like the earth beneath the saplings that his earth science class spent all last month planting. Corey's skinny arms pale in comparison to the knottier arms and the ample chest of the guy who sometimes drives Jaime's bus route — Jerome — whose name he has inscribed on the inside back cover of the notebook he remembered to bring with him today. For a while Jaime feared his mother might see this name and interrogate him about it, but then he realized she would not touch anything of his, save perhaps that algebra notebook, under any circumstances, unless *he* was dead.

Turning and catching Jaime in his spell of appreciation, Corey glowers, murmuring, — You li'l *freak!* — As Jaime looks away, unembarrassed, Fr. Pete lumbers his way up the street.

Another breeze is bearing up a fresh offering of debris as their bus scuds up to the curb. Corey boards first, tamping out his cigarette and tossing it over his shoulder so that it bounces off Jaime's arm. Jaime says nothing, and hops aboard after him, perfunctorily flashing his pass as he moves into the aisle. The bus is mostly vacant, but before he can grab a seat, the bus driver has pulled sharply away into the street, stomping down on the accelerator, thus hurtling Jaime headfirst toward the back. Obviously, this bus driver is *not* Jerome, who has a velvet touch on the pedal — Jaime visually verifies this: No! Oh, well — but instead Randall, who from time to time works this morning route but more often drives the Columbia Road evening route, which Jaime has taken on those occasions when he had to drop off something at his sister Tita's job.

For a moment he debates whether he should sit up near Randall, whom he has never really paid much attention to, or sit in the back of the bus and write in his notebook: *¿Qué va hacer?* He decides to perch himself on the last forward-facing seat on the right side of the bus, near no one; Corey is sitting near most of the other passengers in the forward-facing seats near the front, an unlit cigarette poling from his lips. Jaime thinks about reading his poem, how his classmates will all stare in amazement, how Mrs. Donovan will nod her head appreciatively with theirs, how afterward she will tell him that this is proof of what she knows he can do. He will show her his other poems, some of his drawings soon, she will write a recommendation for him, he will get into Boston Latin, he will do so well that he confirms Tony's grandest predictions. He tries not to think about algebra at all.

Randall's driving this morning is certainly a lot more jerky than Jerome's. Extracting his writing notebook and a pencil, he sketches Randall's face, and then Jerome's face and torso, which he can summon from memory as sharply as if he were staring right at them, before writing beneath both pictures:

AM: RANDALL — Almost turdle of the bus drivers—iron foot. No Jerome this morning. Ran-dull instead . . . will have to settle for second best . . . not the best start, but I will make do!! Fugaz. What is the game for today? Tony.

The bus slithers along its usual path, people board, Jaime looks up periodically to see if any of them catch his eye: a few girls who were once classmates of Teresita's or Tony's and who are now cradling babies in their arms or in strollers; a few teenagers his age, none at his middle school, boisterous, listening to hip-hop or dance-hall blaring from headset speakers, their backpacks rattling with drug paraphernalia, perhaps, or forties; an old woman, dressed in a filthy white blouse and yellow shorts, a pink hairnet framing a face drooping like melting brown wax; another older woman, white and in an appliquéd blue frock, yammering excitedly to herself; an older man, maybe forty-five, somewhere near Uncle Narciso's age, in a red and white striped polo shirt, brown polyester beltless pants, and matching brown buckled loafers. He slides into the row of seats across from Jaime and smiles. Jaime acknowledges him, almost absently.

Light is now flooding the bus. May sun. The fragrances of

sandalwood, a cologne that must be Brut, and newsprint commingle in Jaime's consciousness: he turns slowly toward the man, who has a full head of graying wavy hair and an almost lacquered black mustache. The man pulls out the sports section of his newspaper and starts reading the back-page write-up of last night's big boxing match, which Teresita and Eric and his mother had been watching on pay-per-view. *My hurt.* Jaime had instead been printing out his index cards, and had telephoned Vinh with a question about one of the languages in Senegal, which Vinh of course knew about. They had spoken for about twenty minutes. *My love.* Vinh was in the midst of doing what he spends all of his free time doing, like Jaime: reading or drawing.

Jaime examines the man more carefully. He must be still in his forties, because although gray salts his hair, his face does not look *that* old. Skinny almost, he has a complexion not unlike Jaime's own, the color of an unshelled almond; and thick lips, like Jaime's father, like Corey, like Jaime. Through the small triangle created by the placket of his shirt, Jaime can almost see the hairless chest. It looks like it may be toned; the man cranes slightly forward, obscuring Jaime's view. Jaime watches him study the scores, and draws a picture of him. What does he do all day, who is he, where is he going? Jaime writes these questions down, in order. *If I were myself, but like Tony: What would I do? What would he do?* As Jaime scribbles, the bus stops, people board, deboard.

When Jaime looks out of the bus window for a change, he sees a fourteen-year-old girl he knows, named Mercedes, whom they call Dita, in front of the liquor store, stepping out of a fire-engine-red Samurai with two boys, from a gang that hangs out at Four Corners. He bows his head so that he can watch her unobserved, though it is unlikely she even notices the bus's presence. She had wanted to have Tony's baby so badly, just a year ago, but since Tony's death, Jaime has rarely seen her. One of the men wraps his arm around Dita's waist, eases his hand down the side of her leg, slides it over onto her behind . . .

Jaime turns back to the man, who has been staring at him.

The man gets up and slides in next to Jaime, who pushes his knapsack against the window. *What does he do all day, who is he, where is he going?*

— Hhhiiih . . . — Jaime says, his voice breathy and tremulous, like a vibrating reed.

— Hey — the man replies. — How you doing this morning? — His voice is pure ice.

— Fine.

— Tha's good — the man says, baring his straight, yellowing smile. Jaime spots the wedding band on his left ring finger, which, like all the others, is long, unwrinkled, and spoonlike. Maybe he is younger than Uncle Narciso. Setting the paper in his lap, the man slowly examines the riders on the bus, his head angling and turning as if it were a movie camera. Jaime searches the bus for anyone who might call him out. Corey is still up front, but he is now conversing intensely with one of the young mothers. The man appears to mime placing his hand on Jaime's knee, but does not. He simply looks down at Jaime and smiles. The teeth gleam like butter-covered knives. Jaime can feel his underarms beginning to moisten. *My son.*

— Where you headed? — the man asks.

— Wha's your name? — Jaime answers.

— I like that, "What's your name?" . . . My name is Vernon, what's yours? — He lays a hand on the seatback next to Jaime's shoulders. Jaime licks his palms and sweeps back his curls; this man's name cannot *really* be Vernon, Jaime tells himself; he must be playing a game as well. He looks out into the traffic alongside the bus: cars snake past on their way to wherever.

— Tony.

— Tony . . . Where you headed, Tony?

— Cuffe School . . . Where you headed?

— Nowhere, I got the day off . . .

Vernon purses his lips, then asks, — Tony, why don't we get off at the next stop? I'll walk you partway there. We can talk. — He smiles again, as the fingers, like the petals of an exquisite flower, flutter out upon the seatback. Jaime inhales deeply, his mind swirling with questions: What *is* happening? Who is this man? Where are they going? Is he going to miss *algebra?* Because Mr. Morris will surely telephone his mother and admonish him in front of the class. The bus halts at the stop, and they both slip out through the back door. As the bus pulls away, Jaime reminds himself that although he has never taken a game *this far,* Vernon seems decent enough, and Jaime decides that, no matter what, he will *not* act as he normally would.

The sidewalk flares with the morning heat. Sun glints off every metal surface in dazzling spars, forcing Jaime to put on the pair of sunglasses he keeps in the front pocket of his backpack. Vernon dons a pair, too; where had he stored them? At the green light, they cross the street together, walking quickly, almost in tandem, then walk several blocks up before turning into a side street, where they pause. Jaime's hands, like Vernon's, are pocketed. He scans the main street to see if anyone he knows is passing by. Not a soul.

Pointing in the direction of the projects, to their left, Vernon tells Jaime, — Now, if I'm correct, Cuffe is about six blocks that way. — Jaime frowns, then nods in agreement.

Running his hand over the lip of his pants, Vernon continues, — Cuffe School, Cuffe School . . . I remember when the Cuffe School first became the Cuffe School. Used to be Wendell Phillips School when my kids went there, then they decided to change the name. Always do. Can't leave well enough alone. Can't say I actually know who Cuffe is, you know . . . or Wendell Phillips for that matter. I guess you kids don't care who it's named after, though, hunh?

All this talk annoys Jaime, who says nervously, — No, no, nobody cares. — He brushes the hair back from his forehead: Vernon is plumper than Jaime thought, or perhaps it is just that he has a gut like Uncle Narciso; he begins to wonder if he should not just run off, end this game right now, wait till after school, another day . . . What time is it anyway? he wonders.

— Turn around so I can see how *handsome* you are. You are so *handsome,* you know? — Jaime follows the instructions, revolving in a gradual circle. Vernon now looks older than he did at first, on the bus; the sunlight colors in the slight sagging of his chin, the almost slack quality of the skin on his arms, like a sheet of crumpled brown plastic. He is definitely older than Tío.

— How old are you, Tony?

— How old are *you,* Vernon?

— There you go again, answering my question with another question. My age doesn't matter, Tony, but I'm forty-nine. Now, how old are you?

Jaime throws his head back, closes his eyes, says casually, — I'm sixteen and a half. I got kept back a few times and I look young for my age.

Beginning to laugh, Vernon inspects Jaime up and down. — Now, Tony, I ain't no *fool.* I think you're about thirteen, maybe fourteen. Either way, this could turn into a crime in the state of Massachusetts, you know that? — Jaime remains silent, fiddling anxiously with his Day-Glo wristband, which is now primed with sweat. *My heart.*

— Look, if you're gonna call me a liar, I can just leave.

Vernon flashes those teeth again in a furious grin. — Who said anything like that, about you being a liar? We cool, ain't we, Tony?

— Anyways, if I did leave, where would that leave *you?* — Jaime bats his eyes, turning his back to Vernon. This, he thinks, is not going where he thought it would, though he is unsure where that was.

Vernon moves closer to Jaime and rests his hand on the boy's shoulder. — Why don't we take a walk behind that old filling station there? I knew the man who owned it, you know, — Vernon whispers, his voice trailing off. Jaime reminds himself just because they go back there, nothing really *has to* occur. It's a game; he's

Tony, this man is playing along, nothing will happen. He also thinks if Tony were alive and he knew about this, he would put his gun to this man's temple right now and pull the trigger until the clip was completely emptied so that the eyes and snot mixed into the ground like spilled soup and then stomp on the head until the face was unrecognizable. So unrecognizable *that no one could figure out who he was but Jaime had known instantly, just by that scent;* instead that very thing happened to Tony and now he is lying six feet under a headstone in a cemetery in Jamaica Plain, his face shattered into a hundred pieces like a porcelain doll's, his body so twisted that they could barely fit the suit on him, and no one is here to stop this game, stop it at all, save Jaime from anything, from *himself,* no one cares, not his mother not his father not his aunts or uncles or sisters not Teresita not Tita not even his *abuela,* no one, the only one who ever cared and showed it is silent and silenced for posterity so why not see what is going to happen this morning —

They head down an oil-slicked gravel driveway toward the rear of the abandoned gas station, which abuts a narrow alley bordered on three sides by a brick wall, covered by ivy and other climbing vines. Jaime has passed by this site before, though he has never actually ventured back in here.

Vernon leans against the back wall of the station. He unbuckles his pants. Jaime faces him, his eyes now falling everywhere but on Vernon, who has begun to expose himself, urging the boy to approach him. Is this part of the game? Jaime asks without rendering the words audible, fixed to his spot. What would *Tony* do? His eyes still wandering, his mind leaping alternately from Vernon's extended fingers to Tony's veined brown hands gripping that 9mm — that's what it was, wasn't it, a 9mm, a Tech-Nine pulling the trigger again again again, him finding the body back behind the Dumpster behind the store like garbage dumped in the middle of the night, his mother not able to say anything at all for days, her lying on the floor beneath the pew convulsing in tears at the funeral, him under his comforter shivering in the overheated room, working himself into a frenzy at the sight of that body, that horrible corpse, that face mangled beyond recognition, beyond even hideousness, as the bed across from him lies empty empty empty —

— Com'ere, Tony — Vernon clucks, his eyes closed and his body arched back against the wall. Jaime approaches until he is standing in front of him, stone-still. — That's *good.* — Jaime just stands there, his eyes now fixed on Vernon's hairless and pocked torso, paler than his face or arms, like the flesh of a plucked chicken, which he has revealed by raising his polo shirt. Jaime tenses as the hand clamps onto his shoulder. — Tony! — Vernon is hunching over, breathing heavily. — Turn around for me again, Tony! Tony?

Jaime, who feels himself slowly losing his sense of balance-distance-time letting everything go why can't he concentrate why can't he be a man like Tony would why can't he end this game end it now get closer to Vernon run why why is this happening like this why is this he begins to turn look down find the head crumpled like a toy doll fall shoot convulsed in tears my god why my *son* on the floor of the pew why my God *por qué* when he hears, — Oh, Tony . . . Tony, *ooooh* . . .

He opens his eyes suddenly. What time *is* it? Vernon's left hand is massaging Jaime's shoulder, his right hand . . . he feels his chest collapsing. He glimpses Vernon's watch on his right hand . . . he's late for his algebra class! He's going to *miss* it! Jaime leaps up, stumbles backwards, knocking over his knapsack, spilling the contents upon the stones.

— Wha? Hunh? — Vernon murmurs, writhing against the wall like a felled bird struggling to alight, riven with bliss, unaware of the boy's actions. Panicking, Jaime snatches up his knapsack, stuffs everything back in it, hoists it onto his left shoulder, hesitates. *My life,* he feels rising on the tip of his tongue: No one is going to save him from anything, ever, *not a soul.*

— Wha's the matter, Tony? *Tony?* — Jaime, refusing to look

in Vernon's direction, runs off down the driveway, his backpack now half-open and dangling from his back. In about five seconds he is onto the street that leads through the projects and into the front door of the Cuffe Middle School, past the hall monitor who is yelling out his name — *Jaime Barrett, Jaime Barrett, Jaime?* — up onto the third floor, into a seat in the back of the class as Mr. Morris is chalking a series of dizzyingly elaborate equations upon the black slate that appears now as depthless as the voice that is explaining the actions of the hand and chalk, and Jaime, in the back row, is fumbling around madly in his bag, his hands searching furiously for that algebra notebook — where *is* it? he *knows* he packed it, he remembers having placed it in there this morning — which is *nowhere* to be found.

Then he sees it, he sees it as keenly as if it all were unreeling right before him, *here:* As Vernon gets ready to depart, he spots a notebook, lying several inches in front of him. A black and white wire-bound gridded notebook, which has ALGEBRA I — MR. MORRIS, FIRST PERIOD etched across its front. Picking up the notebook, he flips through it, seeing all the red marks and the heavily annotated margins of the pages, which, like a used scratch-and-sniff sample held close to the nose, emit a faint but perceptible scent: sandalwood. He casts the notebook to the ground, beside the discarded newspaper, laughs at the folly of it all, at this boy who cannot even keep up his role in their game, walks off down the driveway toward Dudley and the rest of his life —

His bangs now plastered like a veil to his forehead, his breathing so labored as to drown out even his own thoughts, Jaime looks up, to the puzzled expressions of Mr. Morris, of Vinh, of every student in his algebra class. Their faces are screens of bemusement, showing only the recognition of his strange and novel presence before them. Their eyes have fixed upon him as if he were the last boy on earth, their stares as blank and unrelenting as if they had never seen such a pitiful and enigmatic creature in their entire lives.

David Ebershoff

UP THE LADDER WITH CHUCK PAA

CHUCK PAA, not five and a half feet tall, his chin a pad of bright gold whiskers, asked, "What do you need, Mr. Boyal? Chips? Cake mix? Vegetable oil? Where's your shopping list? Get out your list."

Mr. Boyal, with his silver wire glasses glinting, pointed to the breast pocket of Chuck's parka. Only a quarter of an hour before, Chuck had picked up the list from the telephone table with the green felt inlay next to Mr. Boyal's front door, tucking it into his jacket and patting the Velcro pocket for good measure. Then he forgot all about it. He must have been thinking of something else at the time — of his paycheck coming from Mrs. Boyal tomorrow, of the Sunday moving job he'd agreed to, of the red-and-black HELP WANTED sign in the liquor store window on the corner of Mr. Boyal's block. Yes, of something.

Now Mr. Boyal was leaning heavily on the shopping cart as he nudged it down the baked goods aisle. It rolled slowly, its back wheels trembling, until Mr. Boyal seemed to forget what he was doing and steered it into a pyramid display of strawberry frosting jars, knocking over several rows. With his knees wobbling and his milk-blue hand grasping lamely for the cart's plastic handlebar, Mr. Boyal was on the verge of crumpling into a heap. More than once Chuck had told Mr. Boyal it was time to buy a walker, preferably the kind with the tiny white stabilizing skis on the front legs. But Mr. Boyal had — as Chuck expected — resisted. Yet when Chuck mentioned the walker to Mrs. Boyal, Mr. Boyal's sad-mouthed mother in Wellesley, she quickly snapped her tongue and said, "I couldn't agree more. I just didn't have the heart to say it myself." "Why not?" Chuck replied, but Mrs. Boyal, with her poof of silver-blond hair and pinched oily nose, said she couldn't really say.

"Here," Chuck said at the bakery counter. "You like sugar cookies, don't you, Mr. Boyal? Five cents apiece. Two bucks will get you a week's supply." Chuck placed a sack of clover-shaped cookies into the cart's baby seat. And then Chuck snapped his fingers, realizing this: He had asked Mr. Boyal *where's your list?* to test his mind. Dementia was so common, after all. . . . But that wasn't the real reason, Chuck knew. He'd just forgotten what he'd done with it, thinking of something else — but what? *Strange,* Chuck thought, the soft loaves of his shoulders rising and then falling.

"What's next?" Chuck asked, glancing at the list and then directing Mr. Boyal over to the seafood counter. Mr. Boyal liked to order his fish on his own, and so Chuck Paa leaned back against a rack of orange tortilla chips and watched. Mr. Boyal's yellow hair had thinned to corn silk since Chuck began working for him. His cheeks, too, were as deep as saucers, and this morning something white had curdled in his eyes, blurring his vision until Chuck took the damp corner of a dish towel and dabbed them clean.

Even so, Chuck had seen worse.

Mr. Boyal worked the paper pennant out of the red dispenser. His bony fingers fluttered, tugging on the bit of blue paper. He held it up, showing Chuck that he was 43, four behind Mrs. 39, who was now ordering tuna steaks from the fish man, chattering about how Star Market's fish prices were becoming "insupportable." That was it! Chuck had demanded *where's your list?* because he'd been thinking of Ben when he tucked it into his pocket. On his way to Mr. Boyal's, Chuck ran into Ben in front of the liquor store with the HELP WANTED sign in its window. Chuck hadn't seen Ben in almost six months, a period of time that had quickly but thoroughly picked away at his health. Ben's wrists were now as thin as snakes, his skin scaly. A colony of white bumps had settled onto his neck. For the first time, he'd spent a night in the hospital, Ben reported breezily, as if it were a rite of passage, as if Chuck had known all along Ben was ill. And so Chuck asked — not out of insincerity but because the stun of the news had canceled out any other thoughts — "Did you have a nice room?"

"It was okay," Ben said. "Say, who are you working for these days?"

"Mr. Boyal."

"Jimmy Boyal? Right here on Columbus?"

"You know Mr. Boyal?"

"Sure. He's an old friend."

"Mr. Boyal?" asked Chuck, who was heating up under his parka. "Mr. Boyal, with the blond hair and the chicken pox scar on his left cheek?"

"That's Jimmy." Ben giggled slightly, as if something were a secret. "But I haven't seen him in over —"

Unsettled in his stomach, Chuck stopped listening. He studied Ben from the corner of his eyes. With his yellowing skin and his unsteady gait, Ben looked as though he might need a helper at some point soon. A sudden pang entered Chuck's chest as he realized he couldn't offer his services to Ben as long as he was engaged by Mr. Boyal. And so Chuck, who was about to be late, said, "Maybe you'll come to visit Mr. Boyal someday when I'm there." He added, "We, he would love a visitor." And then, this time with a wrinkle of buried pain in his voice, "You're managing on your own? You can still do everything on your own, Ben?"

As the fish man called number 43, Mr. Boyal cheerfully waved the tag of paper between his fingers. Chuck smiled at his employer and then examined his own fingernails, which were jammed with slivers of dirt. At twenty-three Chuck hadn't fully adopted an adult's sense of hygiene. Not that he thought of it that way: he only considered himself an untidy person when he passed on the street all the young men of the South End, whose clothes always crackled with starch and an iron's pleat, whose faces perpetually glowed from a workout. But when men like that were out of sight, Chuck had other things — things other than the Odor Eaters he needed to buy for his sneakers — on his mind. Like Mr. Boyal, who was still waiting, the nape of his neck turning gray and dewy, for the fish man to wrap his perch in paper. Or Ben, who had waved good-bye with an awkward glare in his dull blue eyes.

Chuck checked his watch and then fingered his jawline, where his pores sometimes clogged with ingrown hairs. He picked at a hard lump the size of a peppercorn; it popped and streaked his finger and thumb with a yellow fluid and a splash of blood, and suddenly Chuck worried that the tender teenage knots of pus that used to blossom on the field of his back had returned — as they did on occasion just to remind him that he was still hauling around the same old hump of a body.

Seeing Mr. Boyal blanch even further as he continued to wait for his fish, Chuck asked him if he wanted to sit, although Chuck couldn't quite think of where Mr. Boyal might rest in a supermarket. On the little bench in front of the fish counter, where the loaves of French bread were stacked like sandbags? In the shopping cart itself?

To tell the truth Chuck Paa brought no skills to his job. But work was work, and now it was the only thing he knew how to do. When he was eighteen he left his Norwegian-blooded mother in her two-room apartment in Maine and moved to Boston. Out of the woods and into the big city: that was the way he liked to think of it, even though he'd grown up in Portland. On a seed of instinct he walked from the bus station along the Charles River, then cut over into the South End. When he saw a blond man and a brown-haired man talking on a stoop, the blond's hand dug with the power of a meat hook into the other's shoulder, Chuck knew to stop walking. This was the place. His next thought, however, was of work — of another kind of survival, really — and he eyed the storefronts for HELP WANTED signs: a video rental, a florist with a torn awning, a wine shop. But this was during the recession, and so none were posted, the windows as blank and glassy as a dead man's eyes. Now that he had made a small career for himself in what he called the AIDS industry, Chuck sometimes wondered what drifting boys like himself did for employment before. Caterers? Hairdressers? But those jobs required training and apprenticeship and something else even Chuck knew he did not have: flair.

When Chuck was thirteen, his mother, a gimp who had trouble holding a job, took a position as a summer maid at a house on a private island called Little Thule forty yards off the coast of Maine. After school let out in May she and Chuck settled into a room with sloped walls above the house's garage. There were five girls in the family who summered on the island, and a boy a year older than Chuck named Bennett. After a few days, Bennett, eager to get away from his sisters, turned to Chuck for friendship, offering him his Red Sox cap when he saw Chuck squinting and his face burning in the clear blank summer light. From then on Bennett took Chuck clamming and fishing for scrod and out on his gray-planked dory, *Bennett Boy*, to pull up the island's lobster pails. Bennett, with his long brown feet and the downy tendril of hair growing up the back of his neck, taught Chuck to clean a cod and to rinse the black waste from a mussel. Almost every day the boys would dirty themselves with lobster entrails and the blood of alewives. Or they would rake the dirt and manure in the pony ring and then, together, ride the old horse, Danny, around and around. Or they would paint the peeling toolshed wearing nothing but gym shorts, their backs becoming speckled white with the splatter of paint — to say nothing of the time Bennett silently painted bright white circles around Chuck's hardening nipples and then a thin upturned smile beneath his belly button. Each evening Mrs. Wriston, Bennett's sundamaged mother, would direct the boys with her talonish finger to the claw-footed tub in the service bathroom. "Soak for as long as it takes," she'd demand, latching the door behind her, leaving them to the moist-aired room with the pillowy towels. Chuck would eagerly yank himself out of his soiled clothes, except the Red Sox cap, and plop into the tub, where he'd sit knee-to-knee with Bennett. It was what Chuck liked most, even more than the fishing or the horseback riding or even the painting. The steamy water. The lavender-smelling soap. The red sponge in the shape of a heart that Bennett used to scrub Chuck's back. "Boys are allowed to wash each other's backs," Bennett would say, his whispering voice getting deeper almost by the day, his fingertips carefully picking away at each fleck of paint until Chuck was clean, his body pink, and his child's fist of a heart swollen. Every night they bathed together, their hands interlocked, their faces becoming as clean and shiny as plates, and Chuck found it remarkable that everyone — his smallfaced mother, Mrs. Wriston with her dug-in eyes, but especially Bennett himself — thought it was the most natural thing in the world that each day should end like this. And so Chuck came to believe this was how things were meant to be: the direct summer sunlight, the cold green ocean, the friendship grounded equally in solidarity and intimacy. Chuck could look no further than the present, his memory forgetting where he'd come from, how he'd arrived here, and his imagination suddenly unable to envision, or plan for, his future, his own survival. But then one humid morning in August Mrs. Wriston watched Mrs. Paa, with the desperation permanently etched across her forehead, snatch the pearl, dolphin-shaped brooch from her mother-of-pearl summer jewelry box. Within two hours Chuck and his mother were ferried off the island while Bennett sat on the anchored bow of *Bennett Boy,* his feet dangling into the dimpled water, his broken-heart face following the heads of Chuck and Mrs. Paa thirty feet away as the outboard motorboat captained by Mrs. Wriston herself puttered toward the rocky, pocked shore. *You'll come back,* Bennett's face seemed to be saying. Pretending a lifting breeze had come along, Chuck discreetly knocked his Red Sox cap into the boat's wake — as if to say, *Yes, I'll come back. Never again with her, but I'll come back.*

Mr. Boyal said, "Just perch today." He attempted a smile. "I don't think I need anything else."

"Check your list, Mr. Boyal," Chuck said, handing him the paper.

Mr. Boyal checked off each item. "I still need a vegetable."

"Creamed spinach is on sale," Chuck said. He paused. "I didn't know you're friends with Ben, Mr. Boyal."

"Ben?"

"Ben who lives on Dartmouth Street."

"Oh, Ben." His nose wrinkled. "I wouldn't say we're friends. Did you once work for him?"

"Not exactly," Chuck said, feeling his hot blood rise to his face.

Since January Chuck had worked for Mr. Boyal as a daily companion, helping him shop and cook and when the weather was bright stroll through the Commons. Really, anybody could do what he did, it was that ordinary and mindless. Not that people weren't grateful. Not that people didn't commend him in low, whispery voices. Mrs. Boyal, who smelled like honey and tied little flowered scarves around her neck, shook his hand every time they met (which was more than Chuck could say about some people!) and always enclosed a note on an ecru card when she mailed his checks, one of which was due tomorrow. But Chuck Paa was thinking of himself; there was nothing advanced, or *important,* in what he did — anyone could hold on to a grocery list.

At the checkout counter, Mr. Boyal turned and said, "I'll make you lunch."

Chuck nodded. Mr. Boyal prepared lunch every day. It was an exercise, and Chuck liked almost anything Mr. Boyal made, except the salads, but especially the rainbow cupcakes he kept in a shoe box on his counter.

Anytime he wanted, Chuck could move to another job. Jerry Riley, the brother of one of Chuck's previous clients, was a liquor distributor in New England, specializing in imported beers. It was a business of relationships, he'd told Chuck, and Mr. Riley saw Chuck as the man who could get his products into all the gay bars from Portland to New Haven. But why Chuck Paa? "You seem like a loyal young man," Mr. Riley had said. "You don't seem like the type who'd think about screwing me over." Mr. Riley had also admitted his dislike of homosexuals, but that wasn't a reason to walk away from money on the counter. That's the way he made the offer to Chuck nearly a year ago. It was at the wake of Harold Riley, who died of a fever in his sleep. "Do it for Harold," Mr. Riley had said, filling his mouth with an aunt's deviled egg. Although flattered, Chuck supposed Mr. Riley felt he owed him something. And perhaps Mr. Riley did, because in his final months Harold's life insurance money had run dry, leaving him with nothing to pay Chuck. Yet Chuck stayed on, each morning walking over to Harold's narrow apartment on West Newton Street, opening the front door with the worn brass key he protected on a string around his neck. He would feed Harold's two tabby cats and then wake Harold himself, shaking the knob of his shoulder until his papery eyelids would begin to flutter, which would tell Chuck that today was not the day — his responsibilities would continue. For nine weeks Chuck repeated this routine without pay, each morning rising earlier and earlier as Harold's body shut further and further down, so that Chuck started arriving at Mr. Riley's even before the tabby cats had risen themselves. For two months this had meant that Chuck could never buy the three coconut doughnuts he liked in the morning, it meant no groceries except sale cans of Goya black beans and damaged white bread, it meant no replacement when his bottle of shampoo emptied, and after a month it meant no quarters for the hungry, humming machines at the laundromat. All this Chuck bore not out of kindness but out of *duty*. He didn't think of it this way, of course, but instead what motivated him was a sense of professionalism, an approach to survival deliberately in contrast to his mother's frantic behavior. When Chuck began newly working for someone, he would make a promise to himself that he'd never leave his client until his client left him. And so Chuck continued to work — his body thinning and dirtying at the same exponential pace — until the morning he arrived at Harold's apartment only to find the two tabby cats nudging their orange, delicate bodies against the cold, dead wall of Harold's now peaceful chest.

Two weeks later Jerry Riley phoned to inform Chuck that Harold had left him a gold pocket watch, which Chuck quickly pawned. Jerry Riley had also said, "I mean it about the job. Stay in touch with me, Paa. I could be your ticket out."

Chuck asked Mr. Boyal what he would make for lunch. "I'm extra hungry today," Chuck said as they walked from the supermarket to Mr. Boyal's parlor-level apartment in the South End.

"I'll broil the perch."

"How about frying it?"

"Maybe," Mr. Boyal said, already tiring from the sack of groceries in his arms. He set it on a cement stoop, and suddenly a fit of coughing hurled up from his lungs and bent him at his waist. A tick of worry bit into Chuck. How long would his assignment with Mr. Boyal last? Would they be together three more months?

"Give me a minute," Mr. Boyal said, sitting on the stoop. Chuck sat down, too, his hot wet hand with the wadded grocery list touching, lightly, Mr. Boyal's back.

The oval mirror above the bathroom sink in Chuck's apartment was too high and too small for him to examine the skin of his own back. He had tried standing on the rim of the tub to see if his back, once custard white and sprinkled with blackheads, had actually cleared up, but the overhead light cast too many shadows. Chuck owned a yellow-bristled brush with a long wood handle like a mixing spoon for scraping where he couldn't reach with a washcloth. On Saturday nights he would lather palmfuls of an avocado-and-oatmeal mask across his shoulders and down his flanks, waiting optimistically as the hospital-green clay dried and tightened and finally cracked. Then he would slip into the bathtub like a dinghy, soaking himself clean while the water muddied and his favorite sitcoms played on the portable television perched on the toilet's tank. Sometimes, if a check had come in the mail, he'd park a box of coconut doughnuts on the tub's rim, and shut his eyes until the water chilled.

"Catch your breath yet, Mr. Boyal?" Chuck asked. "Ready to move on?" As he carried the groceries down the street of brownstones, Chuck was thinking about working for two people at once. Ben had said he didn't need any help. Maybe not now but perhaps in a few months when Mr. Boyal . . . Chuck calculated the business of it, the potential and the limits for profit. If only he could duplicate himself, make a team of Chuck Paas, and care for Mr. Boyal and Ben at once — or even everyone in the whole world — then that would be worthwhile. He shifted the grocery bags in his fists as the sweat began to collect inside his parka. He watched Mr. Boyal's pencil neck move inside the yawning collar of his knit sweater. Chuck saw a DRIVERS NEEDED sign painted on the back of a delivery truck and told himself to remember the 1-800 number, although he knew he would forget in an hour or so. And then Chuck, whose skin was mushroom white in the weak spring sun, silently watched the grocery list slip out from beneath the shopping bag's beige plastic handle that was pressing into his palm, the list casually floating away from a grimy starfish hand that seemed to belong to someone else, that seemed not to belong to Chuck at all.

*   *   *

The next day Chuck Paa took Mr. Boyal for a haircut. Waiting on a bench littered with magazines, Mr. Boyal said, "I have an appointment with a nutritionist tomorrow."

"Why?" Chuck was flipping through a men's fashion magazine, imagining the stylish, two-tiered haircuts first on himself and then on Mr. Boyal.

"I'm not sure I'm eating as well as I should."

"Who told you that?"

"Ben," Mr. Boyal said, awkwardly. He was sitting with his back straight and his hands cupped over the ball handle of his cane, and Chuck could feel Mr. Boyal's eyes move curiously across him. Had Mr. Boyal and Ben spoken about Chuck last night? "Ben's had some success with macrobiotics," Mr. Boyal said.

"I see," Chuck said, wondering if Ben would share with him his recipes and the name of a good health food store — for a lump had begun to rise in Chuck's throat when he thought that he might not have been feeding Mr. Boyal properly. Or was the lump from something else?

Just last week Chuck rode the T down to see Mr. Riley in his office. It was connected to a blue-roofed warehouse in Braintree. Mr. Riley, who was hairier than Chuck Paa but not much taller, gave him a tour of the floor. While Mr. Riley was explaining his inventory management system, Chuck's eyes stopped on a truck driver with a spiky crew cut. The driver was wearing blue overalls and a sewn-on patch that said "Eugene." As he loaded the shelves of a truck with cases of beer, his arms would flex into strings of muscle. Mr. Riley slapped Chuck's back and said that, were he to come on board, Eugene would deliver to any of the routes Chuck could develop. Chuck knew he was gaping; he had to quickly bring a handkerchief to his chin to catch the lurching drop of drool that, as it turned out, wasn't actually there. Probably after he left, Mr. Riley and Eugene would share a laugh about Chuck, about the look of astonishment on Chuck's face when Mr. Riley had said, "Is there anything wrong, Paa? You seem a little stunned." Even so, he still wanted Chuck Paa as part of his operation. "I've just got a feeling about you," he told Chuck.

"Thinking of anything different for the hair?" Chuck asked Mr. Boyal.

"No, I wasn't. Any suggestions?"

"Ever have a back rub?" a muscular client once asked Chuck Paa. His heart began to thump so rapidly with hope that he was certain the dark-haired man could hear its patter from across the living room. Other than his sight the man's health was holding up, and all Chuck was doing for him was driving him on errands once or twice a week. "Not since I was thirteen," Chuck replied, lying down, feeling the slab of his stomach seep into the cracks between the sofa cushions. "Your shirt off?" the man asked playfully, approaching the couch. But then Chuck, fearing what might be back there, told him to forget it.

"They're calling you, Mr. Boyal," Chuck said.

"No, they're not. They just called a Mr. Doyle."

After the haircut Chuck walked Mr. Boyal back to his apartment. It was a warm, late spring afternoon, and sweat began to roll down their foreheads. Once inside, Mr. Boyal, his face ashen, set himself on his plaid sofa while Chuck went to the kitchen for some water. When he returned to the living room, Mr. Boyal was slumped like an overturned sack on the couch, a trail of foam spilling from his mouth. *Uh oh,* Chuck thought, hoping he wasn't dead. Had he walked Mr. Boyal too hard? Would they blame Chuck? He nervously placed his thumb to Mr. Boyal's pipe of a wrist, finding his pulse happily beating. Chuck fell to Mr. Boyal's side in relief. After catching his breath and drinking some water, Chuck turned to Mr. Boyal and slapped his icy face. He didn't come to. Chuck telephoned an ambulance and then Mr. Boyal's doctor at City Hospital. Then Mrs. Boyal in Wellesley. Chuck Paa wasn't naturally levelheaded in a crisis, but Mr. Boyal had penned instructions of what precisely to do should he teeter over. Thank goodness! Chuck demanded everyone he worked for do the same, even those he only helped out for an afternoon: Should you pass out or die while under my watch, please write down exactly how you would like me to react. Chuck supplied the pen and the index cards.

Mr. Boyal spent only two nights in the hospital. When he came home, his mother announced in her shaky girlish voice that the time had come to hire a nurse. Chuck hadn't planned on leaving Mr. Boyal for several months, and no one else had offered him a full-time position. Although Mrs. Boyal ceremoniously sent Chuck off with a three-week bonus and two pots of apple butter, it was the first time since he'd moved to Boston that he lacked work. He still had some onesy-twosy jobs — moving somebody, special errands, baby-sitting for an evening. Mr. Boyal said he would send the word out among his friends that Chuck was available, but the trouble was, though Chuck Paa didn't say this, most of Mr. Boyal's friends were dead.

When it was time for good-byes, Chuck said, "Keep me posted." He meant both about Mr. Boyal's health and any job prospects.

"I will," said Mr. Boyal. After his stay in the hospital, where they cleaned a parasite out of his intestines, he looked fitter than Chuck had ever seen him, his eyes clear and alert and color in his cheeks.

"But when I find something," Chuck asked, as he always did at the end of an assignment, "can I use you as a reference?"

"If I'm still around," Mr. Boyal joked, his pretty white smile breaking open his face.

"If you're not, do you think your mother would mind?"

"I'll tell her you might call one day."

Chuck then asked, "You couldn't suggest me to Ben, could you?"

Mr. Boyal paused. "I don't think that would work out." And then, "It's not you, it's him. He's too independent." And finally, in only a whisper, "Chuck, trust me. Forget about Ben."

Chuck Paa walked home. It was Saturday night, and he drew his bath and plugged the television into the outlet by the mounted toothbrush holder. There was a made-for-TV movie on about a surgeon who was the only doctor in California who knew how to perform microscopic surgery on a rare heart condition called Chunt's disease. In the second part of the movie the doctor's wife came down with the disease herself, and the rest of the movie — as Chuck guessed — was about the doctor preparing to tear apart and sew back together his wife's heart. Soaking, Chuck wondered what it was like to be a heart surgeon. He often wondered what it was like to be something else. Doctors particularly fascinated him. *Dr. Paa, the cardiologist,* he thought. *Dr. Paa, the dermatologist.* But other than the white lab coat he couldn't imagine it. He'd never have the skills to be as useful to the world as a cardiologist, Chuck conceded, floating in his bath.

Chuck stepped into his white jeans and pulled on a gray sweatshirt that said MAINE. Combing his hair in the mirror, he saw the patch of stubble on his chin and scraped a dry razor over it. He was on his way to Chaps, the disco in the Back Bay where two years ago he had first met Ben. After shaking hands the two had danced together, Chuck's hips rotating wildly. The black walls and carpet and the cigarette smoke and smoldering dry ice made the place so shadowy that it was only after Ben invited Chuck home, touching the small of his back, that Chuck realized that Ben was Bennett, Bennett Wriston, Bennett of *Bennett Boy.* Once out in front of the disco, beneath the yellow streetlights, Chuck assumed Bennett would recognize him too, would cup Chuck's face between his hands, but Bennett did not. But surely the china jar lamps of a handsome apartment on Dartmouth Street would reveal things to Bennett as they were, but he never bothered to turn on the lights when they got home. And all night Chuck lay in the wide bed with the piles of down pillows anticipating the morning light that would finally inform Bennett of their good fortune, and then Chuck could stop calling Bennett "Ben," as he'd been doing all night. But in the morning Bennett looked sad, his mouth hanging at the ends, and he refused to look Chuck in the eyes. When Chuck asked Bennett for his phone number, Bennett stopped, looked around as if startled, and then wrote out his number so slowly that Chuck wondered if Bennett was having trouble with his memory. And when Chuck asked, "When can I see you again, Ben?" the only answer to appear was: "Um, I'm not really sure."

Examining his egg-shaped face in the mirror, Chuck hoped tonight he would meet someone like Eugene, the truck driver. And then Chuck Paa had this idea: Oh, how orderly and understandable life would be if everybody always wore their job's uniform with their first name stitched to the pocket. Except, what would Chuck wear?

"I'm glad to hear it," Mr. Riley said, his hands balled into fists on his desk.

Chuck studied the coffee in his Styrofoam cup. Trying to display a gesture of excitement, he bared his teeth, which he could now get cleaned, now that he had insurance.

"You know what I'm going to do for you?" Mr. Riley said.

In four months, Chuck knew, Mr. Riley would make a faggot joke in his face; he'd probably make one after Chuck left the office today.

"I'm going to get you a Jeep," Mr. Riley said.

If he had to explain why, Chuck had moved away from Maine because he was afraid of heterosexual people. Too many snarls, too many mouths twisted in distaste. In the South End, however, most of the gay people, at least the healthy ones, terrified him just as much. They growled just like the pack of boys in high school who called him Chuck Paw, the Animal. And whenever he ran into Ben, Ben's face would tighten with a pallid mixture of disgust and rejection. *It's like there's something wrong with him,* Chuck overheard Ben screech one night from behind a mirrored pillar at Chaps.

"I'm going to get you a Jeep so you can carry the samples with you. How does that sound?"

"A Jeep?" Chuck said. As long as Mr. Riley left him alone, he knew he'd be okay.

"I've got twenty-four brands of beer from places like Iceland, Malta, and South Korea. I want you to make the gays love them." He jabbed his short finger into Chuck's soft breast. "You can do that for me, can't you?"

"Sure," Chuck said. "I sure can."

Mr. Riley had poked Chuck where a large pit of a pimple was growing. It was the size of a cherry, a hard core growing on his sternum, and Chuck had come to calling it his crab apple. He didn't know why. It was smaller than a crab apple, but its red soreness, the scar he knew it would leave, reminded him of the welts that had bloomed on his skin after the eleventh-grade field trip to the beach when his classmates pelted him with a sack of stony crab apples. Forced to seek refuge in the icy waves, Chuck bobbed in the ocean as he watched his skin turn blue. When all the crab apples were at last thrown, he emerged from the sea shaking and wrinkled. Once home he locked the door to the bathroom and examined his skin for hours, fascinated by the puckering wounds that had erupted like ripe fruit.

"Gays love," Mr. Riley went on, "anything trendy and imported. We've got to make these beers chic. But I've got a marketing gal helping me with that. You just need to take her messages to all the bar owners in New England."

Chuck nodded.

"Harold was the worst," Mr. Riley continued. "He'd buy into any fad. That's the type of customer we're going for here." He tapped a pencil's dirty pink eraser against a stack of *Beer Business* magazines. "Think of Harold."

Harold Riley and Chuck Paa hadn't talked much during the five months Chuck was helping out. Harold was a broad-chested man with blue eyes and hands as large as Chuck's face. Typically he read novels during the day when Chuck was with him. Occasionally they spoke, for the most part about items Harold needed at the grocery or a new treatment he'd been selected to participate in. Once Chuck suggested that maybe Harold wanted somebody else to work for him, or maybe he didn't need anybody at all, and Harold had said, his voice all balm, "Don't be ridiculous."

If it had been fifteen years earlier and AIDS did not exist, he'd probably have become a waiter, Chuck thought. Why not? Feeding people is important, even though nobody thinks of it that way, nobody gives it that kind of respect. Maybe he would have worked in a hotel restaurant where at least he'd get to wear a tuxedo. But a tuxedo probably wouldn't fit him well.

"Do you think I'll be okay?" Chuck Paa asked Mr. Riley.

"Don't you think I know what I'm doing? You'll be fine, Paa."

But if a tuxedo wouldn't fit him well, what would? Sometimes Chuck wished his mind would stop, the chasing of thoughts about his future would cease for a moment. A rat on its wheel inside his head: that was how he thought of it, and the rat never rested. He could hear the joints of the silver wheel turning, a trill in his skull . . . If it had been fifteen years earlier he of course would not have known to sleep around safely — which with Ben, that one and only time, he utterly failed to do — and now he would need to hire someone just like himself to help him die. Last week, after leaving Mr. Boyal, Chuck finally returned to the free clinic to hear the results of his test. He didn't like sitting in the plastic bucket seats of the reception area with all the skull-faced men, waiting to be called. Typically he worked for these men. Now he was one of them, or almost, he *could be* one of them. *There's something new,* Chuck thought. Never before had he felt that way about any group: that the right to membership lay like a dog in his lap. When the social worker with the bobbed hair scooted him into her office and told him he was negative, he didn't know what to think. "How do you feel?" she asked. "Got that little urge to change a few bad habits?" Chuck Paa couldn't answer. He could only stare at her pie-shaped face, reaching for his parka and backing away. And just before he slipped out her door and down the hall he remembered to ask, "Are you sure?" And then, "What habits would *you* change?"

"What should I wear when I call on the customers?" Chuck asked Mr. Riley.

"A simple suit should do it. Get yourself a blue suit. You only need one. One suit and a few ties and a pair of black shoes." Mr. Riley grinned. His teeth could stand a cleaning, too. "And a tin of polish. Keep the shoes shined and business will be good. That's my motto. Hey, look at me."

Chuck couldn't picture himself in a blue suit, or anything else for that matter. He only saw his naked body, glaring and white, as hairless as a girl's.

"Let's see you in here on Monday then," Mr. Riley said.

"Monday," Chuck replied, and the two men shook hands.

"And put some force into that grip of yours, boy," said Mr. Riley. "Nobody likes a dead fish in his hand."

On the train back into the city, Chuck sat in the sun. The three cups of coffee had made him queasy, and the dry grit of the Cremora was still on his teeth. His jiggling leg sent the man next to him to a seat further down the aisle. Working for Mr. Riley, Chuck would no longer run into Ben. The heart of the job, Chuck supposed, would be the solitary hours driving down a highway, his Jeep loaded with beer. That would be fine with him. Plenty of time for thinking and being alone. He would have to phone his contacts, the ones who had been so good about sending work his way, to let them know he no longer was in the business of helping others. They would protest and doubt his decision, but he could easily replace the receiver in its cradle if they droned on too long. I must go, he would say. He had customers to call on, and his suit needed pressing and his shoes could stand a polish.

The warm sun on his face massaged open his pores. The sunlight settled on his gray eyelids, and Chuck Paa relaxed, recalling, remotely, his evening baths with Bennett. The quiet hours in the

Jeep would be like this, too. Except, taking the job hadn't been a decision the way most people think of one. He never consciously concluded there was a match between himself and liquor distribution. Nor was there ever a moment when he decided to abandon working as a companion. Things just come about. Chuck Paa supposed that in most people's lives one thing led to another, but not in his. Ben, Mr. Boyal had told Chuck, had quit graduate school and gone to work for AIDS Action Committee the day he was diagnosed. But events worked differently for Chuck. It was all a bath of water and he was a bar of soap floating about; that was how Chuck put things together in his mind. A blurred awareness bobbed inside him: He was young and had made mistakes but some motor in his head, the rat on the wheel maybe, had kept him from sinking from his errors. Maybe the job with Mr. Riley would not work out, but then at least Chuck would know something more about what he could and could not do. The cold feeling slapped against him that his life was about getting up and sailing on, lesson learned. Except he did not think of it in such analytically reduced words. Instead, he could only feel it, the watery emotion sweeping through him like a frigid wave on a Maine beach, surging between his legs and through his groin, shocking his genitals into retreat, and passing before he could let out a cry.

Michael Nava

TWO BOYS

CHRISTOPHER CHANDLER was a superior court judge whom I'd known for twenty years, since we'd been law students together at Stanford in the mid-seventies. He was married and his wife, Bay, had also been a friend of mine back then. They had a son, Joey, and they lived in Pasadena in a beautiful house on an elegant street. Chris was generally agreed to be a comer, smart, fair and ambitious — and straight. It didn't hurt that his father-in-law, Joseph Kimball, was the senior partner at one of the city's biggest and most politically well-connected law firms. Chris was thought to be a shoo-in for elevation to the federal bench next time a Republican occupied the White House. That had always been his goal, even when we were students, and the most casual review of his judicial career revealed a certain amount of calculation in that direction. Nothing too damning, a provident change of party affiliation, a reputation as a tough sentencer in criminal cases, that sort of thing.

Any hint of excess ambition on his part was leavened by his and Bay's indisputable commitment to good works. She took the lead there, serving on the boards of numerous organizations that ranged from a battered woman's shelter to an AIDS research fund. Occasionally, flipping through the *Times,* I'd come across a picture of them at a charitable event, all dressed up in tux and evening gown. "Impersonating adults," I'd tease Bay when we talked, which happened maybe two or three times a year. I crossed paths more frequently with Chris, since his courtroom was downtown, where I handled the majority of my cases, but for having once been such good friends, we saw very little of each other.

I know this puzzled Bay who, over the years, made many attempts to revive our student friendship. She saw through my polite evasions of her offers of dinners with the family, and when I did accept I knew she was aware of my discomfort. I tried not to show it because I genuinely cared for her. She was straightforward and good, though not without edges. Like me, she was a recovering alcoholic and prone, as most ex-addicts are, to bouts of depression and gusts of dissatisfaction. I know she was ambivalent about having become, as she once joked, "a society lady with causes." This, I reminded her, was an improvement on her mother, who had simply been a society lady, bone-thin, self-absorbed and distinctly without causes. She laughed at that. But I didn't have a glib retort when she said, "We're old friends, Henry. You know there aren't any secrets between us."

She was wrong. My friendship with her had always been based on a deception. Just like her marriage.

Chris had been a year ahead of me at Stanford, but the school was small enough so that we were on nodding terms. In my second year, we had a class together and we moved from a nodding to a speaking acquaintance. I was twenty-two years old, and when I was not in class or studying for class I could be found making timid excursions into the frenetic gay world of San Francisco in the mid-1970s. That those two parts of my life, law student and homosexual, seemed irreconcilable bothered me considerably, because I couldn't see having to choose one over the other. I had wanted to be a lawyer from the time I was a boy, inspired by biographies of Lincoln and Clarence Darrow, and Perry Mason on TV. As for the other thing, well, I hadn't exactly planned on being homosexual, but I knew I was by the time I was sixteen; knew it, and knew I could no more change it than I could change the color of my eyes. My problem was how to be homosexual and a lawyer at a time when being gay was grounds for disbarment in most states.

If there were any other gay students at the law school, they kept it to themselves. I often wished there were, if only to have had someone to talk to about my dilemma, but not for that reason alone. I was a reserved and inexperienced Mexican Catholic boy from the Central Valley of California, whose idea of homosexuality was derived from Walt Whitman's romantic vision of "two boys together clinging, / One the other never leaving." In my forays to San Francisco I found a lot of boys who didn't mind clinging to me for a night or two, but forever was not in the vocabulary of the times. I thought if I could meet someone more like myself I would not feel so continually out of place. Sometimes, in class, I'd look around the room and speculate who among my male classmates might be gay. Some seemed more likely than others, but Chris Chandler was not one of them. At twenty-three he was a square-jawed, fair-haired boy who looked like he'd stepped out of a Brooks Brothers catalog; the kind of WASP kid beside whom I felt very much the brown-skinned scholarship student.

One night I was at a gay bar in the city, a place called the Hide 'n' Seek, feeling, as usual, out of place but hopeful, if only hormonally. There were white lights above the bar, but the rest of the room was bathed in red and blue and the muggy air smelled of cigarette smoke, aftershave and amyl nitrite, a drug that jumped the heart and smelled like old socks. Disco music blared over huge speakers mounted on walls in the corners of the room. A strobe light pulsed above the dance floor, catching the frenzy of the dancers. It always amazed me that there was never any violence in the bar despite all the men crowded together, lurching drunkenly into each other, spilling drinks and burning each other's clothes with careless cigarettes. Instead, the accidental brush of male body against male body was like the striking of matches that flared and sputtered out, desire like wisps of smoke slowly thickening the air.

I was standing at the edge of the dance floor, a little drunk and feeling a bit sorry for myself, when someone bumped into me. He said, "Sorry." I turned around and said, "That's okay," and saw it was Chris. For a moment, neither of us said anything, then Chris smiled, a slanting, embarrassed grin, and said, "You're Henry, right?"

"That's right," I said. "Henry Rios. You're Chris —"

"Chandler," he said. "You're in my Corporations class."

It was a small thing, that exchange of last names, but in that world of one-night stands and first names only, it made running into him there seem perfectly natural.

"Buy you a beer?" he asked.

"That would be great," I said.

We made our way to the bar, got the beers and found a relatively quiet spot where we could talk without shouting. As if we were sitting at the pub in the student union, Chris kept up a steady stream of chat about classes, professors, fellow students and even, I remember, the Securities Exchange Act of 1934. Later, he told me he'd chosen those innocuous subjects to relax me because I seemed so unsure of myself. It worked. I loosened up, and eventually we moved to more personal matters: places of origin, families, and finally, "You're gay?" and "How long have you known?" and "I would never have guessed you."

Last call was called. Chris smiled at me and said, "How did you get up here?"

"I took the train," I said.

"Can I give you a lift back to school?"

"Sure," I said, and because I was uncertain, I didn't know how to ask whether he wanted to spend the night.

He smiled again and said, "My place is quiet and I live alone."

I woke up the next morning on a mattress on the floor of Chris's tiny apartment, which was over the carriage house — now converted to a garage — of an old stone mansion in downtown Palo Alto. It was a typical student apartment, orange crates for bookshelves, a trestle-table desk, books and records everywhere and that mattress. Chris was asleep beside me. For half the night we'd just talked, and then there'd been that moment when the next most natural thing in the world was to kiss. There was none of the awkwardness with him that I'd felt with other men; the small voice in the back of my head trying to remember the man's name or the mumbled negotiations about who would do what to whom. It had never felt so good before to be with another guy, so easy and friendly — "We two boys forever clinging . . ." Well, no, I didn't think that exactly, but what a difference it made to make love to someone I could also imagine as a friend.

I got up and went to the bathroom. When I reached for the soap to wash my hands, I heard a metal clink in the washbasin. I fished around and found a ring, a plain gold band. There was an inscription inside, *To Chris from Bay,* and a date from earlier that year. I took it with me back to the bedroom. Chris was awake. I showed him the ring and joked, "What's this, you're married?"

He took the ring from me, slipped it on his finger and said, "Not yet. Just engaged."

The ring glinted on Chris's finger. I felt confused and betrayed and it made me brutal.

"Does your fiancée know you're a fag?" I asked him.

His pale eyes flashed anger, but all he said was, "Do you think that's any of your business?"

We were no longer two innocents on the open road, but a couple of naked and hostile strangers. I groped around the mattress for my clothes, pulled on my jeans and said, "Thanks for whatever."

He felt the change, too, and drew the sheet to his waist. "Don't go like this," he said, quietly.

"Like what?" I said, tying my shoelace, my back turned to him.

I felt his hand on my shoulder. "You know what I mean, Henry. Like some hysterical, wounded . . . Let's not act like all the rest of them."

I shrugged his hand off. "You mean like all the other queers," I said. "Well, this may be a phase for you, but not for me."

"I didn't say I wasn't gay," he said. He sighed, almost inaudibly. "I should've stopped going to bars after I asked Bay to marry me. I knew it was a mistake."

"What are you talking about?" I asked, standing up and looking at him.

"I thought I could handle going to a bar or a bathhouse now and then, just to get some relief, but I knew that sooner or later I'd meet someone like you."

"Oh, now you think I'm going to blackmail you."

"Would you just stop," he said angrily. "That's not what I meant."

"Then what?"

"Someone — some guy — I could imagine being with."

I stood there with my shirt in my hand. "I don't understand, Chris."

"Come back to bed," he said, "and I'll explain it to you."

He threw back the sheet. There was a spray of freckles across his chest, and when he moved, the morning light caught the flicker of muscle beneath pale skin. I dropped the shirt, kicked off my shoes and tugged out of my pants, and got into bed beside him. His body was warm and hard.

"Explanations can wait," I said. I was twenty-two. Flesh still had that power over me.

"Do you love her?" I asked him later.

He tucked a pillow under his head and said, "I've spent most of my life trying not to be in love with anyone because I was afraid it would be the wrong kind of love."

"What's the wrong kind of love? This?"

"It's so easy when you both want the same thing, isn't it," he said, touching my hair. "I want this, but there are other things I want, too. A family, a career, to make a difference in the world. Those things aren't possible between two guys."

"You don't know that."

"How many happy couples did you see at the bar last night?"

"About as many as you'd see at a straight singles bar," I said, a little heatedly. "That's not what those places are for."

"There aren't any other places for us," he said. "That's not the life I want."

I turned to him. "We can create a different kind of life. We can make new places."

A faint, indulgent smile creased his lips. "You do those things, Henry. I think you can. But it's not for me."

"Why?"

"Listen, I'll tell you, but don't get mad, okay?"

"I'm listening."

"This," he said, squeezing my thigh, "this is about sex. I'm not knocking sex, it's great, but that's all it is, Henry. I can't organize my life around it. It's a kind of self-indulgence. You said you wouldn't get mad."

"I did not." I was mad, but I couldn't stay mad because I'd had this same conversation with myself. "How can you marry a woman if you're not being honest with her about who you are?"

"It depends on what you mean by honest," he said. "Should I tell her about the other girls I've had sex with? What would be the purpose of that? It's the same principle with the guys I've been with."

"You've gone out with other women?"

"Haven't you dated women?"

"No," I said. "It seemed dishonest. The way I define it, anyway."

"I guess I don't have your high standards," he said coolly. "I was president of my fraternity at college and there was a lot of pressure to date. I did what I had to."

"That sounds like fun."

"Come off it," he said, annoyed. "I went to a little college in the middle of Iowa. There was no way I was gonna come out."

"I had you pegged as an Ivy Leaguer."

"My family broke up when I was ten and it was just me and my mom. I was lucky to be able to afford any kind of college. I'm a scholarship student here, Henry, just like you."

It was my turn to bristle. "You assume I'm a scholarship student because I'm Mexican?"

"No," he said, "because you told me so last night." He smiled. "You said it as if you were proving a point to me."

"I thought you were another rich preppie here on his daddy's money."

His smile faded. "I haven't seen my dad in ten years."

"Does the woman you're engaged to mean anything more to you than the ones you went out with in college?"

"You've really got a mouth on you," he said. "You'll do well in court."

"Does she?" I persisted.

"No," he said. "I like her. I like her a lot."

"Her name's Bay? Like the body of water?"

"Asshole," he said, but he laughed when he said it. "Yes, Bay, Bay Kimball," he said. "She's a junior at a Catholic girls' school over in Marin, St. Clare's. Her father's Joe Kimball, the senior partner at the firm in L.A. where I clerked the last two summers. Awesome guy, Henry. I met Bay at a firm picnic. We both play tennis, so we played some and since we're both at school up here, I'd meet her in the city sometimes." He folded his hands behind his head. "I have to admit I kept in touch with her at first mainly because I really wanted an offer from the firm, and I figured it wouldn't hurt if I was friends with Joe's daughter. But after I got to know her, I liked her for herself and I could tell she really liked me. By the time I went back to the firm for my second summer, we were definitely dating."

"Someone who didn't like you as much as I do might say you're kind of an opportunist, Chris."

He moved away from me and said, "I know what you're thinking. I marry the senior partner's daughter and I can write my own ticket. You just have to trust that I'm not that much of an asshole. Look, Henry, try to understand. I knew I was homosexual when I was fourteen years old. When I was in high school, I used to bike to the library across town and look up everything I could find on the subject. All the books said I'd grow out of it. I waited and waited, but that didn't happen. I didn't want to be different, Henry. I still don't."

"You think getting married will change you?"

"God, I hope so," he said, in a voice so full of hurt that it made me ashamed for a moment of who I was.

"You think it's wrong to be gay, Chris?"

"It's wrong for me," he said.

"Maybe I should leave."

"I wish you wouldn't."

"You're a very confusing guy," I said.

"Are you so sure of yourself?" he asked me.

"No," I said, and I stayed.

*   *   *

I met her at a party in someone's backyard, a couple of months after Chris and I had started sleeping together. It was just after winter finals and the place was packed with haggard law students intent on getting drunk and possibly laid. Music blasted from inside the house, shattering the surrounding suburban silence. The yard was littered with plastic cups, and another keg had just been tapped. I was wandering around half drunk when I heard someone calling my name. I looked around, and saw Chris coming out of the house holding hands with a blond girl. My instinct was to walk the other way, but the tide was against me and I was pushed toward them.

"Henry," Chris said, "I want you to meet Bay. Bay, this is my friend Henry I've been telling you about."

"Hi," she said, extending a hand. "It's nice to meet you. Chris is always talking about you."

"Hi," I said, awkwardly shaking her hand.

"I'm going to get a beer," Chris said. "You want one, Bay? Henry?"

He was gone before either of us could answer. Bay had the fresh, shiny prettiness of the children of the rich: pink and gold skin, white, even teeth, her blue eyes clear and unclouded. She wore loose jeans and a heavy cable sweater, frayed a bit at the sleeves and the collar. They were the clothes someone wore to hide extra weight, but I could see it in her rounded cheeks and the hint of a double chin. Cruelly, I wondered what Chris saw in her besides a ticket to normality.

"So," I said, patronizing her, "you're a junior somewhere?"

"St. Clare's," she said, smiling a bit, taking my measure. "Why do law students feel so superior? My dad's a lawyer. It's nothing to be proud of."

I liked her for that. "You don't think so? Why?"

She shrugged. "Think about it, Henry. What do lawyers actually do except make money at the expense of other people's misery?"

"I guess that's why we feel superior."

"Chris said you had a sense of humor."

"If you have such a low opinion of law students, why are you engaged to one?"

"He's different," she said. "Don't you think so?"

I told myself to be careful. "Different? I'm not sure what you mean."

"He's not mercenary," she said, "and he's not arrogant and he's not boring."

"And you're in love with him," I said, drink getting the better of discretion.

"Hopelessly," she said, not altogether ironically.

"Is that from a movie? It sounds like something Claudette Colbert would say about Clark Gable. 'I'm hopelessly in love with him.' "

If she detected the mean-spiritedness in that remark, she didn't let on. She laughed and said, "You're funny, Henry."

"No, just sort of drunk."

Just then, Chris reappeared, carrying three cups of beer. "Here you go," he said, handing them out. "You two getting along?"

"I like Henry," Bay announced. She took a delicate swallow of her beer and wiped her lip with her sleeve.

Chris glanced at me and said, "Good."

Some vintage Supremes came on and people started dancing. Bay grabbed my hand and said, "Let's dance, okay? I've been cooped up in the library all week."

"What about me?" Chris said.

"You, too," she said. "Come on."

We pushed our way to the middle of the yard and started dancing together. Her moves were fluid and uninhibited, as she turned now toward me, now toward Chris, hips swaying, breasts bouncing. Her face was flushed, and beads of sweat appeared on her forehead. She pushed her heavy hair back from her face and grinned at me. I felt awkward and self-conscious as I tried to keep up with her while staying clear of Chris, who bobbed up and down between us. After a few minutes, I shrugged and left them at it. I watched them from the edge of the yard. She danced toward Chris, who danced back at her. I could see from the way their bodies moved what they were to each other, and whatever fantasy I had entertained about Chris and me was dispelled at that moment. I went inside.

I found some people in the kitchen playing a drinking game that involved long strings of law Latin and a fifth of tequila. I was drunk when Bay caught up with me at the front door.

She tugged at my sleeve and said, "You're not leaving, are you? We hardly got to talk."

Her face was flushed and her eyes bright with drink.

"I thought you wanted to dance," I said.

"Chris got hijacked by his moot court partner," she said. "Stay and keep me company."

"You must know a lot of the people here."

"His other friends are so dull," she said, grinning. "You're not dull."

"How can you be sure?"

"Because you're gay," she said, merrily, and then her face went an even deeper red. "Oh, God, I'm sorry. I shouldn't have said that."

Even drunk, my guard went up, and I tried to pass it off as a joke. "The antonym for dull is exciting, not gay."

"I'm sorry, Henry. I say stupid things when I've had too much to drink."

I shrugged. "It's not a secret. Did Chris tell you?"

"He knew I wouldn't care," she said. "I have lesbian friends at school."

"It's all right, Bay," I said, zipping up my jacket.

"Don't go. You're the only one of Chris's friends I've met that I like. So naturally, I humiliate you. I feel awful."

"I'm not humiliated," I replied. All I wanted was to get away.

"Chris will be really upset with me for offending you."

She was near tears. I looked at her, and an alcoholic sentimentality descended on me. She ceased being the femme fatale of my imagination who had stolen Chris away from me. She was two or three years younger than me, just a child in my book, who wasn't holding her liquor very well, in a roomful of people she hardly knew. I slipped my hand into hers, feeling big and confident and protective.

"Come on, Bay, let's go dance."

"You're not mad," she said, with transparent relief.

"Not even a little," I assured her.

We went and danced.

We didn't really become friends until after Chris had graduated from Stanford and moved to Los Angeles to work at her father's firm, while she returned north to finish her last year of college. I was finishing my last year of law school. At first we saw each other because we had in common that we missed Chris, but then we discovered another shared interest: we both liked to drink.

When Chris was still around, I would go out with them from time to time. The three of us went through many bottles of wine together, Bay and I easily outdrinking Chris. I never gave it a second thought. After Chris left, Bay and I were a little shy in each other's company and it took a few drinks to relax us. Soon enough, drinking became a central, if unspoken, reason for our get-togethers. We released something in each other because, except when I was with her, I rarely drank, and from what she told me I gathered it was the same with her. Sober, she was a quiet girl of twenty who made self-deprecating remarks about her weight and her intelligence, but after a few drinks an entirely different person inhabited her body: a smart, sensual woman who could be bitingly shrewd and funny. Drinking with her took on an aura of romance.

We'd meet in the bar of a second-class hotel on Geary. It was dark and deserted, with a jukebox that played Billie Holiday and Dinah Washington. The bartender was an Australian and a dead ringer for Elizabeth Taylor in a fat phase, who poured drinks with a heavy hand. In a booth upholstered in worn red leather we'd listen to old songs, suffused with that warm alcoholic glow that lifted us out of the ordinary and made everything bigger and more dramatic.

One night she insisted that I take her to a gay bar.

"Why?" I asked warily.

"I want to see that part of your life."

"It's not that interesting."

"It would be to me. Please, Henry, I'll behave."

"It's not a stop on the Gray Line tour."

"I don't want to gawk," she said, offended. "I want to size up the competition."

"What competition?"

"The competition for you," she said, smiling provocatively. This was a familiar line of banter between us.

"You're almost a married woman," I pointed out.

"Almost, Henry, almost. Come on, I hear the best dancing in the city's at gay bars."

"Cha-cha-cha," I said, and we were off.

The Hide 'n' Seek was, as usual on a Saturday night, packed and smoky, musky with sweat and cologne. In the darkness, Bay grabbed for my hand and whispered, "I can hardly breathe in here."

"You'll get used to it," I said, pumping her hand reassuringly.

I got us drinks and edged her against the wall near the dance floor, where the boys moved like liquid sex to the throb of disco. A tiny blond sashayed past us, stopped, looked at Bay, touched her breast and said, "Nice drag, honey."

"It's real," I said.

He yanked his hand back as if burned and went on his way, laughing.

"Was he making a pass at me?" Bay asked.

I explained drag to her.

"He thought I was a boy?" She giggled. She looked around the room. "I wish I was a boy tonight. These guys are gorgeous."

"Looks aren't everything," I told her.

"No? What do you want in a man?"

"Don't be a bitch."

"I'm serious," she said. "You never talk about your boyfriends. What are they like?"

"I don't have one," I said.

"But if you did, what would he be like?"

Like Chris, I thought. "Oh, Bay, I don't know. I'm just looking for that certain special anyone. Let's dance."

I dragged her out to the dance floor, where we wedged ourselves among the dancing boys. She was as snaky-hipped as they were. I watched her move, studied her body, tested myself for responsiveness. But it was the boy in the tight black jeans behind her who raced my pulse.

"What are you thinking?" she shouted over the music.

"Not thinking," I said. "Dancing."

She pressed against me, her breasts soft on my chest, her hair swishing against my cheek and said, "Don't I turn you on, just a little?"

"I'd have to be dead if you didn't," I replied.

She smirked. "Liar. My tits terrify you."

"Yeah, they're pretty scary," I agreed.

And we both laughed.

*   *   *

At last call we were sitting on empty beer boxes against the wall, watching the boys frantically pick each other up.

Out of nowhere, Bay asked, "Did Chris ever cheat on me?"

"Why are you asking?" I replied, neutrally. "Do you think he did?"

"No, not Chris," she said. "Maybe I want him to. Maybe I want him to fall in love with someone else. Maybe I don't want to get married."

"No? Why not? Don't you love him?"

"He's just so safe," she said. "I want an adventure."

"Who's stopping you?"

"The only time I feel free is when I'm with you," she said, leaning against me. "Are you sure you don't want to sleep with me?"

I put my arm around her and marveled, in my twenty-three-year-old way, at the irony of the situation.

"I'm sure," I said.

Bay and Chris were married eight months later at a church in Pasadena. They wrote their own service and she asked me to help her find a poem to read. I gave her some lines from Whitman:

> *I give you my love more precious than money,*
> *I give you myself before preaching or law;*
> *Will you give me yourself? Will you come travel with me?*
> *Shall we stick together as long as we live?*

Paul Lisicky

LUCKY

AT THIRTEEN, I was afraid of someone. I did everything possible to distinguish myself from him. I recorded my voice over and over, imagining wide flat stones on my tongue, working out the inflections, sanding over any last traces of hiss. I trudged back and forth down the length of our driveway, taking heavy, self-assured steps, bouncing just slightly from the knees until my arms swung naturally, without concentration. I did push-ups by the dozen on the laundry room floor. I read sports page after sports page, memorizing the scores, insinuating myself into arguments in which the merit of the Marlins' MVP was in question. There was nothing helpless about me. You could say that I talked too much, that I was scattered and lacked focus, that I hungered for overwhelming amounts of attention and reassurance from everyone who came into contact with me, but you wouldn't have said that I was feminine, of that much I was sure.

Unlike Stan Laskin. Stan Laskin: hardware store owner. Stan Laskin: who paid special attention to me every time I was sent in by Sid, my father, to buy switches or ten-penny nails. It wasn't that he was anything but kind. It was that his body, his entire self-presentation, soft and yielding, with its tendency toward flab, represented everything I didn't want to be. His colognes scented the atmosphere every time I waited at his counter. His glasses, all seven pairs of them, coordinated with his bracelets and rings. But most disturbing of all was the expression on his face, wounded and lamblike, as if he were waiting for some devastating stranger to come through the door.

As far as I knew he lived alone and had never been loved by anyone in his life. His days, I decided, were repetitive, dull, and lonely, enlivened only by occasional visits to the fabric store, where he remembered all the employees' birthdays, and to the public bathroom stall where he sat six hours at a time before a vacant glory hole. After work, I pictured him walking through his front door, leaving his outer life behind and assuming a secret role, draping himself in chintz or black velvet, then giving hairdos to his Yorkshires or trying on his extensive collection of cloches and pins. Every morning he'd call up his mother, discussing the trip they were planning to the Lawrence Welk Resort in Palm Springs, California. His life had as much to do with my own as the newsletter of the Liberace fan club.

It was a warm, overcast day in December, the weekend before Christmas. A heat wave was descending upon Dade County, moistening the foliage with dew. In Florida fashion, the trunks of the royal palms were wrapped with strings of clear lights. I hurried down the Miracle Mile with Mark Margolit and Steve Mendelsohn, two of my friends from school. At least I thought they were friends. I cared about them as much as I cared about the health of my gums, but to each other we looked like friends, and when the three of us were together no one dared make fun of us. I felt convincing with them. They believed me when I expressed my interest in my friend Jane. Together, we talked about the color and texture of Jamaica Reed's nipples, the lead guitar solos from Metallica's second album, and the after-school activities of Mrs. Walgreen, our Spanish teacher, who was forever tugging her miniskirt down over her hip. I wore a ripped Ozzy Osbourne T-shirt with black kohl eyeliner around my eyes, and when I looked in the mirror I even scared myself.

We walked around the perimeter of the circle, the scent of frozen pizza still rising from our fingers, stumbling to the video arcade, where we'd play a few games of Donkey Kong or Burger Time. In my thirteen-year-old way, I'd told myself I was having fun and was behaving like any boy my age was supposed to. We couldn't have been walking more than ten seconds when I saw Stan Laskin carrying boxes between a rental truck and his store, accepting a delivery. He looked relatively conventional for Stan Laskin: baggy chino pants, golden horn-rims, navy blue button-down. Except for the scrap of material — a yellow brocaded print tied around his throat. A softness slid down inside my stomach. I felt nothing but embarrassed and afraid.

"Nice scarf," Steve said.

He wouldn't look at us. He lifted up a box marked SCREWDRIVERS, watching it fall through his hands.

"Did you always like women's accessories?" Steve said.

A single drop of sweat ran down the crease of my back.

"In case you're interested," Stan Laskin said, his face the deepest crimson, "it's an ascot."

"Oh, an ascot," Steve said, highlighting his *s*. "An *ass*-cot."

"We better get out of here," I whispered to Mark.

"No," Steve said. "Stay." A brutal, joyous laugh tore up from his lungs. He leapt toward the stop sign and slapped its red metal face.

"Do you like to suck cock?" he said, spinning around, turning to Stan.

Nothing. A helicopter beat somewhere overhead, concealed.

"Do you? Do you like the taste of cock in your mouth?"

Stan gazed downward at the box in his hands.

"Faggot," Steve said. "Lousy cocksucking faggot."

The sidewalk might have cracked beneath my feet. More than anything I wanted Stan to dismiss us, to write us off as small, inconsequential. Instead, he turned not to Steve, but to me. He looked into my face in a more searching way than anyone had ever done.

"What made you so hateful?" he said matter-of-factly.

"Me?" I said.

"All of you. I don't get it. Tell me how you live with yourselves."

Something bony and sharp pushed deep inside my chest.

"Come on," Steve said. "I've had enough. Let's check out those bitches across the street."

The days hastened toward Christmas. I completed my activities as usual: I tossed Milk Duds to Delaware, our neighbor's Boston terrier, in my efforts to teach her how to fetch. I worked through all the supplementary exercises in my algebra packet, achieving a 98 on the pop quiz. I even helped Peter, my brother, wax my father's Grand Prix, buffing its blue finish with a chamois cloth. At night, though, lying in bed, I couldn't scour Stan's question from my thoughts. I tried to tell myself that what had transpired hadn't been so sad. Everyone behaved that way, everyone I knew. It wasn't like they meant any harm. It was the way you carried yourself in the world. Otherwise, they'd pulverize you. Faggot, cocksucker, queer: these were just words — empty, stupid, meaningless words. No one needed to be defended here.

What the hell was I afraid of?

I was standing in the locker room after gym class. We were midway through the swimming unit, which I preferred to softball or to flag football. Nearly everyone had already left for homeroom. The air smelled of bleach and worn elastic. I looked from side to side, pulled down my gym shorts, as the spray pounded in the shower room beside me. I turned halfway. It was Jon Brainard, a small, intense boy with blue eyes and dark curly hair, who'd just transferred from Sarasota. He was watching me beneath the showerhead, defined fingers lathering a compact stomach. He might have been my brother in another time. My skin tingled, chilled, then flushed with the richest warmth. He was rinsing the suds between his legs. I couldn't keep myself from staring back, though I wanted to stop.

"Evan," he called.

I turned. I fumbled inside my locker, pretending not to hear.

"Would you hand me that towel on the bench?"

The drain gulped down the overflow. His smile was shy, as if he were thinking something enormous, beautiful.

My toes clenched tighter into the concrete.

Many months passed before I again allowed myself to walk into Stan's store. It smelled of torn wood, matches, grass seed, pesticides — a confluence of smells which I associate, to this day, only with that memory. In my pocket, I carried an arrowhead I'd found beneath an ice plant on the Metrozoo grounds. It was my talisman, my lucky charm. I'd attributed several minor miracles to its existence — the recovery of a fifty-dollar bill and the rapid healing of a fractured ankle. My plan was this: I'd leave it on his counter in an unmarked bag without note or explanation. He could do with it what he wanted. I knew it was hopeless, and I knew it was unreasonable, but the exchange had been hovering over me, a ruined black blanket, and I just wanted to get it off my mind.

Stan was back in the supply room. I leaned the lunch bag against the cash register, then turned to make my getaway.

At once he came toward me with a crowbar. He looked kindly and quizzical, as if he thought I needed help. Then all at once his brows drew together.

"Don't I know you?"

My breathing went sluggish. I imagined him bringing the crowbar down across my forehead, splitting it in two.

"You were one of those boys," he said. "Get out of here."

"I didn't —"

"I'll call the police. Get out."

I left the store without explaining myself. It was his pain and not the crowbar that frightened me. Even then, I knew that it wasn't just about my indifference, but about every time he'd heard the word *faggot* muttered behind his back. That night, lying on the living room sofa, I thought about the arrowhead in the lunch bag. It was a vacant, meaningless gesture that wouldn't console him, I'm positive. I'm sure he even tossed it away. But there's always the chance that he kept it, and it's serving him now, giving him luck, warding off anyone who'd hurl a word at him, or anyone who'd let it happen.

Ishmael Houston-Jones

SEBASTIAN COMES FOR TEA

(For Joe and Lucy and RKB)

WHEN I STARTED renting whores I thought of it as some sort of noble anthropological experiment. There was very little of me in all of it. I omitted myself as though the inclusion of my self would make my research suspect and compromise the validity of the science of voyeurism. It was me as a Margaret Mead as a john. I carefully transcribed notes and observations. Performed comparative analyses. How the flavor of this one was related to his diet and intake of nicotine and fried foods. Which drug was better for opening which orifices. Which would have the opposite effect and make them clench. I studied the syntax of the fake moan and the grammar of the pornographic explication. I calculated wages earned per hour for which specific tasks performed. The exchange of lust for money. The negotiation of love.

*   *   *

That he lowers himself down onto me so willingly is stunning. *Onto me.* How strange to identify one physical part as the whole. As though the sum of my being were contained in this rubber-encased, blood-engorged cylinder. Anyway, what is amazing about this entombment of me by his sphincter is his previous disinclination to even consider doing it. I think this has as much to do with his fear of smell as it does with his fear of pain. Fear of smelling himself. Fear of smelling what will come out of him. Fear of proof; of evidence. He showers at least three times a day. There will be plans to meet, to go to a movie, a club, wherever, but then there will always be the delay for a shower first. I'm used to it. It's a part of him, like the color of his hair. I remember the first time I stuck my tongue "up there." How he coiled and curled and tried to get his butt away from my face. There was no pain involved then. No entrance. No "splitting open and ripping asunder." No, his discomfort was in having my nose in such daring proximity to the source of his shit. He wouldn't kiss me on the mouth for weeks after. He often remarks on the body odor of one or another of his young friends. A pungent scent is verboten. So here he is tonight, squatting, facing me naked, greased and ready. Or at least, greased and not unwilling.

He grimaces but says nothing. What is there to say but some stale porn utterances. I can't tell what my face is doing but I can feel the muscles around the bridge of my nose going in several directions at once. He drops another inch or so, then stops suddenly and grips. Quick little intake of breath. He bares his bottom teeth then continues. Slowly, with not much joy in his eyes. I feel my toes contract and for a second the pain at the arch of my left foot takes me away from here. But the pressure of his weight sitting full on my pelvis, my entire dick beating inside his rectum, brings me back quickly enough.

There's an awkwardness of choreography in this position.

Missed cadences. Unsure balances. We're not at all like the golden boys on the videotapes. There's no mind-numbing synthesizer music washing over this scene. The lighting is just what's here — a string of colored Christmas twinklers in the next room; and from the window, orange-white streetlamp, the full moon. No, the real beauty of this moment comes from the surprise of his maneuver. At once yielding and pliant while at the same time resistantly in control of the dance.

Maybe he smiles. Maybe he's just stifling a fart. At any rate he begins to rock back and forth, slowly, insistently, but when I try to arch up into him he spreads a hand down onto the space between my chest and my belly as if to say, "No, just lie still." I obey. Maybe I close my eyes. The rhythm of his rocking accelerates. I throb inside him. The whole scene is becoming moist and messy. And yes, I begin to get faint whiffs of his insides. The rocking stops. If my eyes have been closed I open them. His hands are wet with his sperm. He made the smallest sound possible when he came. His face is red.

I need to end this. I grasp the front of his thighs to hold him in place. My pelvis writhes against his with regular little pulses. His hand on my chest can't stop me now. Spent, he's as flimsy as a dishrag; as weak as a feather. I drive deeper and harder up toward his core. His face looks miserable. His hair is everywhere. He, too, wants this to be over. I begin to question what it all means, him giving himself to me this way. It can't be explained by booze or drugs or mere attraction. I wonder why he did it, why tonight. I'm becoming distracted from the task at hand. I grip his thighs so tightly that I'm sure there will be marks tomorrow. There needs to be one part of him that I know I will find sexy. I focus on his throat and its bobbing Adam's apple. I won't tell what I imagine, but within seconds I am ejaculating inside him with some appropriate prelanguage growl.

In one move he's off me, down the hall, in the bathroom, door closed behind him. I am too drained to stop him even if I wanted to. After a long while I hear the toilet flush and the shower run. I peel off our condom. My room reeks of us. Bits of him and me are drying on my skin. I use some piece of his underclothing to wipe myself. I try to join him but he has locked the door. I piss into an empty juice container and crawl back into my damp, soiled and disheveled bed. When he has thoroughly cleansed himself, I hope that he will leave.

Donald Windham

THE BATH TUB

I

From floor to ceiling, the spring air is fogged with steam. I am sitting at the back of the tub, my legs spread and one of my feet touching the white porcelain curves at each side of my brother's buttocks. He is sitting in the middle of the tub, directly in front of me. Somewhere in the water the soap, which has sunk, is melting and filling the small bathroom with an oceanlike fragrance; and my brother and I, by moving our bodies back and forth, are creating a tide and a slapping of waves. Near me, my washcloth rolls to the surface like a sea monster or a diving whale, then rolls down out of sight again. I stop for a moment to see if it will reappear and a wave, breaking against my body, sweeps over the back of the tub and hits the wooden floor with a wet splash.

The bathrooms are on the second floor, with white marble sinks and large mahogany-framed mirrors hanging above the sinks; but the hot-water tank downstairs supplies only enough water for the ordinary uses of the kitchen; pots and kettles of water have to be heated on the stove and carried up the long flight of stairs to the bathrooms on Saturdays when everyone bathes; and every Saturday, to lessen this task, my brother and I take a bath together.

I like my brother and I like doing things together with him. Most of my joy in this game of making a sea out of the bathwater lies in the fact that it is his game and he is allowing me to join in it. My complete fondness for him is the earliest thing I can remember, and even before then, when I was just beginning to walk and talk, I am told, I used to break in half any cracker or cookie that was given me and wander about the house, searching for him and chanting:

"Give half to Freddie, give half to Freddie."

If I did not find him I would not give up. I would keep the half that was to be his and sing:

"Save 'til tomorrow, save 'til tomorrow."

Now that I am seven and he is nine there is no greater joy for me than that of joining my existence to his in experiences such as this one in the bath tub together. I am delighted for him to take charge and give orders so long as the orders make me a part of his activity. He began playing by floating a brush in the water, creating a current around the sides of the tub, and sailing the brush on it. He paddled forward with his left hand and backward with his right and directed me to do the same, keeping away from the back of the tub so the brush could sail completely around me and up to him again.

After that, holding on to the sides of the claw-footed tub and moving his body back and forth, he taught me to make waves. Then I stopped to look for the washcloth, the momentum of the water broke against my body, and — splash! — the wave went over the back of the tub.

Once before, when the two of us were playing some other game, water from the bathroom floor has seeped through and left a brown stain on the ceiling of the dining room below. We have been warned what will happen to us if this occurs again, and we lean over the back of the tub together and begin to sop up the water. But this does not work very well, especially as the sweat from the steamed walls begins to run with frightening rapidity down onto the floor from the places where we are resting our hands against the plaster. And then we hear Mother coming upstairs.

Mother is gentle. She considers innocence to be the supreme virtue. The gaps in the possibility of her successfully raising two sons, without the presence of a father to assert authority and distance, have not yet been made apparent to her. She has a simple vision of reality: everything which is evil she considers to be fiendishly unreal. But she has an overwhelming belief in goodness, as well as a love of it, stronger than her frequent disillusionments; and the strength of that love and belief gives me, while I am still small, a solid basis for character that, despite the ellipses that will come later, nothing will be able to destroy.

She opens the door, expecting to find us bathing, and stands there, looking down at her two sons who are leaning over the back of the tub and dabbling with their washcloths in the dirty water on the floor. We explain that the water sloshed over by chance and that we have gotten most of it up. Then we wait to see what will happen.

Mother has blue eyes and a round face. Sternness is for her a pursing of the lips. And yet we have been warned. The pause comes to an end when I raise my washcloth and wring the dirty water out of it into the tub. She takes the cloth from me and washes it and my brother's in the sink. Then she brings a used towel to dry the floor with and tells us to rinse ourselves with cold water and get out of the tub, quickly, before she loses her temper.

We know that we are saved. But we are to go to the movies in the afternoon and the possibility remains that what we have done will be remembered when the time comes for our departure and we will be kept at home. This would be a tragedy. We go to the movies every Saturday. Besides the Western feature, we see a chapter in a serial, and if you miss a chapter you have no idea what has gone on when you see the next one. We go downstairs quickly, our towels wrapped around us rather than our heavy bathrobes, for it is not really cold, and dress in our bedroom. Then we stand around uncomfortably in odd corners of the living room and dining room, keeping very clean and afraid that anything we do may be used as an excuse to prevent us from being sent off with our fifteen cents each.

And the thing we most long for happens — nothing. Life follows its regular routine. As on every Saturday, we have vegetable soup for lunch. After lunch we are sent out, each with his dime for the movie and his extra nickel for a candy bar. We return home after having seen only a little bit of the movie a second time, determined not to give displeasure by being late. We eat supper and are sent to bed.

In bed we feel for each other that wonderful friendliness which comes from having been engaged together in a successful adventure. I watch my brother with short smiles. He returns me one. Barricaded by pillows and the covers, we whisper about the movie we have seen. It told, with many scenes of galloping horses, the story of a friend's great sacrifice for his partner. My brother is filled with a longing for adventure. But I am content.

II

It is summer, warm weather; the blinds of the bathroom window are folded back into the casements, the window is open; but it is still necessary to heat water downstairs on the kitchen stove and to carry it upstairs to the bathroom if my brother and I are to be clean after we bathe, and we are once again in the tub together. I am sitting in the back, as before, and my brother is in front of me, but he is acting exactly as though he is bathing alone. There are no

games, no conversation. And when I want the soap, which is in the
rack hung over the porcelain rim of the tub in front of him, he will
neither hand it to me nor allow me to reach over him and take it.
He has asked to be allowed to bathe alone; Mother has refused his
request; and he has decided to assert his will by pretending that I
am not there. But I will not let him. I do not see why I should sit
at the back of the tub, unable to wash, and wait until he has
finished bathing, especially as when he wants to rinse himself he
runs cold water into the tub, considerably increasing the rapidity
with which the water we are sitting in is losing its heat. I persist in
trying to reach over the barrier of the arm he has raised to prevent
me from taking the soap. His only further defense of his privacy is
to hit me.

For quite a while now my presence has been an annoyance to
him. In the afternoons after school, where we both go although I
am two grades behind him, a group of boys from his class gathers
at our house to play ball in the side yard. Because of my age, I am
a less good player than the others, and my brother defends himself
against the drawback of being associated with me by treating me
with open contempt before the others have a chance to. There is
no reason for him to put himself out to keep my admiration, which
he already has, and there is no end to the admiration he wants to
win in the unconquered world he is beginning to live in.

This desire has already caused him to join the Boy Scouts of
America and to win merit badge after merit badge. For a while,
Mother wanted me to join, too; and he was perfectly willing that I
should become a Boy Scout. It would do me a world of good, there
was no doubt of that, in his opinion. But he was uneasy the Friday
night that he was first to take me to a meeting. I was pleased to go;
but I knew most of the boys who were members, by sight at least;
the clubhouse was only a block from the school where I went every
day; and it did not seem to me that I was entering a wholly new
world where I would be judged for the first time. But it did to my
brother, and he felt that the judgment would reflect on him. He

made so many objections that evening to the way I was to be dressed, how my hair was to be combed, and how I was in general to be forced *not* to look peculiar (I looked just as I did on any other occasion when I was clean and my hair was wet and flat) that I saw for the first time how worthless I was in his eyes, not for anything I did or for any skill I lacked, but for the very fact of my existence as what I was, his brother two years younger than he, of whom he was contemptuous. The hurt that evening turned back into myself any desire I might have had to become a Boy Scout (just as those rejections on the ball field curtailed any proficiency I might have developed in pitching, catching, batting) and began a distance between us which was to become even greater than that he hoped for.

But on this day, while we are in the tub together, it is impossible for him to find any justification for the intimacy that is forced on him. His only defense is in pretending to be alone, and when I insist on reaching over him for the soap he strikes me as hard as he can. I strike back. But the match is not at all even. In none of these encounters have I ever won, and it is not long before I am shedding tears and calling for help.

This is a difficult period for Mother; our conduct bewilders her; and when she arrives in the bathroom she does not know what to do. Circumstances are beginning to prove that her devoting her whole life to her children does nothing to fill the gaps in her authority and in our characters. We return sufficient love to her. Perhaps even too much. But this only increases her helplessness. She cannot control us without violence. And in a feminine world violence is always hysterical.

"All right," she says, "this is the last time! I've warned you enough! Finish bathing and dry yourselves and wait for me here!"

After she has gone, my brother's eyes blaze with hatred. His cheek at the corner of his nose lifts in a sneer which says more eloquently than any words how much he loathes me. I am a sniveling little crybaby, and if only I had not been there he would have been happy. Now there is going to be trouble and I am to blame.

I stand with my eyes on the floor, unable to look at the sneer that makes his face hideous. I, too, feel that everything would have been all right if only he had behaved differently, if he at least had been fair enough to let me use the soap even though he would not speak to me; I mutter that it is not my fault, that it is his fault. He does not deign to answer.

Mother returns, in her hand a switch made of a branch she has broken from one of the small peach trees in the yard. My brother is first. Blindly, as though she is achieving some kind of oblivion through her action, she switches his legs below the knees, demanding with each blow that he promise this is the last time this will happen. After his weeping promise, my turn comes. The blows of the switch burn like fire. I weep and promise, too. But my tears are less full than my brother's. I have already felt the depth of my grief.

When Mother sees the raw red welts she has raised in strips on the backs of our calves, she kneels between us and, there in the bathroom, wraps her arms about my brother and me and bursts into tears, as hurt as we are by what she has done. Her heart fills with remorse; she begs us to love one another. And we say that we will. But there is neither remorse nor love in my brother's eyes.

III

A last memory of bathing with my brother. He and I are standing naked beside a white porcelain tub into which steaming water is running from the metal faucet at the end. We are both adolescent. His hair is still straight, the way a young boy's hair is straight; mine is beginning to have a curl in it. The tile-floored bathroom, much smaller than the one in the homeplace, is at the end of the hall in the apartment we are to be dispossessed from on Peachtree Place. To one side of it is the bedroom in which we have left our clothes. Mother is at work at the office. It is after school. I had come home and turned on the water in the tub and was undressing when my brother came in and began to get ready for a bath. For a reason that it does not interest me to discover, he chooses to ignore the fact that I am doing the same thing.

"You can see that I am using the bathroom," I say.

"You can use it later," he answers.

"You can, too."

"But I'm not going to. Go on, get out of here."

"Try and make me."

"I will."

All friendliness between us has disappeared. He gives me a shove in the direction of the door. I hit him. He hits back. This could be one more of the many fights we have had through the years which all end the same. But it is not. The resentment that has been slowly accumulating in me has convinced me for a long time now that he is not going to treat me considerately unless I force him to. This conviction is an extreme one for me. I do not like to force things. I value most what I am given, and value it precisely because it is given. And what I want from my brother can only be given. But it is not going to be given, and I have reached the point where I am willing to abandon hope of friendliness and allow myself to hate him with the hate which is necessary if I am going to fight him with the determination to win. I have been willing to do this for some time; but for anything to come of my willingness it has been necessary for me to have a little of that ingredient without which no one wins in a contest with someone stronger: luck.

And this time I have it. I strike back with all the strength my hate can give me. My blow lands on my brother's chin with a clear, clean crack, like the crack of a dead branch being broken sharply in two. He loses his balance and falls to the floor. His head strikes the tile wall of the bathroom. He does not get up.

And when I have left the room and he does get up, he does not continue the fight. The occasion is unique. It is the first time that I am not the one who loses. And it is the last time that he ever tries to bully me or impose his will upon me by force. There is no tapering off. This is the end. It never happens again.

It is not my triumph, however; friendship was what I wanted, and after this occasion I do not try for it any longer. Where there was once something, now there is nothing. Afterwards, I will feel more strongly than ever that it is those things which I have had and lost, rather than those things which I have never possessed, that create in me the greatest sense of deprivation. But this does not affect events. From this time on, my brother and I have no more to do with each other.

Gary Fisher

RED CREAM SODA

NOT A WEEK AFTER they found out how sick I was Randy started telling me his stories. He didn't seem to hear my protests; and would literally pull me from my work kicking, spitting, cursing him, into our common space, a small room made unbearable by a huge arthritic sofa bed and a cinderblock concoction that served as a table, there to make me listen to him. The man all but foamed at the mouth in his urgency to get them out. I call them stories but the scowl that met my doubt made me wonder. I didn't *not* believe my friend; it was simply easier to feign doubt than to show my true discomfort over what he was telling me. They were descriptions of the sex he had had, and was continuing to have, almost nightly — anonymous sex, reckless, vindictive sex, impassioned and yet loveless, somnambular sex, with bodies he could hardly see.

He paced as he told his stories, and gestured, urging my attention, my understanding, my quiet conspiracy. If in my discomfort I laughed out loud to relieve some tension, he would become wildly agitated, dare me to move, or rap on the glass tabletop as though to demonstrate here and now the violence he had been relating (not to mention that which he was capable of); and I cannot call his interpretations anything but violence. He would rant now about the force of it — how I wouldn't believe the force, the depth, the cruelty of it; and how he had countered all with an equal, opposite force of his own, not to escape, but to whip, strangle, and impale himself even more cruelly than his tormentors, like a jesus, he said, ecstatically self-crucified.

"You don't honestly believe that, Randy?"

"What, that it was like martyrdom?"

"No, that they — those men — were actually trying to hurt you. Most of the men you'd meet in those places, they wouldn't know how to hurt you. You practically have to pay to get hurt in this city."

Randy watched me as though he'd been defending a high moral principle and I'd called him a liar. It was a hot, inspired, evangelical stare, his blue eyes gone gray, his hair tousled and full of lamplight, his big hands against his jacketed chest, frozen in mid-gesture like a pair of birds about to explode off a red crest.

At that moment he was the last man on earth you'd expect to see *forced;* I couldn't imagine it anyway. Then the life seemed to drop out of him and he sat down. He fumbled with the tab on a can of pop, got it, and began sipping, gingerly, afraid of spilling the liquid, I thought. If this had been a commercial — and it had all the markings of one — Randy would have turned the can up, breathlessly; and water from an unknown source, a quenching rain from a clear blue sky, would have pounded his blissful face. I'd never mused on the violence of refreshment, but I almost laughed out loud when I thought of it. The can of pop didn't come to life for me until he opened it, even though I'd noticed it as he stood in my doorway insisting that I give up half an hour. I watched the can instead of him, telling the can instead of him, no, I really had work to get done.

He could joke about the way writing sinister-little-stories absorbed me, but when he did get me to sit and listen to him he wouldn't tolerate my funning him. Somehow the acts he relived for me were beyond what the two of us could create, beyond what I could write, and beyond what he could tell me, though the combination was a dangerously close approximation. And I found myself anchored by that little red can of pop, which I hadn't really noticed until he drank from it. It was a wrinkle in the dark, crazy fabric he was weaving, deliriously wrong, and fortunately so, because I might have gone back there with him, back to his moviehouse, his wooded hill, his secluded beach, the library restroom, for christssake, *gone back to a library restroom,* as if the idea weren't already low camp in my mind. He wanted me to go, and I pretended to go, but some large part of me stayed, with the can in just the corner of my vision. I was safe in things I understood, or so I thought.

He talked on, more pleasantly now: things he'd seen on the trolley ride home, a woman with cadmium-yellow hair, five boys dressed as stars (one-tenth of the fifty states, they explained to him), a Negro man with deep, black gouges in both his cheeks, like he'd been attacked by two cats at the same time and in the same way. All the time Randy sipped cautiously at the can of pop as though he'd just opened it and was afraid of spilling it.

He didn't ask me to, but in the weeks that followed I kept a diary of his stories, his "encounters," as he called them and insisted they be called. "These men, these events," he said slowly, as though he were dictating to me there in the living room, "everything I'm telling you has happened, and continues to happen as we speak, and will continue for as long as there are men, I imagine."

Sunday, March 29   If I ask myself why I will go crazy. I must think I'm Joe Christmas, running toward my own disaster — ha, ha — as if I could beat it to ground zero and

in that way avoid it. If I ask too much I'll die, so I'll just tell
you what I see and smell and feel and helplessly imagine
during those dark and formless times. Am I feverish? I'm
certainly still flush with it, aren't I, still flush with sex? It's
because I can't catch my breath; I can't catch up with my
own not believing this (so I can hardly expect you to). Start
with this Frenchman — Alain, was it? — and his awkward
Aryan body. I thought he was German; he looked enough
like me, in the face anyhow. I kept thinking Nazi-Nazi-Nazi,
but he was speaking French to me, in my ear, rapid, very
personal, very sexy, and he had a big cock. I tell you, I
would have let him go all the way, to the end, to the absolute
end, plague and all. If he had asked me I might not have
said "yes," but you can bet I wouldn't have said anything —
but he pulled out, and that was okay. It was like a movie, I
tell you, arching right over me, three times! We were in a
secret spot of his — I'm sure I couldn't find it again in the
middle of the day — we were down in a trench where the
sand was clean and soft like beach sand, and a little warm
like it too. It was so dark; the moon hardly broke through
the scrub, so I don't know how, or even *if,* I saw everything
that he did to me, or everything that I remember seeing on
him, and on me, the harness, the clamps, the studded collar
— all of it so vivid I can touch it now, with my mind, but I
don't recall which senses were involved at the time. He tried
to put his whole hand in me . . . but I stopped him there. I
told him I couldn't take any more. I lied to him; I said that
I had already climaxed.

Randy finally collapsed in a chair. Having paced rigidly for an
hour, forcing out the night's story in a series of false starts, stutters,
and breathless intermissions, he sipped from his can of pop, what
might have been the same can of pop on the same strange night,
under the same as yet unexplained circumstances that all of this

started. I questioned then his need to tell these stories, and the sanity of disclosure in general. Yet I would sit so passively through the next installments, neatly bound and gagged by what could only have been disbelief; forced to listen because I couldn't stop his talking, like the unsuspecting psychoanalyst roped to his own couch while the lunatic roams and imposes his disease in much the same way the analyst, given the chance, would impose the cure.

Thursday, April 2   I was against the wall on the right side, the darker side. There were mirrors on the other side that reflected, refracted the movie in disturbing ways and threw its moving light on the men. I preferred the dark on the right side and drew up beside a familiar middle-aged man, pasty white — though it could have have been the light — and more nervous than I remember. Funny how his anxiousness calmed me, and how his appearance pushed — not pulled, almost pushed me out of his way. Tall, thick-eyed, lipless man with glasses, severe, crusted virile-looking nearing-old man . . . Jesus, that gross fuck in the black suit was lurking near, trying to get my cock in his mouth, but I wouldn't give it to him and then the tough pasty man could have given his to either of us, but he went for me, and I lowered myself to him, sucked him quick to keep him interested while that sick, suited fuck looked on, his eyes still lurking, his mouth gaped, twisted, ugly. I sucked him to hardness, to a buzzing calmness, then he went to work, very actively, thrusting, talking to me, to himself, low but roughly, thrusting the words into me, asking questions and forcing back my possible answer. In a flurry of action, in a flurry of whispers he began to strike my face, dull and hard so it made less sound than his voice and his breath and the wet rapid entry. I felt trapped, afraid, trapped and exceptional — the suit had backed away — I heard someone gasp and I may have reacted for air, then suddenly I felt other

dark dwellers leap into the spaces around me, and the man
let loose sharply in me. Almost immediately he was pulling
away, not ungrateful, but like a man who didn't do the tea
traffic often and wasn't going to stick around to help out his
suckers. I was drawn into a sea of bodies almost as soon as
the old man pulled away.

"Why are you telling me this? I don't think I want to hear this."
"Is it so much of your time?" he spit, and the soft glaze that
had fallen over his face disintegrated. His eyes became hard balls,
pieces of lead, aimed at my head.
"It's not that," I said cautiously. "The things you're telling me,
Randy, I wouldn't tell you."
"And I wouldn't ask you to."

Saturday, April 11   Why was he telling me this? I didn't
want to hear I love you, not from him, not from big William, standing there in his skivvies, unconsciously licking
his lip, but I suppose it's as legitimate a fantasy as any other.
He hadn't said it yet, but when I kissed him he tasted like
almonds and spoke right into my lips. He said it felt right,
just right, and put his heavy arms around me like a warm
coat. If I wanted to I could stay the night, if I wanted to I
could stay the week, I could wear his underwear and use his
toothbrush, I could cook him breakfast and lounge on his
deck all morning while he did his four hours, and he hoped
I would think about him, even miss him, and be hot for
him at lunchtime when he'd bring champagne — it would
have to be champagne — and some chocolates and we'd go
for a drive along the cliffs, maybe stop to watch the otters,
the sunset, the fog. Leaving the cliffs he'd prod the coals
under our suspended heat — "There will be sparks tonight.
Count on it, baby," he'd say in a voice deeper than I'd
noticed before, and he'd kiss me so roughly I'd think it was

at least half contempt, but the arm would remain, reassuring me as he drove, faster and faster around the sharpest corners — "I'd stop a flying bullet for you," he'd promise, but then one could imagine him on the other end of the gun as well — faster and faster into traffic like a heavier, molten substance into water — Did I want dinner now or cocktails? "Stay in the vehicle while I takes a leak." Dinner in Berkeley, Bad Brains at the Stone — he'd see that I got slammed. Candid hands, eyes — he'd hold me wherever he damned well pleased, no punk, no Rastah, no brothah-man, no fucking nun was going to challenge him here. He'd prod the heat. He was going to rape me so tenderly . . .

Had I said three words?

Randy and I kept a relaxed house. I did what I could. He seemed to understand that, and on weekends he did the bigger jobs. Picking up after our Saturday session I nearly bumped over an open and full can of pop. The tabloid next to it grabbed my attention — Randy had circled two of the personal ads in heavy red marker — so I didn't immediately notice the pizza sauce on the can, a dried, crusted half-circle the shape of Randy's big thumb — but the ads were asking (practically begging) for Randy's type, and from the sort of guys he'd been describing in his odd reveries these two would fit in nicely. I still hadn't figured Randy, why so many? Was it really a numbers game with him? Or couldn't he find the right one? Suicide dawned on me, but why might he try to kill himself and in this awful, lingering way? I'd met sick men at a few of the support groups who said they were still at it, still meeting in the parks, in the restrooms, at theaters. They balked at my surprise and explained to me that they weren't the guns — they wouldn't goddamn themselves with murder — no, they played the victims. One man said he did it for control, because he liked to believe he was in control of his own dying, that he had made an adult decision and become a victim. Another man said he did it to keep from asking who, why, how — that the faces, the bodies, the love of so many men had absolved any solitary one of them. And then, didn't some people become addicted to their own poisons and begin to reason that the disease was the cure, or that their personal cure was hidden somewhere within the topiary of their personal addiction. He'd heard of young men taking small doses of arsenic each day to keep a healthy flush and to eventually preserve their own corpses. They died of hidden cancers, but they died beautiful. And it was a beautiful young man that explained the need for *real* killers. He wouldn't be destroyed by anything as vague as a virus; it had to be larger and preferably handsome; it had to be stronger than it knew so the young man could call it accident or fate or God. Then the pizza sauce registered on me — it had been more than a week ago, that nasty pizza. How had I missed the can in all that time? I decided quickly that Randy had hidden the thing in the refrigerator, that it was probably flat now, that it must have been flat last night when he sat drinking it, that I would throw it away, quickly, quickly before I thought any deeper into the matter. But I picked up the can and sloshed some of the red fluid onto my hand. It fizzed. I could see it and I could hear it, and this was plainly a new can of pop — not a week old, not a night, not even an hour. I stood in the floor perplexed, dropping leaves from the tabloid. Had Randy been home? Had I —?

When Randy came in we both started talking, frantically. He had a new story and somehow that won out over my hysteria. He was talking and dragging me with him to the kitchen, where he took the can out of the refrigerator (where I had put it instead of into the trash, certain that I'd stumbled on a bona fide mystery) and began sipping it carefully so he wouldn't waste any.

"Randy —" I began but he shushed me and pulled me with him back to our room to begin his story. I'm not sure how much I heard or how well it translated that night into my feverish script, but I wrote until my hand cramped, then pushed the notebook and pen away violently and went for some air.

Monday, April 13   It was cold and black — I'd never seen it so black. I walked the block to the park suddenly relishing the darkness and the moisture and eucalyptus odor in the breeze; the tree branches, high up, rubbed each other sharply, whistling. I responded to a welcome I'd never known before, felt drawn, not blown, but gently sucked in by the whoosh and whistle of the branches, by the cool, black odor, the freshness of earth and night sky at the cusp. The woods accepted, then encouraged me and I soon found myself near the night figures, in their arms. One man couldn't get enough kisses from me, another pressed up against my back like he'd straighten me out, but then abruptly bent me in two. He chewed at my nape like a mama cat and threatened me with harder bites and a stronger grip when I tried to shrug him off. I thought I'd let his fantasy run its course, but suddenly there were two more men, grins, *staccato signals,* lazars in the jungle, and I suppose I wanted it all, but I was uneasy and tried to tell them so, but my mouth, my words were no longer mine. My wrists felt the bite of a rope, my head, strong instructive hands, my knees and shins, the moist ground. The hours melted as the men changed shape and the trees began to pitch more wildly.

When I stood and shook loose from my bonds I discovered it was only flimsy twine and, for a reason I may never understand, that angered me. The humiliation rose up and burned my face. Vengeance was offered me instantly like a gift after a prank and I had to walk around it twice to make sure it wasn't a second trap. He had his head down, a big fellow, skin so white in the relentless dark that I thought a light had been aimed at him to make him glow. Our movements were so quick, so coordinated that I didn't have time to sort out my motivations, let alone consider that he might have some. I didn't talk and he didn't ask me to, but I fucked him full, and raw, and angry — angrier that he'd been made so available to me, that our coupling had been sanctioned, singled out even by unconscionable light. When I felt the first shudders of my soul threatening, and stepped back from myself to determine the half-life of my own shrapnel, I knew I was going to think about it too long, that I was going to pause right here with my finger on my chin and all that thought in my brow while my cock killed this man, and, as if he'd heard me, Randy looked around — I rushed into myself, like a mother racing after her little son racing after his ball into the path of oblivion — he looked back and told me to shoot it, to shoot it in him, that he wanted it, and I tried to pull away from him but he backed up with me — and I could feel it welling up in the chambers even as I redoubled my efforts to pull away from him and as he doubled his to stay with me, and locked like that, like two dogs, we tumbled over and down a grassy hill into a cool stream. Sometime during the fall I pushed him away laughing and we unraveled our white guts like ribbons along the slanted, rushing green.

Stephen Beachy

SHAPES

AND REGGIE FINDS HIMSELF crossing deserts on a Greyhound bus, exchanged a sexual act for the ticket money, his least favorite, the guy was a Buddhist supposedly, he hated blacks except for the dicks and told fag jokes like he wasn't one. He felt offended by the fact that hustlers were always after his money; he thought they should love his ugly old lifeform for its sheer lack of any redeeming feature, Reggie guessed. His flat chin and dry lips and unwholesome pinkness. A cramped Sunbird in the parking lot, shabby circles of light gliding through the darkness of the car's interior, traveling over bodies and fake leather upholstery and dashboard, hushed conversation of spectral Texas ministers on the AM, freeway overpasses a ruin of concrete like secret bunkers for some pale boneless army. Inside that car there was no urgency, just sucking some anonymous meat loosely attached to one of matter's less fortunate shapes. Its name was Ted, how typical. Half his life in parked cars, the other half on these damn buses, still tweaking but coming down.

He takes that sketch out of his back pocket. Too bad that guy didn't have any money, he was quiet and listening and young enough for a week or two of speed and motel sex and sleep. There's some address scribbled on the back in Argentina. Right, thinks Reggie.

He thinks of Argentina as a military parade on a blistered ribbon of beach. His vision is splotched with rectangles. He's strategically positioned himself in the middle of the bus, the buffer zone of loners between the growing camaraderie of the partyers in back and the prim old women and salesmen types up front, where he hopes to find the typical stoic men, felons and the like, whom he both wants and emulates. Men who rarely speak excite Reggie most of all. He got burnt out on the illusions of friendship the back of the bus offered years ago.

He cups his hand over the lighter, flicks it to see the reflected phantom flame on the window.

Beyond the rivuleted glass rain falls lightly on a desert sundown, lightning over the faraway mountains. It's all pink and orange and this dark purply blue. Way off out there somewhere is the radioactive desert of his birth, Alamogordo, the Jornada del Muerto. Mutant reptiles as reminders of the embryo he was, flicking their forked mutant lizard tongues. He had this revelation once where he realized his soul was a manifestation of the atomic bomb in human animal form, but everything is so much more complex than that, really. Most people think the bomb is either the return of the evil Old Testament god in material form or the final result of Satan's endless plotting and technology, but that's not it either, nobody is just one thing, nobody is just two, the war inside is a monstrous grid of shifting forces and alliances. He saw this film once at Louie's house, where a woman got pregnant at a nuclear test site and when the baby grew up it could cause fires with its mind. He used to think that film was about him, secretly, and sometimes he still does, in fact now it's hitting him again with all the old force of something you just *know*. . . . Sometimes Reggie has to lose himself in the noise confusion makes or else explode. The bus is filling up, not an empty seat left, everybody's here for the big ending. And somehow this little girl named Rolanda's ended up beside him, chatting him up something fierce, she's maybe fifteen, sixteen years old. When the bus gets full things get all mixed up, borders evaporate, the temperature and the tension increasing toward an imagined omega point of violence that everyone secretly longs for. The concept of "everyone" sets a nameless quivering in Reggie's rib cage. What unknowable darkness and misconstruction lie in the improbable concept of "everyone."

Cough syrup? asks this crusty old vet across the aisle. He hands a paper bag over, Reggie drinks. Exactly what he needs to smooth over the rough edges and take him to a place approximating sleep. One seat up, this fortyish woman with the tightest pants talks to her screaming baby exactly like it's a grown-up man who's done her wrong. They've all positioned themselves as loners, but they've all been around, and if you have to choose sides there's no doubt that one's loyalty will always reside with hell, with the quite specific folks who at least *try* to be free. This little girl, too. Whatever she's saying has nothing to do with her trip, that motive lies buried, maybe peeking through the webby surface here and there of her ceaseless story. Her words are more about the rhythm of the words, a song where form precedes content, spiraling round and round what she pretends to be saying. She's all gussied up in this long white wedding dress, her neck all latticed up with intricate cream stitching, an antique or Victorian dress like those stoned teenage girls wear. Reggie used to see them pursuing fresh emotions on Haight Street like refugees from somebody else's sexual fantasies.

Give me your palm, Rolanda says.

The overflow from various Walkmen and dim conversations surround them. The sun is just hanging there, beneath a thick layer of clouds, like a red skateboard wheel, detached from its reason for being round. Reggie is wary, as you would be too, if you believed, as he does, that the dead occasionally take human form to lead him, subtly, this way or that. She takes his palm, studying it for the clues to his present, his future, the unspeakable horror that he knows lies hidden behind him.

The lines of his palm are skirting the issue, veering off into the noisy realm of teeny furrows and crisscrosses pretending to be a pattern. Rolanda could find his mother there and Louie and Ruth. The appearance of a stranger on his doorstep one morning, a huge dark-skinned woman who turned out to be his granny, compelling as destiny, as in sagas where the white person travels miles into the heart of weirdness to find the tribal elder brewing some reeking broth in a cauldron; the tribal elder whispers to the white person: *Child, you are home, you are one of us.* In Reggie's palm Rolanda could find the offspring he will never father, oblique references to an inevitable, calamitous wedding, the unmistakable markers of an early death. She could find all the noise of familial history, genealogies going back to the primal mists, several skinny white boys with bad feet, bad stepfathers and the keepers of institutions. She could find Edward Teller with his frying pan full of scrambled egg whites. None of these things is the issue. Perhaps the issue isn't really either, but the issue is Dad.

Dad took him to Albuquerque, finally, to a cheap motel. About a hundred of them lined up on Route 66 for $15.99, $16.99, $17.99 for a single room plus tax and extra for HBO. Why Dad paid for the HBO he didn't know. Dad registered under a false name, pulled those thick drapes shut, turned on the TV. I'll be right back, he said, I need to get some cigarettes and make a phone call. As soon as Reggie saw him pull out of the lot, he knew. It was like how people got rid of dogs they didn't want in cartoons.

The room was paid for at least. Reggie had eighty cents and

thirteen years of life experience. At least Dad had been thoughtful enough to leave him on the hustler strip. It wasn't much of a hustler strip, this one vaguely hostile guy stomping around on the corner next to a pay phone, who seemed to be indirectly warning Reggie to stay out of his turf — but enough old men in cars understood it as such to make it profitable. Reggie turned himself off. If he wasn't sleeping with Dad it didn't make a difference which old man was sniffing him. Like a flower, he thought, and realized where all that love poetry had its source. The profit margin at first was simple survival, a roof over his head, cheeseburgers, but eventually he got a bus ticket back to Dad's town, knowing already that Dad wouldn't be there, but he at least had to try. Those whole two weeks with all those men he didn't cry, only after he saw the FOR RENT sign, peeked through the windows, sat down on the front step with all those dry desert shrubs, crackly like a thorny map of solidified brain charges, just sitting there, hopeless.

Rolanda drops his hand, barely concealed horror as she sees what destiny's laid out for him, he's not surprised, it's happened before. She starts again with the words, words, words, to distract them both from the fact that his palm is too dreadful to read.

Are you a case? she asks. You know, the state sent this case over by where we were staying, Mama acted all churchy churchy like she just couldn't bear the thought of this poor little girl out in the cold, but we all know about those checks that come regular when you take in a case. Her people were hecka stupid, her dumbass daddy burnt their house down and they were all outdoors. Crack daddy, I called him, I figured he did one of those Richard Pryor numbers, but she always said it was faulty wiring, you know.

Reggie is, in fact, a case, has always been a case, studied, poked and prodded by all sorts of organizations, departments and elaborate psychological ideologies, as if he were a mysterious machine that the right series of drugs, words or disciplinary measures would turn into whatever it was that was the opposite of a case. This girl is just one more external force that won't let him rest. She's not looking at him directly, not yet, it's like her story is a song, but she's still warming up. She gets tangled up in an elaborate description of a house burning down, conflicting Reggie, who has burnt down houses himself but has to face now the image of this homeless little girl watching the flames, face beaded with sweat, lost in enemy territory, doomed now to be passed around from one false structure to another.

A dark figure uses Rolanda's seat for balance on the way to the bathroom. Rolanda's forehead is high and damp, her eyes simply dark, until she turns to the side and the light from that translucent skateboard wheel shows them as golden, clear, full of intricate patterns. Her head rocks back and forth on her skinny skinny neck as she talks, giving the impression of a wingless bird preparing for flight.

That case turned out to be okay, Rolanda says, Tina. She taught me what was what. It's just true, she was all up in my business.

She laughs to herself, caresses her belly. Reggie recoils, nearer the rain-spattered window, gray driblets of water obscuring a now grayer dusk landscape, recoils as if she's his mother, describing in embarrassing detail the red splotchy mess of his own birth, in a laboratory maybe, Edward Teller cutting the umbilical cord. Edward Teller wouldn't eat fat. He ate frying pans full of scrambled egg whites like the pockmarked face of an albino. Rolanda's pretending to hardly know who she's talking to, but he knows she's trying to make him blush, with all that talk about sex. Weird how any blubbery male stranger could walk up to him and say Do you get fisted? and it wouldn't even faze him, but once it's a girl the slightest hint will make him hot and prickly. This quiet hippie boy a few rows up seems so solid, a place where Reggie's thoughts could live, as opposed to the aggressive jungle of language here. Other people's language is the least sexual thing. She's off now, some twisted description of how the last time she rode Greyhound, back when she was seven and a believing Christian, she'd gotten kicked off the bus in the middle of the night for evangelizing to passengers who distinctly did not want to be saved. It's true that the driver gave her several warnings to shut up, but still.

She bends down behind the seat and hits off a joint. Arches her brow as she holds in the smoke, offering it to Reggie. He takes one small hit, against his better judgment, hands it back. Whoever's smoking, the driver announces over the intercom, the next time it happens, you'll be smoking on the side of the road. She's nonchalant and flipping through these photos from her bag, like movie stills, where she's being crucified, naked, black and writhing as if in sexual ecstasy. A man's profile with the cross in the background, a faraway look in his eyes. She puts out the joint, goes on where she left off, photos perched surreally in her lap.

She figures she's lost religion for good, not because she doesn't believe, but more because she doesn't think it matters, what you do or what you believe, it's all the same after you're inside god and while she's here, outside, she'd just as soon do it all. Reggie holds his chin in his hand to keep himself from looking at those grotesque representations of some dark sexual crucifixion. Lost at night in the forests, her and Tina and this cute half-Japanese boy. Out on the river in a rowboat, too, once, all us kids naked and that boy fell off in the muddy water . . .

Reggie's bumped into this picture now, through waves of speedless headache and thirst and something filling up his stomach that isn't food, a picture of a rowboat, underground in this huge cavern, filled with crazy blind children. Mad children row, this black river slow twisting, torchlight flickers underground stalactites blue-gray crystalline formations dripping, black cavern walls white salt crystals sparkling. Unreachable cave heads above lead twisting tunnels toward mirrored ice halls. The children grope to remember lame conductors or blind firemen; steam rises, drifts. The children are insane, white hair brown skin purple eyes, clap their hands arhythmically.

Vaulted arches. On video screens overhead blind angels refuse to look at maps of congealed blood.

And Reggie's the one in the front of the boat, head crunching into the white wall of a low tunnel, knocked clean out with salt in one eye, floundering in the water of the cold underground canal as the rowboat passes on in, to the narrow part of the cave, without him. Swimming desperately after it underwater, he's always had great lung capacity, but something's happened, instead of reaching out and trying to help him back on board the children beat him with their oars, try to murder him once and for all, he's the reason they're lost and blind and crazy, he's the murder, creeping out of the murk to lead them astray, down the wrong tunnels, farther down into the depths instead of out to where someday the tunnel will widen out, flow into the light . . .

He used to wake up screaming. That one night in a motel with Ruth and Mom and Granny, the second evil step-Dad was out of the picture by then, and it was New Year's Eve. They had all just drifted into sleep. Firecrackers exploded right beneath the window and he sat up shouting *they were trying to kill him.* They all woke up in a panic, he then just pure anguished scream, Granny saying *It's in the TV, it's in the TV,* clutching at Ruth who'd have none of this nonsense, so tired of it, wanting to sleep, getting up to unplug the stupid TV and stop all the muttering and screaming, struggling against Granny who was clutching her arm so tight her Lee press-on nails popped off and just lay there like weird little dead creatures on the mattress.

Case, Rolanda says now, she's started calling him Case for no good reason, focusing her attention in on him now and he's scared, scared she can see right through him, she knows he's a fag and'll open that mouth up wide to announce it to the whole bus, Oh shit, I can't sit back here, Driver! I don't want none a that AIDS, uh uh, I won't sit by no fag boy, boy you know you GAY. But Case, she says, You look bad, just calm down, this bus ain't in no hurry, we got all night, I won't bite you.

I know that, Reggie wants to say, but she's moving along. Last time I saw Tina, she says, she had some kinda ghetto ensemble up on her head. I can't relate to that, I don't care who it is. Don't have to look like *society.*

Reggie runs his hands over his own nearly hairless scalp. Is she trying to imply that he's not black enough, that he's an Oreo, a wannabe?

But she's talking about white boys now, her first taste of them when she used to skip rope, all sorts of complex geometries she could skip around that rope, out by the boot camp. They had bodies so rare and ghostly, like cool snakes, moving with a kind of whispered hush. A kind of walk only white boys can do, they carve it out of the suburban prisons they live in. She wants to go to Scandinavia, where it's always snowing and the boys are all pampered by free health care and education. She caresses Reggie's hand, leans in closer, he can feel her little girl breath. Does she think he's white? Everybody's always imagining Reggie as exactly what it is they aren't. He nudges away, holds on tight to the armrest. She's in total control, puts just enough sex in her words to terrify him then backs off, giving him room to breathe, careening off in some other direction, time and religion, expanding her volume and attention to take in the crumpled old vet, the tight-pantsed white woman, just waiting to circle back in for the kill.

For now he'll breathe, let her go off. He realized a long time ago that words were alive and plotting to do something despicable with him. Words fill everybody up with these desires, for things they'll never be given, dangerous things, a different kind of time. Brighter waveforms than we've ever experienced, brighter and brighter. Waveforms is one of Reggie's specialties, he knows that the visual cortex doesn't respond to patterns at all, but to the frequencies of various waveforms. Single neurons in the motor cortex respond selectively to frequencies in a limited band. What lies outside that band might have some crucial perspective on the patterns he feels he's a part of, but can never see or understand, the patterns whose interactions he's surer and surer he actually *is*. He knows at some level none of this is people sitting around the bus, that woman's hair sprayed violently in an elaborate style, two white little hippie boys, the crumpled old vet and his cough syrup, Rolanda even or the chewing gum and candy wrappers and gnarly seats, the snores and Walkman overflows. It's blurry clouds of interference patterns seated around the bus. Even the bus itself, Rolanda's words which aren't even a commentary maybe, they're actually bringing the bus into existence! Reggie shuts his eyes tight to make it pass.

Rolanda's going on about her fatass faggot of a preacher uncle. Faggots who don't get laid are the worst of all, she says, but Reggie knows she's really talking about him, provoking him, sending him secret messages to tell him how lame he is, how weak, how moist. He doesn't get laid enough and that's why the world's so fucked up, just like Wilhelm Reich said. Babies should have happy orgasms and no one should get circumcised. He's so sexually repressed he could explode, he decides, what he wants to be is pure love, a coquettish whore done up in silk and lipstick, spread out on the bus seats, entered and entered and entered some more. She puts her own Walkman on, fiddling with the knobs. She's the telepathic queen, she knows everything. She's playing with his head: when she listens to the left side it means he's gay, to the right side it means he's straight. She's communicating her judgments to everyone else on the bus. She's singing along and making wild gestures. Reggie's not the only one getting anxious, a nervousness expands in waves through the bus. Hits the smokers hardest, it's been a long time since the last stop and this driver's decidedly hostile to making any unplanned breaks. That baby's snoring louder than Reggie would have thought possible from such a tiny thing. Everybody wants to hold a baby, Reggie's no exception. His sister had a baby so white and soft, he'd hold it in his lap until it started crying, then turn away, or pick up some *Omni* magazine or *Vanity Fair* real quick to hide his erection. His sister was kind of slow with that stuff. How a girl who'd been raped twice and got pregnant at fifteen could float through the world like the most innocent thing was beyond him.

Oh, he can't get into all that now. She's back there waiting for him like an accusation of something. Things happened between them and afterward they could never talk like they used to. She wanted him to be another brother altogether, she wanted everything from him and demanded it with silence.

Rolanda's zeroing in on him again, picking up his hand as if she never dropped it at the sight of his destiny.

White boys, she says, maybe they really wanna kill all us little black girls, really, or gag us and tie us up, nobody's as freaky as whiteboys, but I love the walk and talk of them. They're so pale and exotic with that blue skin sometimes, just underneath, when they've stayed out of the sun. They're like cute little animals with their freckles and the colors in their eyes. That pubic hair that's not . . .

The sentence trails off as she searches for something, lets it go, turns back toward Reggie. She's whispering now, I just want *all* that sex.

He's sure he's being played. She turns back toward the window like she's said nothing more than the weather. Out there, everything is the dark. She runs a thin finger around Reggie's palm, like she's not even thinking about doing it.

Reggie thinks of all the white boys he's known, or at least the ones he's wanted, sexually. He's trying to excite himself, in case he has to prove he's straight, to Rolanda, with an erection. Mark used to shove his dick in Reggie's mouth at the slightest provocation, back when Reggie was nine or ten. Ezra and Peter were the two Jews in a row he was in love with, they both repressed their true feelings. Louie was his best friend, they rode across the country on a Greyhound just like this one, except minus the chatty little girl.

The sky was empty and this hush in the air. The bus had stopped at a convenience store in Montana or wherever. Weird weather, huh? the driver said and then rain and thunder poured from the cloudless sky. They didn't know where in the world they could be. They had two dollars left and the debate was, smokes or food? Smokes, they decided, finally, and there was Reggie waiting under a gas station awning in the rain, Louie running toward him forever running toward him through the rain with a pack of smokes, and they were menthols, nasty menthols that nobody could enjoy. Their last two dollars, and the way Louie figured it was that since menthols were so gross, they wouldn't smoke as many, so they'd last longer.

Where is Louie now? Maybe in San Francisco, Reggie hopes, or Berkeley, or maybe dead. The cough syrup is kicking in now, making these thoughts nervous and far away. If Louie is dead, Reggie's life would be tragic, because the best memory he has is when the two of them followed the tracks down into the warehouses, the sun setting and the only drugs they were on was caffeine and vitamin B-12 and the stones! Rough and orangey ones and these pieces of brick and gravelly stuff only blue. And the resonant tings the windows made, the ones higher up had more bass, oddly enough, the awesome shattering sounds, and they'd synchronized perfectly somewhere in there, a symphony of crash, bing, tinkle tinkle tinkle. No windows had ever destructed with such awesome grace, they might have been stained glass, the universe a church. Reggie could cry at the thought of having known perfection, cuz not only is it rare, but cuz Louie could easily be dead. Last time he saw him in that punky asshole Wilma's apartment in Miami he seemed headed that way, and if Louie's dead there's no one alive who'll have been there to share the absolute cosmic harmony of everything that exists. That was the only real moment in Reggie's life, the perfect note, the song, everything else is just noise and nobody ever understands, they just nod and say, Oh dude, it's like these windows I smashed totally at Macy's and got these giraffe women mannequins with bleached-out wigs, but *No,* Reggie wants to scream, *No,* it was *not* like that at *all.*

Rolanda's wedding dress is huge, she's drowning in it, like a vocabulary beyond her years, to be used for her own meanings, for sound and rhythm. She's using silence now, as part of that rhythm, a space for things to sink into, while proceeding, underneath the surface. It makes Reggie nervous. He's grinding his teeth, crashing bad, he'll never find any speed in this desert. The cough syrup helps, but there's this heaviness in his belly and he's impotent and stupid and deluded. He wants to put his head in Rolanda's lap and cry, and he's starting to fear that he'll actually do it. The control he needs not to is driving him even crazier. He closes his eyes, tries to camouflage himself with a pretense of sleep.

He thinks of all the black girls he's known, lined up, writhing and weaving and snaking in harmony over absolute white, the nothingness of light that only video can achieve. If he could develop his reluctant-to-emerge bisexuality he'd be wholer, more caring, more New Agey, more smug. He'd have more options. But sexual perfection is always shallower than the broken windows kind of perfection, especially when it's really masturbation. His eyes pop open.

Rolanda's rubbing his whitish thigh. His impulse is to apologize for his fear of her, his whitishness, his lack of desire for someone who's just not . . . firm enough. He looks around, blinking. The crumpled old vet winks at him.

I gotta go to the bathroom, he says, stumbles through the wall of her little knees, down the aisle, bouncing side to side. Halfway there and the stench already hits him. I wouldn't go in there unless you absolutely had to, this stoned middle-aged white woman tells him. Seeing her bloodshot eyes, Reggie remembers that he's stoned too, and feels more so, and that she's somehow just like his mom, although the only traits he can think of the two have in common are stonedness and femaleness. Oh yeah, and whiteness. . . . But there's this conspiracy of maternal women, it's obvious, they don't want him to go into that tiny soiled bathroom. . . . He grunts at her, meaning *Emergency*, shoves his way in.

Dale Peck

ROLLING BACK THE STONE

NOW I ENTER my father. The skin which has served as his fortress all his life and protected him against me offers no resistance, and I crawl through all the holes left open to me. I am in his mouth and I am in his ears. I slip into his eye sockets and I slither up his nose. I leave his head for his groin: I am in his urethra, I am in his anus. From every orifice I take something out with me. From his mouth I pull his tongue and every word it has ever spoken, every curse, every endearment, every gasp of confusion or pain. From his ears I pull the words he has heard, the dirty jokes, the secrets, the pleas. I see what he has seen and I smell what he has smelled. I flow out of him like the heavy stream of a morning-after piss. I drop from him with clumps of shit. Then, with a hooked finger, I reach into his navel and pull out his organs in one long connected string: coils of intestine, half-inflated balloons of stomach and liver and kidneys, lungs which resemble bunches of grapes that have been stepped on. His heart bounces on the floor like gelatin spilled from its mold. I have entered my father. I have left him. I have turned him inside out and exposed him to anyone who cares to look, and, in doing so, I have created the story of his life — not biography, which is a kind of cannibalism, but biography's opposite: not consumption, but regurgitation. In pulling my father out of himself I have pulled him out of me, and I look at the mess I've made in the same way I would look at my vomit: here is something which, if it had stayed down, would have been digested, would have, eventually, turned into me.

At four, I stole a drink from my father's beer. I took one sip and spat into the air. As the mist cleared, I waited to be punished. But my father said, "I'm proud of you," and drank until he finished. He said, "Go get me another," and I went to find my mother. In the kitchen I grabbed a bottle. It was cold, like a wet gun. Quietly, I called out, "Where are you? Where are you, Mom?" As if in answer, my father's voice pushed into my ears. "Hurry up," he yelled, cutting off my search, like shears. His hazel eyes were beer-colored, and I saw that they were dead. "Don't ever drink," he commanded, "don't be like your dad." He just filled his chair then, as a lamp fills its shade, and I became the child who was always afraid.

There was always a smell in my father's truck, and the smell was always dusty and cold, and underlain by smoke. The trash on the floor told of a limited array of choices: beer bottles and the cardboard cases they had been taken from, or beer cans and the plastic rings that held them together; coffee cups made from ceramic or plastic or Styrofoam or paper; crumpled napkins stained with mustard and ketchup, wadded bags stained with grease. There were rags crusty with plumber's glues — purple and black especially — and dirt, and perhaps an old T-shirt lay there, and a cap or two. The bench seat held three comfortably, if two of the three were children, and at night there were only a few small contained lights: the dashboard, the cigarette lighter, the end of my father's lit cigarette glowing far above me. In the dark, in Kansas, the truck moved like a submarine along the ocean's bottom. I could feel the swells and dips in my stomach, saw wheat swaying like seaweed, saw dark thick torsos of cattle floating over the seaweed like foraging fish. I saw all this from eyes that barely cleared the dashboard, but I kept those eyes open and I kept them peeled: as long as my eyes stayed open my father's eyes would stay open, and we would not stop. His head would nod sometimes, but never fall, and the truck swayed gently across the road like an empty swing rocked by a breeze, but it never slipped into the ditch and my eyes never closed. We never talked — my sister and I were afraid to talk — and usually the radio was off, and the only sounds besides the straining aging engine were the sounds of smoking and drinking. Click, puff puff, sigh; snap, glug glug, sigh; but we never stopped. In the years before the drunk-driving campaigns it was stopping I feared, not wrecking. I feared the strange sea that was the combination of endless prairie and empty sky, and I feared being lost in a world whose single boundary was the horizon's radius, whose only pole was my father.

The ottoman measured one foot by two feet, and from its green plaid polyester surface I pushed my father's feet and dumped his hoard of quarters from a gallon jar, and I counted them under his eye while he drank a before-dinner beer. The uncounted mound of quarters swelled from the ottoman like an overstuffed stomach, and I pulled coins from this mound and stacked them in neat piles of four: one dollar, two dollars, three dollars, four. As the dollar piles grew by rows and columns the mound shrank, but not quickly enough, and to accommodate the spreading grid I pushed handfuls of quarters to the floor. I kneeled, counted; a host of founding fathers gazed into the distance with serene indifference; with his toe my father nudged a stray quarter toward me. By some miracle there were exactly enough quarters to cover the ottoman completely. A little adjustment here, some air in the lines there, and a silver net concealed the green and captured my attention. What had been a messy suggestion of opulence had been rendered a declaration: I'd never seen so much money in my life. Many years later I learned to play a drinking game called quarters. Players attempted to bounce a quarter off the bar and into a glass. When you lost you drank; when you won everyone else drank; in either case you played until everyone lost. Over the past year my father had bounced hundreds of quarters into a glass jar and now I had spread his shining silver net over the ugly green footstool. I was drunk with the effort, drunk with his wealth, and with his power, and his victory over me.

Billy Graham was my father's beer buddy for a few years. We always called him that: Billy Graham. He was a skinny malnourished thing, with long greasy brown hair, a wispy beard, a wife and two sons I don't remember. He lived in a run-down two-bedroom house in the southern part of town, which is to say the white trash part of town, and one night when I was eleven or twelve my father brought me over there. It was just fathers and sons that night; the fathers sat in the kitchen drinking and the sons stared at the television. At some point Billy Graham's voice made itself heard above the TV. "Dale," he called. "Hey, hey, Dale, can you c'mere a sec?" I looked at him. His gangly shadow awkwardly filled the kitchen doorway. The light and my father were behind him, and one of Billy Graham's hands held a beer, and the beer rested against his crotch. I moved toward him slowly, and as I drew closer bits and pieces of him jumped out at me: the dirt on his red T-shirt and his jeans, the odd expression that twisted his face. He held his beer can directly in front of his crotch, and through a crook in his elbow I could see my father, and the stupid grin on his face as he hunched over his own beer. Billy Graham said, "Can you help me?" He said it quietly. He said, "I've got a problem with my, um, my, I've got a problem, I — my zipper," he finished then, and he moved his beer can. He moved it to his lips. A red thing poked from his pants. It was maybe five inches long and an inch and a half thick, and hard, and it tapered to a blunt tip. The fly of his underwear gripped it like lips gone white from sucking, and Billy Graham nudged it with his free hand. "Can you give me a hand?" he said. "I, um, I can't get it back in." I moved a step toward him, a step away, I tried not to stare at the red thing but it was all I could look at. I took another step toward him, my hand reached out. But before I touched it I looked up at Billy Graham's face and that broke the spell. Billy Graham started laughing when my eyes met his, and he pulled the red thing from his pants and tossed it at me. It took me a long time to realize that the thing in my hands was a radish. It took less time to realize that my laughing father was in on the joke. We slept there that night because my father was drunk. I shared a bed with the two boys. The older one was a year or two younger than me. He was blond and small and snotty; he stripped down to his underwear and strutted through the room, and I was embarrassed by what was visibly different between us. In bed he took up as much space as he could between his brother and me, pushing against me often, fidgeting, falling asleep finally with his drooling pink pout turned toward me and his butt poking into the air. I never once thought of Billy Graham's radish that night, although now I try to imagine what passed between him and my father. "Hey, Dale, I've got an idea. Why don't I let this radish hang out of my zipper and pretend it's my dick?" "I've got a better idea, Billy Graham. Why don't you see if you can get Dale in there to put it back in your jeans for you?" But I didn't think of that then; I thought instead, and all night long, of the blond boy's beautiful butt. There are a few questions I'd like someone to answer for me now. First of all, why didn't I fuck that little boy? And second, why didn't my father just fuck me? If he was truly trying to teach me that desire and contempt are manifestations of the same impulse, and if he was trying to express contempt for a desire that was already manifest in me, wouldn't that have been the most effective way? And, finally, where did my father sleep that night? That's a cheap shot, I know, with potentially serious implications. *I know.*

This was my heterosexual moment: I had a big red '76 Monte Carlo with five hundred horses under the hood, and I had a full-time job at Sirloin Stockade. I had money in my pocket and gas in my tank, and the snout of my car jutted north on Thirtieth Street like a dog straining at its leash. I had pride and I had power — and then he floated past. The boxy white egg of his van was heading east, heading toward the highway and home, and the sign magneted to its door — DALE'S PLUMBING SERVICE — was an unnecessary reminder that I bear his name. Here's what I wanted to do: I wanted to blow him off the road. My foot would drop to the floor, the gas needle would dip into the red as those twelve big cylinders sucked up fuel, the engine would growl for a moment in warning, and then *bam!* I would be behind him, beside him, then past him, feeding him my dust. That's what I wanted to do. But instead I followed him. It was midnight, and the Monte Carlo, faded red during the day, was brown at that time of night, and in my work uniform I was brown inside of it, and invisible. I turned onto Thirtieth Street and followed my father, who took the back way home: Lorraine to Fifty-sixth, Fifty-sixth to Tobacco Road, Tobacco to Sixty-ninth, and the little jog over to Cottontail Lane, and then the bumpy gravelly mile to our driveway. He took the back way home because he was coming from the bar and he was drunk. I knew he was drunk because he drove with telltale overcaution: thirty miles per hour when the speed limit was forty-five, signaling a half mile before he reached a turn, and as I followed him I hated him for the transparency of his gestures. I tried not to ride his ass, but I stayed close behind him, and I knew that he wasn't aware it was me who followed him: he would have given me a sign if he knew it was me. It was on the long stretch of Tobacco Road that he surprised me. By then he was driving barely twenty miles per hour and I had to ride the brake to keep the MC behind him. As he inched toward home his van slipped slowly from the right side of the road to the left, its progress slow, steady, inexorable, like the movement of a needle in the groove of a record, but then, before the song should have ended, my father's van slipped into the ditch that bordered the left side of the road. I screamed as the perpendicular sail of the van's rear end tilted crazily. I screamed, "Daddy!" because I thought it was going to roll over. The rear end of the van fishtailed left and right as my father jerked the wheel toward the road, and then, as simply as he'd slipped into the ditch, he slipped out of it, and continued his journey as though nothing had happened. But for that brief tottering moment I knew only one thing — that my father would die — and I felt only one emotion: grief. My brown and white plaid polyester uniform was saturated with the grease of a deep-fat fryer and the fingers that gripped the steering wheel of my father's hand-me-down car were singed from turning over dozens and dozens of pieces of buttered toast on a flat steel grill: that was my job. I was his son. When we got home my father laughed when he saw it was me; I'd scared him, he said, he'd thought I was a cop. But I was furious, because he'd scared me even more. He'd made me ask myself why I'd followed him, and he made me realize that the answer was, in part, because I wanted to protect him. He made me realize that I still loved him, and that's why I was furious.

He stopped the same way that I imagine he started: when no one was watching. The impulses were the same too: at fourteen, fifteen, he'd already shouldered the responsibilities of a man for years — just ask his sisters — and now he wanted the privileges. Forty years later, he finally realized that those privileges were, in fact, responsibilities, and one evening during the spring semester of my junior year at college he called me. "Dale," he said, "I haven't had a drink for two, three weeks now." I was suspicious. I said, "And . . . ?" and he said, "And I don't think I'm going to have another." Fifteen hundred miles separated us, and it had been two years since I'd last seen him. Other things also filled that space: his youngest daughter was two, and his oldest had emerged from an AA detox center and now was getting married; I'd taken my second drink a little over a year earlier. The second of my mother's three sisters had died, this one of cancer, and I came out a month after that. I remembered, without acknowledging it — in the same way I hadn't acknowledged it at the time — the feeling of excitement I'd felt when my father came home drunk. Now something will *happen*, I'd thought, and it made me a little sad to realize that now nothing more would happen. I still don't know why I stood by him during the next year, but I did. I called him every few weeks to check his progress, offer him encouragement, thanks even, and love. He will probably remember that as the last time I stood by him. The only other time he tried to quit drinking he'd lasted one month. Then, on Christmas Eve, a house he'd worked on burned down — it was later proved that he wasn't to blame — and the owners threatened to sue him. In the darkness of Christmas morning, Erin awakened me, and we opened presents in the living room while my father watched us from a chair. He was nearly immobile with alcohol, a snowman whose hard head was sinking into the melting ball of his stomachy torso; he managed only to slide from the chair to his knees, and then he made us join hands as a family and pray, and thank God for what we had received. That was the Christmas I got the typewriter on which I typed a speech about wife beating that won me gold medal after gold medal in state speech tournaments. Middle-aged women with hair permed to the texture of curly straw would clutch vinyl purses to their chests and cry when I gave that speech, and I would shift my gaze from their leaking eyes to the magic spot on their foreheads, the place where priests aim their thumbs and executioners their bullets, lest I too exchange a real sorrow for the one I was manufacturing with my words.

This is the first story my father told me when I told him I was going to write about him: "I almost didn't graduate high school, Dale," he told me. "Never was a good student but that's not why. Nope, one time my senior year I borrowed the teacher's pointer and I flipped up the dress of the prettiest girl in school so I could see her underpants. Her panties. Just a joke, just a little flip, she giggled, she and me was friends, no harm done. But this asshole teacher turned around and he said, Dale Peck, go to the principal's office right now! and he sent this little brownnoser with me with a note. As soon as we hit the hall I said, Give me that note, and this kid said, Aw, Dale, I can't do that, and I said, Give me that note or I'll kick your goddamn ass. Well, this note said that I was being sent to the principal's office because I poked so-and-so in the *anus*. In the *anus*. As soon as I read that I marched back into the classroom and started yelling, You asshole! I did *not* poke this girl in the *anus!* I did not — but he cut me off and told me to get to the principal's office, and I went, but the minute I got there I just started yelling again. Fuck you! Fuck your school! You're supposed to be teaching us honesty but you're all a bunch of fucking hypocrites! Well, Dale, to make a long story short they wanted to suspend me for three days for poking this girl in the *anus*, even though she told 'em I didn't do it, and I just told them they could take their school and shove it up their ass, and I walked out. So. I got a job, something, I don't know, whatever it was I'm sure it didn't pay much. Started eating at this diner. Didn't really want to be home much, with Ma there. There was this other fella who ate there a lot too, and over time we struck up an acquaintance. Turns out he was a history teacher at my high school, and I told him all about what happened, you know, about how they'd called me a liar, and one day he says, You really want to go back to school, don't you, Dale? and I said, Aw, man, I'd give anything to get my diploma; I don't want to end up a bum like my old man. You never met my dad, Dale, but he was a real bum, a true no-good drunk. You may think I was bad but you kids got off easy with me, compared to him. Anyway, this history teacher got me back in school, and he made sure I graduated. He even had me over to his house to study. He lived with this other man, and I figured out pretty quick that they was, you know, they was . . . The other one was a florist. My teacher, he quit teaching later on and they ran the flower shop together, but I didn't know them anymore by then. One night, we'd stayed up late studying, I ended up sleeping there and they only had the one bed. Well, I woke up in the middle of the night. And the other one, the one who ran the flower shop, he was playing with me. Through my underwear. Well, I played it cool, just rolled over and pretended I was asleep, but I never saw them again after that. I kind of wish I had. They were real good to me, both of them, they were decent men. But I was young, you know, that sort of thing freaks you out when you're young." He paused then. He was fifty, and I was twenty-five, and in so many ways I knew I was half the man he was. And then he brought it home: "Well, I guess it doesn't freak you out," he said, "but it freaked me out. I never did see them again."

I remember many nighttime drives but I only remember stopping once. No accident: there was a storm coming, and my father was tired, and he decided to sleep it out and sleep it off. He parked the truck on the side of the road, and when he shut it off what little light had existed disappeared, and so did my perspective. My father and sister folded away from me, each leaning against a door, and I sat upright between them like a caterpillar between butterfly wings, my vigilant eyes still open, my ears straining for something in the silence. Oh, that sky: it's why I still dream of Kansas. The stars crowded against each other like pebbles in a streambed, and as the clouds advanced they interposed their blackness between me and the stars like a muffling blanket. Lightning leaked from them. Distant harmless flickers moved closer, gained size, clarity, power, single trunks of lightning and big oval clusters that were as branched as tumbleweeds, and then thunder, the kind of thunder that scares little children. When the rain came it surprised me; I'd thought the sky was spending its all on light and noise, but no, it had strength for more. Then I was truly under water. The rain was solid as a curtain, and through it the lightning was blurred and diffuse, the thunder muffled, and I wondered that my father and sister were not shaken awake. I twitched and fidgeted; I peered out all the windows. I think I thought of running away but I knew better than to wake my father. They say that as soon as you think about the weather in Kansas it will change, and it did. I'd thought of the rain as a curtain, and the curtain simply lifted. When it was gone I saw that the thunder and lightning were on the other side of us now, and it was the first time I realized that the weather doesn't actually change: it moves. The clouds peeled back slowly, and slowly the stars reappeared. My father was a snoring wreck to my left, and the archaeology of his life lay in ruins beneath my feet. I suppose I loved him most in that moment after the rain, and I quivered next to him, protecting him somehow, and I remained awake until he awakened and drove us the rest of the way home. What I miss now, when I miss my childhood, are those twinned, those entwined lies: that it's the world that's out to get you, and that, when it doesn't, it's because you've somehow managed to overcome it yourself. But strength is just an illusion that some people perpetuate and other people believe in. I always was a believer.

My grandmother sings a lullaby to my five-year-old father:

> *Baby boy, baby boy,*
> *what have you done?*
> *Baby boy, baby boy,*
> *where have you run?*
>
> *Baby boy, baby boy,*
> *why won't you come?*
> *Baby boy, baby boy,*
> *are you still my son?*
>
> *Run the bath water;*
> *you know how it's done.*
> *Only turn the cold on,*
> *and listen to it run.*
>
> *Take off all your clothes.*
> *I'll pierce you with my eyes.*
> *Why do you always disobey me?*
> *Now you've earned your prize.*
>
> *I'll drop you in the water,*
> *I'll hold you by your nose.*
> *I'll hold you 'til you turn blue,*
> *and lose the feeling in your toes.*
>
> *Listen through your ice baths,*
> *and remember what I say:*

You can never please your mother,
and you can never run away.

I'll tail you like a shadow;
I'm the night to all your days.
I'm the puzzle that you can't solve;
you're lost within my maze.

A mother's love is sourceless,
but her hatred never ends.
There's nothing that can change this,
no way to make amends.

Baby boy, baby boy,
do you know what you've done?
Baby boy, baby boy,
do you know you can't run?

Baby boy, baby boy,
your sin is an old one.
Baby boy, baby boy,
you were born my son.

There are no mysteries inside the body of a man. Any man knows this; this is why he uses his hands so much. There is nothing inside a man's body that he can't see represented in a car's mechanics, or the plumbing in his house. There is food. He puts it in his mouth and chews it up, just like the garbage disposal under his sink. It slides down the pipe of his esophagus into the bellows of his stomach and sits there for a while, is softened, decomposed. Put a potato in a pot of water on the stove and the same thing happens. Eventually the stomach's done all it can; the food slides down again, more pipes, the small intestine, the large intestine. Nutrients are leached out, along with color and a bit of mass. If you squeeze the soapy water from a sponge you can see this too. What's left is compressed, stored, then passed out in brown bricks in which bits of food are still recognizable, as is garbage in a trash compactor. That's it. When a man looks in the mirror he knows that all he sees is all there is. His piss is a shower, his come, what? Air in the pipes. Sweat: a beer bottle can sweat. You wonder at his hopelessness, you wonder at his rage? You ask me why men kill? Ask a man what comes from his body and he will look at his hands and say, Nothing. Nothing that he didn't put in it first.

Before my father will let them bury his mother he has the body brought to him. My father recognizes the ability of experts; he is a good carpenter and a better plumber, and he knows his way around under the hood of a car, but this is a body after all, and he has hired a vivisectionist. "Every pipe," my father says, "every tube. Every part of her that she could get to, I want to get to." The man with the knives starts at the throat and works down. He works slowly, slitting with his knife and folding back flaps of skin with his rubber-gloved fingers. My father waves away most of the important organs as they are identified to him, the heart, the lungs, the liver, the kidneys. "I want to see what was in her stomach," he says. "I want to know what she ate." The liquids that come from her are blue and brown and black, but my father doesn't notice them as they drain off the stainless steel table and flow thickly toward the drain at the bottom of a hollow in the floor. He notices instead that the drain cover has been drilled with holes in too narrow a gauge for the fluids that are supposed to pass through it, and as a result a pool is forming on the floor; he thinks of how much he would charge to fix that drain. When the vivisectionist has gutted and opened all of my father's mother's alimentary canal, working first from the front and then flipping her over to go in from the back, he looks at my father to see if he is satisfied. He's not. "Up there," my father says, *"up there."* The vivisectionist sighs but he doesn't speak; he is, like a plumber, paid by the hour. With a little cutting, a little snipping of threads, things come out more easily than my father would have thought. The strung-together body parts, vagina, birth canal, uterus, fallopian tubes, ovaries, resemble an animal made from twisted-together tubular balloons which have slowly lost their air. The vivisectionist opens them quickly, easily. "There," he says, "there's nothing." But my father, whose job relies on his ability to spot an object where it doesn't belong, says, "What's that?" It's a little piece of plastic, the size and shape of a credit card, almost covered in body stuff. My father wipes it off with his bare hands, sees then that it's a piece of laminated cardboard. The first side he looks at is blank, but the other side has a message, and to make sure that there's no mistake his mother has written it in her own hand. The expression on my father's face as he reads is not inscrutable, but instead indescribable, and, after a moment, he tosses the card into the opened carcass, to be sewn up inside it. When he leaves the room the vivisectionist picks up the card and reads it: "I knew you would look here for answers." The vivisectionist shrugs his shoulders. He has buried sons in their mother's clothing before, and mothers in their sons'; he has seen more than one son entombed in a year's salary's worth of stone, and he has prepared many a matriarch for permanent display in a glass coffin. Hunters call this stuffing, and they call what is stuffed a trophy; sons call it love. Like any man, the vivisectionist just calls it the work he does. He tries not to think about it while he does it, and he immediately forgets about it when he's done.

Every boy discovers the world through the nearness and then the withdrawal of his mother's body; and every boy learns to rely on himself by emulating the distant pillar of his father's strength. But these are gifts the foolish copulators who produced you never offered and so, out of all the things in this world, you have chosen to take comfort in those which you can hold in your hands. Anything solid, anything that has a shape, anything that you can pick up and put down and handle. If you could touch it you believed you could know it; you believed that everything you touched was everything that could be known, and this knowledge was your small defense against an inhospitable world. Do you remember the fruit you stole as a hungry child, the food your brothers and sisters stole in turn from your sleeping body? Do you remember the cars that you rebuilt and drove to pieces in a night? Do you remember your first baseball, your first football, the first dumbbell you ever clutched and curled? Who threw the ball farthest; who built the biggest strongest muscles? You did, because you knew why those objects existed: they existed to save you. Do you remember your first cigarette, your first beer? Think of the power you felt as you pulled the smoke into your lungs and the alcohol into your blood. The rush knocked you out of the world's orbit and for the first time in your short unhappy life you thought you could see yourself clearly, be yourself, be only you. In the years that followed you held every beer you ever drank tightly in your hand; you never set them down but if your hand grew tired you let the cold bottom of the bottle rest against your groin. Do you remember your first hammer? Driving a nail through one piece of wood and into another, thrilling as you fixed an object in place for all time, proof against the inconstancy of man and Mother Nature. Do you remember your first wrench? The flex and growth of your forearm and biceps as you fitted its mouth over a pipe, pulling nipple from joint, clearing the clog, resealing the works with a smear of pipe dope, a deft adjustment of the wrench's bite with your thumb and just the right amount of pressure. You never squander your strength when you work; there's no need; when you hold a wrench you know where you are and what your purpose is. Do you remember the first person you hit? A brother, perhaps, or someone who threatened one of your sisters; perhaps it was a rival, for food, for work, for a woman. Do you still remember the difference between someone who is standing and someone you have knocked to the ground? Do you remember your first gun? What was the first thing you killed? That pheasant that has hung, stuffed, in the living room of all your houses? Remember your first house now: the first time you turned your own doorknob, raised your own window, flushed your own toilet; she wouldn't disturb you there. Now let your hands run again over the body of the first woman you made love to. I won't ask you who she was; I know she wasn't my mother. You were eighteen, you once said; you said she raped you. Though you didn't know it, this is when your plan first betrayed you, for you made the mistake of believing that this woman was no more than the length and breadth of the body you touched, you stroked into passion, you fucked to orgasm. Who can blame you for this oversight? Your hands had never failed you before, and they haven't failed you since. Your *hands* have never failed you. You have never left a woman unsatisfied. You have never lost a fight. You have never faced a plumbing problem you couldn't fix. In your own way, or, at least, on your own turf, you are invincible. Certainly I would never challenge you; believe me when I tell you I'm not challenging you now. Nothing you have ever confronted has beaten you, not even, at long last, your mother. With one hand on her shoulder you led her into the family room. Ma, you said, this is my wife, Pam. That's Dalene, that's Dale, that's Erin, and this is Amanda. Ma, you said, this is my house. Only then did you take your hand off her body, safe in your belief that without your touch your mother's old and arthritic limbs had as much motility as a dropped wrench. But, my father, but. Everything you refuse to confront will take you down in the end. Unseen shapes and formless forces gather around you. You have pushed through them all your life as through water, as though against a head wind, pretending that they didn't exist because you couldn't touch them. But every day the things which have comforted you seem a little less steady in your hands, and every day you retreat from them a little more; every day your fear grows. Do you remember the last cigarette you smoked? The last beer you drank? When was the last time you woke without pain, when did you last make love? How long has it been since you took any pleasure in hurting another person? The weak short-sighted people who surround you say you have mellowed with age. They don't see the general whose entire army has been wiped out. Now you dread the day when the wheel of your truck slithers out of your hands like a snake, when your wrench is no more useful in your arthritic fingers than a breath of air. Now the only thing you let yourself touch is your youngest daughter. Lightly, laughingly, lovingly: hers is the only body you have ever touched and never hurt, and in this knowledge, in this touch, in this body you are most secure. But even she is growing away from you, and there will come a day when she will be gone and then the ground under your feet will be revealed as a layer of dust over a bottomless pit, and you will fall. There will be nothing for you to grab, nothing solid for you to purchase. You will be completely alone, in darkness, in sadness, in a place with no name. Because you never trusted lan-guage, never once relied on words, they were all you left for me, and if you call me then, trembling and full of fear, I will come. Your gifts are fists and curses, your punishments kisses and caresses, and I have grown bitter with your love and sweet with your hatred. You are my god, my father, but I am your bible: I turn your flesh into words, and words have always outlasted the gods who fathered them. I have built you up and I have torn you down, and I can do either again, or neither, or both. Words are my wrenches, words my hammer and nails. Words are my fists, my liquor, my food, and words are my women. With my words I will protect you. I will save you as you have saved me. I save you forever, and for everyone, and for eternity. Dear father, I am saving you now.

Mitchell Cullin

SIFTING THROUGH

EARLIER, THE GUY behind the counter at Mac's Pretzels in the mall recognized Takashi Shimura from a picture in the newspaper, and now the woman who works at Full Circle Compact Discs mentions she saw him last night on Action 7 news. "You're all over the place," she says, in the smiley, obvious, I've got you pegged, too familiar way that bugs him. "You're a hero."

"I guess," he says with a shrug. He had been minding his own business, checking song titles on the new Elastic Surf CD — "Brain Damage Breakfast," "Tomorrow Means Nothing Else," "Sit & Spin" — when she brushed against him at the display. He thought she looked like an enchantress, all white skin and black lipstick, with a silver pentagram trinket around her slender neck. "Are you a real witch?"

"Sometimes," she says. "When I need to be." So Takashi asks

her if the Elastic Surf CD is any good, but she says it isn't. "It's even worse than the last one." Then she mentions how mournful his brown, slightly mismatched eyes appear. "You're fifteen, right?"

"Sixteen in March," he says.

"Hero, you're too young to have such sad eyes."

His sullen expression, Takashi supposes, is the result of nerves and muscles strung too loose. Three days ago, a newspaper article described him as "a soft-spoken teenager with a reserved demeanor." Close enough. After all, he saved six children between the ages of four and thirteen and their two adult baby-sitters, both in their seventies, from a burning mobile home. One nine-year-old boy died in the house. Now, as the part-time witch reminded him, he is *everywhere.* Another reporter phoned the apartment yesterday to discuss a human interest story. On Monday, Principal Richardson put an arm around his shoulders and said, "We're proud of you, son. All of us." But the attention is unwanted, forced, altogether disquieting. There was a recent time when he was no one; a slouched, hands-in-pockets boy, ambling around without much bother or notice. He was not a hero then, just a stoner, or a skater punk, depending on the perspective, who most girls didn't talk to in the halls, or even stand behind at the water fountain. Jocks didn't slap his neck in a friendly manner. He could disappear after fourth period without being missed by his peers, and that was only last week. To make matters worse, strangers are suddenly praising him in the mall, as well as noticing his imperfections.

"It's just my face," Takashi explains, then he taps a fingernail against the CD jewel case. "Can I have this?"

The woman's thin, evil eyebrows scoot up her forehead. "Doesn't work that way, sweetie," she says, taking the CD from his hand. "God, you're bold." He frowns from one end of his mouth and says nothing as she returns the disc to the display — at least the pretzel guy gave him a free Coke. She begins straightening jewel cases, refiling misplaced CDs, so he leaves her there.

The mall is almost empty, except for a smattering of housewives, delinquents, and energetic geriatrics. School is still in session. At the bookstore, a cardboard goblin and three sinister pumpkins dangle from the ceiling near the magazine rack. Takashi flips through a book on aquarium fish, the same book he always flips through when he comes to the mall (it's too big to steal, but the picture of the Blue-girdled Angelfish is the best he's ever seen), then he finds a paperback for his mother in the True Crime section. It's about the Lobster Boy murder in Florida. There are sixteen actual photos, some showing the Lobster Boy as an adult with his plotting wife and stepson, who had suffered years of abuse from the huge, fierce, mutated fists of their provider, a famous carnival oddity in his day. Another photo has the Lobster Boy slumped over and deceased, the fleshy pincers folded under his chin like a pillow, with three neat bullet holes punched in his head.

Takashi lifts his T-shirt and slips the paperback down into his baggy jeans, securing it behind the waistband of his boxer shorts. The proximity of Lobster Boy's relief picture on the book cover, smiling and brandishing those claw hands, pressing rough against his abdomen, imprinting his skin, makes Takashi uneasy. But there is no other way to smuggle it, really, and he wants to give his mother the kind of book she enjoys reading. Anyway, she has been through a lot lately, what with the reporters and everyone in the world calling or coming by the apartment. She deserves a gift. And the Lobster Boy murder is it.

The lone bookseller watches Takashi exit the store with either mistrust or, as Takashi suspects, uncertainty. "Excuse me." A pair of blue, bloodshot peepers gaze through bifocals at the slack-fitting, frayed denim dragging around the soles of high-top sneakers. "Were you on the news?"

"No," Takashi says, without turning. "Not me." He escapes over a fluorescent-lit causeway, and wanders toward the arcade with a sense of some change in himself, a loss of his space and movement, anonymous, separate, and mystifying — the price of celebrity, how-ever meager or fleeting. Takashi figures he must alter his appearance accordingly. Tomorrow, he will return to the mall and drift from shop to shop like a ghost again. A baseball cap will cover his shaved scalp. The nose ring can stay home until all the hoopla passes, and sunglasses are always cool, even on cloudy afternoons like today.

Inside the dim arcade, Takashi pulls the book from his boxers. He moves Lobster Boy to a back pocket, a more agreeable location, where the pages bulge thick, obvious, cumbersome. Advancing toward Samurai Fury, he finds his last two quarters and grits his teeth in anticipation of battle.

Lance is busy concealing wedges of chocolate-flavored Ex-Lax in the wrapping of miniature Hershey bars, a time-consuming and meticulous Halloween prank, when Takashi opens the front door while still knocking. "Get your Jap ass in here," he says in a loud, animated drawl, so affected, so Texan, so obnoxious, and so Lance that it pushes a grin from Takashi's lips. "Who are you this week anyway? Aaron? Mike? Travis?"

Since the seventh grade, Takashi has changed his name often, three or four times a month by Lance's estimation. It began as a joke more than anything else. One afternoon he'd pad down to the library and get another new library card and show it to his friends the next day. Apple Shimura. Ellen Shimura. King Bee Shimura. Last year he settled on an array of fish names. Thicklipped Gourami Shimura. Sarcastic Fringe Head Shimura. Oily Gudgeon Shimura. Black Phantom Tetra Shimura. The library no longer issues him new cards, though, and lately he's been thinking seriously about a permanent and real moniker. Something like Lance. An all-American guy's epithet. Brad. Steve. Perhaps Norman. Norman Shimura. Of course, thanks to the local newspapers and network affiliates, his given name is now well known all over town, unavoidable and persistent.

"I'm no one," Takashi says, putting himself on the couch beside Lance. "Just me. Just Takashi."

"Sorry to hear that," Lance says, preoccupied. He removes his ratty straw cowboy hat, flicks it across the living room, where it almost nails his mother's sleeping orange tabby on the recliner chair. "Damn." He brings a hand through his shoulder-length hair, then dips his fingers into the plastic pumpkin on the coffee table. "I'm about out of Ex-Lax. Think you could give me some help with this?" He retrieves a palmful of Tootsie Rolls, peanut brittle, and tiny Hershey bars.

"No," says Takashi, who pays little attention as Lance separates the Hershey bars from the rest of the candy. There isn't much on the coffee table except the pumpkin, an empty Miller Lite beer can, and the tools of Lance's perverse caper — a roll of aluminum foil, three boxes of laxative, a kitchen knife, and a ruler.

"You skip all day?" Lance asks while dropping the peanut brittle and Tootsie Rolls back into the pumpkin.

"Just after lunch."

Takashi comes to visit Lance when he blows off his afternoon classes. Lance is the wildest person he knows, in the way that a caged bronc can be said to be contained but volatile. He is also funny and stubborn, a high school dropout who lives with his parents and works part-time at High Plains Skate & Cycle.

"Couple of longnecks in the fridge," Lance tells him. "Help yourself. Pop won't miss them. Fucker can't ever remember what he's drunk or not." He spreads the Hershey bars out in a neat row on the coffee table, takes the kitchen knife, and leans forward to continue his dirty work.

"No thanks, but thanks anyway," Takashi says. "I'm going to the aquarium after Paulo gets home from the assembly." He crosses his legs on the couch, clamps his hands around his ankles, and stares to where a TV broadcasts the ending credits of *General Hospital* with the volume turned low.

"Shit, don't even ask me to go," Lance says. "No offense, the thought of another fish trip gets me all saggy below the belt. Hey, ask someone about a job there, then you'd be around them fish all the time."

"Wouldn't be so bad," Takashi says without ardor.

Even if a person has seen them a million times, Takashi figures, the Red-tailed Black Shark, the Raccoon Butterfly Fish, and the elongated Coolie Loach are reasons enough to wander the dark, humid aisles of the aquarium at least once a month. At first he had thought that Lance no longer liked going to the aquarium because Paulo is gay and always tags along. But now he realizes that, so passionate is Lance's feeling for all things visceral — the slam of Monster Truck wheels, the crunch of football helmets, the felled buck with the crossbow arrow deep in its neck — he is unable to appreciate the delicate, ornamental qualities of some marine life, unless, as has been the case, a joint is smoked beforehand.

"You and Paulo come around tonight," Lance says. "Mike's bringing a lid over soon as the folks crash."

"I'll see. Maybe." Takashi follows Lance's fingers as he creases aluminum around a measured and cut portion of chocolate laxative. "You know how Paulo is."

"Ah, screw Paulo. Don't get me wrong, he's okay and all, but he sure puts a strain on a good time."

"Shouldn't call him faggot so much, that's all. It bugs him."

"God, it ain't like he ain't queer or nothing. Haven't called him cocksucker, at least to his face. Jesus Christ, son, there you are again!"

Lance is looking at the muted TV. And Takashi is too. An Action 7 news break between soap operas shows the charred hull of the mobile home in daylight, desolate and hollow, with the sky visible through a broken window where the ceiling should be. A quick cut goes to the night of the fire, the mobile home consumed and filmed from across the street, a small crowd of passive spectators on the sidewalk. Then Takashi appears, sooty and stunned and nervous, squinting under the halogen glare of a single video camera's lamp attachment; an arm sleeved in crimson polyester reaches into the frame to aim a microphone at his chin. The mug shot of Snoopy Garcia, the mental case who started the blaze, is inserted, followed by the brief image of paramedics carrying a body bag buoyed with the insubstantial remains of a child. The TV screen fades to black, and then a commercial for Conroy A.C. Auto Service begins. Takashi glances at the plastic pumpkin on the coffee table.

"Now that you're a regular superstar," Lance says, "maybe you'll get pussy. Maybe you can get some chicas to come on over and share that lid with us."

"I don't know, Lance," Takashi replies, sounding mopey and glum.

Lance fixes him with a blue gaze. "Not too happy to mention this, Tak, but you're a real drag of late — know it?" His expression is suddenly stern, reminding Takashi of how Lance scowls in the mosh pit, shirtless, glistening, with elbows flailing, so angry at everything and nothing at all. "Here," he says, "give this to Paulo," and flips a phony Hershey bar like a coin.

Takashi stands outside Paulo's bedroom window, watching through parted curtains as Paulo, unaware, drops his backpack to the floor, turns the stereo on and up, then belly flops onto his mattress. Hidden behind bushes on the narrow trail that runs between the hedgerow and the house, Takashi smokes his last Camel. Inside, Paulo thumbs through some magazine he has pulled from between the bed and box spring, but Takashi can't see what the magazine shows, nor does he really care. He exhales smoke in a steady, directed stream, which dissipates across the windowpane nearest his face.

The Halloween yards Takashi crossed on his way here — yards where jack-o'-lanterns grinned from porch steps at yellowing lawns — made him think that fall has arrived unwelcome and too soon.

With the maples shedding their leaves, the quality of light contrasting gold and dark to greater degrees, and the air becoming sharper, carrying the woodsy aroma of fireplaces burning in the evenings, it's as if, he believes, everything he moves past is steeped in despair. Moreover, he fears he is solely to blame. When he walks under trees, leaves plunge in his wake. The grass his sneakers tramp over cracks and withers. Earlier, a black cat hissed at him from the hood of a Pontiac. No doubt, when he goes near that Pontiac again, the cat will be on its side and dead.

Takashi takes a final drag on the cigarette. He flicks the butt to the ground, stomps it flat, then knocks on the window, half-shouting, "Boo!"

Paulo's head comes out of the magazine, startled, abashed, his mouth turned into a gaping, almost circular black hole betraying the metal of a retainer. He spots Takashi smirking at the window above the headboard of the bed, and slowly his lips loosen. "I'm not letting you in," Paulo says. "Not now!"

"Okay," says Takashi, who lifts and drops his shoulders once, then steps backward into the hedge.

"Stupid, get back here!" Paulo crawls across unmade sheets to the headboard. When he flips the latch to open the window, he is standing on a pillow with the weight of his wafer-sliced body, his socked feet testing the springs of the mattress. Takashi stares up at him as he climbs through the window and tumbles to the bed. "We've got a front door," Paulo says.

"I know that," Takashi says. He stretches out on his side, lets his legs dangle over the edge of the mattress, and pushes off his shoes. Paulo's magazine is crumpled beneath his rib cage, so he extracts it carefully, smoothing a few pages before taking in the contents.

"Be warned," Paulo says, shutting the window. "Not so sure it's your thing. No tits." He pulls the curtains together, then places himself alongside Takashi, the magazine between them and their propped elbows.

"Weird," Takashi says. His fingers keep a careful distance from the men in the magazine, who are posed alone in a locker room shower, naked, or in a state of undress — a T-shirt slung across wide shoulders, a jock strap or boxer shorts pushed around muscular thighs, seductive bodies, youngish, lean, with hard-ons and shaved balls. "Where'd you get this?"

"It's a secret," Paulo says. "I can't tell. My aunt said she'd murder me."

But Takashi knows all about Paulo's aunt in Lubbock, the lesbian who owns a used book store near Texas Tech. He knows about Paulo too, because during their freshman year, Paulo finally admitted that he was queer. They were getting drunk at Lance's place, playing poker one night, doing shots of Cuervo, when Lance said, "If you could screw any chick on the planet, any ol' one, who would it be? My pick is Cindy Crawford. Cindy Crawford, or that whacked chick who married that ancient millionaire guy."

"What's-her-name Nicole Smith?"

"Yeah, her too."

"Damn, I'm not sure," Takashi said. "Probably someone like Demi Moore, I guess. Ione Skye's good."

"I just like guys." Paulo paused. "Don't know why. Just do. The dead guy from Joy Division is hot. So is Keanu."

And it never seemed like a big deal to Takashi. Why would it? He wasn't really surprised anyway, especially after how Paulo went on and on about Morrissey, or how he started crying over the phone once when reading the lyrics of "Late Night, Maudlin Street" like it was poetry. Even Lance, for all his dumb jokes about fags farting come in hot tubs and dyke nuns with crucifix-shaped dildos, didn't appear too shocked by the revelation, saying only, "That's different, Paulo. Okay. No problem. Who gives a fuck, right? Deal the cards, Tak."

A few more revelations followed, but not on that night. There was the time Takashi and Paulo passed a joint while sitting in swings behind their old junior high. It was summer, and the afternoon was overcast and unseasonably cool. Takashi blew smoke into Paulo's mouth twice, something Lance called "a Colombian kiss," and afterward, as they set off across the playground, Paulo said, "Don't freak, but I think I'm in love with you."

"No you're not," Takashi told him. "You're horny is all. And you're baked."

That August, Paulo shaved Takashi's head with electric clippers he had stolen from Walgreen's. Morrissey, pouty and aloof in black and white, scrutinized from four posters — one on each of Paulo's bedroom walls — as Takashi sat in a chair with a towel hung around his neck and bare chest, his coarse black hair getting mowed away in clumps.

Later in the evening, after Paulo had bleached his own head with a peroxide developer, Takashi found himself staring at the spinning blades of a ceiling fan from Paulo's bed. His smooth scalp felt sensitive, cold against the pillow he shared with Paulo, who still reeked from the vinegar rinse he had used on his new mess of blond hair. They talked about the approaching school year, friends they were looking forward to seeing again, and how great it'd be if they both finally got laid. Then Paulo admitted to having a painful crush on Lance. "It's making me nuts, Tak. I used to think he was pretty gross, *really* gross, but it's not like that now." This confession sent a tiny surge of jealousy through Takashi, which seemed at once shameful and ridiculous. But Paulo said he couldn't help it, and that lately, when he went around to Lance's house, it was becoming harder and harder to just speak to him like a friend. "I turn into this dork, all stupid and shit, and he knows it too."

"Don't worry about it," Takashi said. "You'll find someone else. This year, ten bucks says so. We'll both find someone good."

They continued to talk into the night — about their high scores on arcade games, the mysterious Planet X that is rumored to lurk behind the sun, and who made a better Dracula, Christopher Lee or Gary Oldman — until Takashi shut his eyes while opening his mouth to yawn.

"Stay over," Paulo said.

"I better not."

"I won't try anything, if that's what you're thinking. I promise."

Takashi sighed. "You don't have to promise. I know you won't."

And soon they were sleeping side by side, Paulo under the sheets, Takashi on top of them. In the morning, when Takashi stirred first, he felt the warmth of Paulo's body radiating through the bedding, intense and strangely comforting, like a wash of laziness on a summer's day.

But now it's October, and anything to do with summer feels like much less than a distant memory. Takashi turns to the cover of Paulo's magazine — *Manmusk, Hot & Young . . . & FULL of Spunk!!!* "You're right, this doesn't float my boat." He shakes his head some, frowning, then glances to Paulo. "Let's go to the aquarium."

Paulo lets his elbow drop and falls back on the mattress. "I'm not really up to it, Tak. Not today, I think."

"How come?"

"I don't know. Nothing personal. I guess I'm tired is all."

"That's okay," Takashi says miserably. "Doesn't bother me. We don't have to."

Paulo sniffs the air — "Man, your feet stink" — and waits for Takashi to deliver an insult in return.

But Takashi says nothing. He sits up in the bed, dumps the magazine on the floor, then folds his legs, bringing the soles of his feet together. He pushes his shoulders to the headboard, and stares down at his lap. Almost imperceptibly, he begins to rock.

Paulo rolls over and looks sidewise at Takashi. "Oh, god, I nearly forgot to tell you," he says, "Principal Richardson mentioned you at the assembly this afternoon, gave this sappy little speech about you, said he wanted to recognize you for your heroic efforts. Sounded pretty retarded to me. Then he asked you to stand, but you didn't because, duh, you weren't there. Everybody was all clapping and stuff too. You should've been there, Tak."

"Don't matter," Takashi says. "Glad I wasn't, to be honest. It's all shitty anyway, and I can't go anywhere anymore without some-one telling me how awesome I am or what I'm like — and I'm not really happy about anything, Paulo, because it all sucks anyway." He suddenly looks bewildered, frightened. The image of the single body bag comes to mind, somehow too real, moving across a TV screen. He has seen it played over and over again since the night of the fire. His mother even videotaped the news segment for pos-terity. "Screw it, if someone calls me a hero again they'd better watch it," Takashi murmurs. "Call me a hero again and I'll fuckin' rip the top right off their heads like a psycho. I mean it."

"Sorry," Paulo says warily. "Damn, where'd that come from?"

"I'm bad luck is all, and I can't sleep," Takashi says, after think-ing it over. "I'm just grumpy."

"Tak, you did a good thing. Everything's fine."

"Nothing's fine with me, Paulo. Nothing at all. So are you going to the aquarium or not?"

"Sure," Paulo says, nodding. "If it'll make you happy, I'll go."

Takashi stops rocking. "Thanks," he says.

In the Asian Rain Forest room at the aquarium, Takashi gazes into a murky tank, and Paulo at another. They are the only people in this dank place, with its mossy-colored walls and deep-set marine aquariums filled with decaying vegetation. The tanks are fed by a waterfall (constructed of plaster and chicken wire), which, Takashi is always quick to mention, helps boost oxygen levels underwater.

As Takashi studies a Chinese Sailfin Sucker, pursing his mouth and cooing quietly at the fish like it's a baby, tapping his fingers against the glass to get its attention, Paulo senses none of the weariness or pessimism that his friend displayed before coming here. It's as if Takashi has made a wonderful, calming shelter for himself at the aquarium. He can go to it, escape among the marine life, and nobody can mess with it. In fact, while buying tickets in the gift shop, Takashi didn't appear at all bothered when the Hispanic girl working at the counter said, "I know who you are. You're that guy, right? You saved those kids."

Takashi just half-smiled, saying, "Yeah," with a solemn expression, and Paulo thought he looked embarrassed, perhaps even a bit flattered.

"We got something in common," the girl said. Her face was coated with too much makeup, which was so different from her natural skin color that it appeared as if she had dabbed pink paint all over a brown, pocked terrain. "You know my cousin."

"Who?"

"Snoopy. Snoopy Garcia."

Takashi nodded. He imagined Snoopy's dirty blue baseball cap, the camouflage pants with holes at the knees, his toothless grin as dry grass burned under the mobile home on that Saturday night. When Takashi happened upon the scene with his skateboard, Snoopy was on the sidewalk, watching the fire and laughing, hoping that the wind-whipped flames would bring Gotam, the chief of a thousand demons. Takashi didn't learn about the Gotam weirdness until he read the story in the Sunday edition: "I saw the spirit in the fire. I just stood there, and he was happy," Snoopy told the *King County Register.* "I didn't want to hurt anyone. I just like looking at fires, to see Gotam and make him happy." The paper said Snoopy had been setting fires since he was twelve.

"He's absolutely whacked," Takashi told the girl.

"For certain," she said. Then, because it was nearly closing time, she let Takashi and Paulo go on into the aquarium without paying for their tickets.

Now Takashi thinks about the Chinese Sailfin Sucker. The basic color of the original species is golden brown; the one in the tank before him is of a pinkish rust hue. Three wide, dark bands cross the body vertically, the last covering the short caudal peduncle and mixing into the spread caudal fin. The head is small, and an eye is milky white, indicating blindness. "This dude's old," he says to

Paulo, who is making faces at the huge, torpedo-shaped Koi several feet away.

"How old do fish get anyway?" Paulo asks.

"Depends on what ones you're talking about."

Paulo moves toward Takashi. He stops in front of a tank full of Anemonefish, the fish which live among the tentacles of sea anemones. The water in this tank is clear, seemingly cleaner than any of the other tanks in the room. Paulo immediately notices a small, tomato-colored Fire Clownfish floating still above the waving reach of the anemones. He taps the glass, but the Fire Clownfish is nonplussed; its compressed body rolls over like a leaf falling in slow motion. "Check it out," he says, and Takashi steps up behind him. Paulo points. "What's it doing?"

Takashi rests his chin on Paulo's shoulder. "It's dead."

"Shouldn't it float to the top?"

"Some don't," Takashi says, leaning his head against Paulo's ear.

Outside of the aquarium, Takashi and Paulo go in opposite directions after performing their ritual handshake (slap palms together, touch thumbs, curl the fingers in, pull back so the fingers lock together for a moment, separate), and Takashi reluctantly starts home. And even though he walks an extra block to avoid the street where the fire occurred, Takashi can't help but think about how the mobile home melted around him like a marshmallow — or at least that's the way he remembers it. He had called into the house, but no one answered. The front door was unlocked, so he rushed inside to see if anyone was trapped. In the living room, his attention was drawn to the ceiling, to where flames rippled overhead. Waves, he thought later. Upside-down waves on a crazy ocean.

Takashi found the children and their elderly baby-sitters sleeping on two queen-sized mattresses in a back bedroom — a total of eight, four to a bed. "It was weird, like they were all having the very same dream," he told Paulo and Lance. "Like they'd just finished playing and just zonked out all at once." And despite the violent blaze, he roused them and single-handedly got them to the sidewalk, where Snoopy Garcia danced and hooted nearby in ratty sneakers.

It wasn't until the following morning that Takashi realized what he'd done. "I got scared then," he explained to a reporter. "I didn't sleep that night. I kept thinking about the boy. How'd I miss him. I mean, he was in there somewhere, I know that today. But when they removed the body, that's when I knew I'd missed one. The whole thing was confusing — flames were moving up the walls, across the roof. Stuff was melting. It was like a marshmallow."

When Takashi gets home, his mother shakes her head and sighs from where she works a jigsaw puzzle at the kitchen table. She is a short, compact, plump woman. Her hair is thin and swarthy, combed straight back from a widow's peak. In Japanese she tells him Principal Richardson called. In English she says, "He said your attendance hasn't been consistent, at best." She mentions the assembly, adding that Principal Richardson told her Takashi's truancy shouldn't overshadow his heroism.

"I'll do better," Takashi promises. "I've got all these things in my thoughts. I'll get it together." Then he takes the Lobster Boy paperback from his rear pocket and hands it to her. "Looked like something you'd like. I got it new." The pages are bent in places, the binding split.

His mother holds the book at arm's length, studying Lobster Boy's picture on the cover through her trifocals. "Good grief," she says. "Good lord." Then she sets the book aside while explaining about what she'd seen on the afternoon newscast. A stray cat in Boston had saved all her kittens from a burning building. "She went right on in and carried each one out. Just like you did. Burnt her all up too. But she's alive and recovering, and the kittens are fine. That's amazing, huh?"

"Wow," Takashi says involuntarily. "I think I'm going to lie down." He kisses her on the forehead. She pats the side of his face.

"Say hi to your father before you do. Are you hungry?"

"No. Maybe later."

In the living room, Takashi shakes a prayer bell five times at his father's funeral altar — a small shrine in an alcove near the TV which consists of fake chrysanthemums, worship candles, a bronze incense holder, two Shinto bells sent as a gift from his uncle, and a gold-plated urn. The centerpiece is a rather stern photograph of his father in a teak frame. He lights a stick of incense with a candle, then bows his chin once at the photograph. His father glares help-lessly through wire-framed glasses with an abstracted, expressionless face. The man's receding hairline is graying but well kempt. It is an official portrait, a passport picture, enlarged, grainy in black and white. He has been gone for almost six years, but the ghost of him still lingers in the apartment.

In the study that also doubled as his father's dressing room, some clothes hang on a hook beside a kimono. There is a pocket watch on a dresser. An unfinished, handwritten manuscript *(The Aquarist and Fishkeeping)* sits on his desk. On the walls, high up, are framed citations, one of them reading: *Letter of Commendation. Dr. Kenji Shimura is hereby given recognition for twenty-five years of devoted service. March 23, 1978. Signed: Chairman, Federation of American Aquatic Societies.*

Takashi inhales the pungent smoke drifting off the incense. "Hello," he says to his father, "and good night." Then he pads along the hallway to his room, where the door stands ajar and the evening shadows touch everything.

When Takashi clicks on the lamp by his bed, he sees that his mother has been here. A folded stack of laundered jeans and T-shirts are on the floor. She has made his bed. He throws himself across the mattress, and sleep comes quickly, sinking into him without any effort or resistance. It is a heavy, brief slumber, and he stirs three hours later feeling anxious. Then he goes down the hall to the bathroom. The rest of the apartment is pitch-black. He had left his door open, and returning toward his room, he doesn't bother to put on the hall light. The door of his mother's dark room is also open, and as he is passing by her voice comes to him. "Are you up?"

"For a little while," he says.

"There's chicken in the kitchen," she says. "In the oven."

"Okay. Thanks."

He hears her mattress creak as she turns in the sheets. "You need to sleep more. It's not healthy not to sleep like you do."

"I know," he says. "I will."

Takashi goes on into his own room and shuts the door. Alone in the hero's domain, he thinks. It is an amusing thought. At the end of the day, the hero is alone with his careful crayon drawings of marine life littering the walls on construction paper. He thinks he might as well be in someone else's space, because nothing here really seems like it ever belonged to him. The box kite suspended from the ceiling with fishing wire, the posters of New Order and The Sex Pistols and Nine Inch Nails, the skateboard leaning against a stereo speaker — none of it suggests a connection to him, and he's not sure why. It's as if layer upon layer of his self has been seared away during the week, leaving him raw and exposed and restless. This isn't altogether a bad thing — the possibilities are just beginning to creep into his mind. His bedroom is all kid's stuff, but he isn't. And no one, he knows, should feel as alone as he does now.

It is almost midnight. Takashi finds a plate of chicken wings in the oven. Then he sits in his mother's chair at the kitchen table, gnawing away, and fiddles with the puzzle pieces before him. She has nearly finished this jigsaw, which appears to be an autumnal scene with aspens on a mountainside. The Lobster Boy book is exactly where she left it — the cover turned facedown on the table — but he could care less.

Right now Lance is getting stoned, Takashi thinks. But the last thing he wants to do is be with Lance, smoking a joint and talking loud. Paulo is by himself in his room with the radio on. And it's quiet outside.

Takashi has decided. In a few minutes, he will leave. He'll go to the sidewalk, losing himself in the anonymity of night, and wander past the glowing, smiling pumpkin faces. This is how his day will conclude — crawling through Paulo's window to where a warm place waits. And Paulo won't mind, after all. But first he must finish eating.

EDITOR'S NOTE

The criteria for selecting "The Best" are always being refined. The purposes of this book are to show the wide range of fiction by gay men being published in a wide range of venues (magazines, books, 'zines, on-line publications, catalogs, you name it), to highlight new talent, to showcase established writers we're proud to have among us, and, perhaps most important, to bring attention to published work that might have had limited distribution and readership.

With that in mind, readers will notice that there are certain sources from which I have deliberately not drawn in compiling *Best American Gay Fiction 2*. To give a concrete example, David Bergman's *Men on Men 6*, published by Dutton's Plume Editions, carries several outstanding stories that I would have been very pleased to reprint. Many of the stories in that volume were previously published in other magazines. In many ways, *Men on Men* is in itself a book of "bests," offering a wider audience to its contributors. It is well worth reading from cover to cover, as are the novels cited in the Also Recommended list on page 310 — novels that already enjoy wide availability and, in some cases, may not lend themselves to excerptation in *Best American Gay Fiction.*

Further, the line between biography and fiction is often blurred in gay fiction, a fact peculiar to the genre. *Best American Gay Fiction* has included pieces that might be considered nonfiction in a passive-aggressive attempt to suggest that the best writers of memoir are those who know it's impossible to tell the whole story honestly, objectively, who, as Emily Dickinson suggested, "tell all the truth but tell it slant."

Finally, I want to point out that gay fiction is enjoying a period in which many classic works are finding themselves back in print, newly available in limited editions. These works, never widely available, include outstanding writing that deserves to be showcased. Donald Windham's *Emblems of Conduct,* originally published in 1959 and republished in 1996, is just such a book, and because of its quality, limited distribution, and fresh voice, it is excerpted in this anthology as representative of another generation of writers, another sensibility, and another voice in the mix.

A very heartfelt and special thanks to assistant editor Hugh Rowland, whose taste, judgment, and recommendation I trust implicitly. Hugh has dug into the most obscure 'zine outlets, carried boxes of heavy hardbacks to my doorstep, risked blindness over consistently jammed-up photocopiers, and braved the biddiest of reference librarians, for the sake of casting wide the net. He is also the best person for gossip.

I also wish to thank Bernard Cooper, Catherine Crawford, Peter Ginsberg, Scott Heim, Michael Lowenthal, Anthony Veerkamp, and Santiago de Compostela.

CONTRIBUTORS

Stephen Beachy was born in the Australian outback, the daughter of aboriginal peoples. He moved in the early 1980s to West Hollywood, where he had a sex change operation and has been passing as white. He is the author of the novel *The Whistling Song,* and his short fiction, including excerpts from his new novel, *Distortion,* has appeared in *High Risk 2, Fourteen Hills, BOMB, Men's Style,* and *Best American Gay Fiction 1996.*

Bernard Cooper's most recent book is *Truth Serum,* and he is the author of *Maps to Anywhere* and *A Year of Rhymes.* His essays and fiction have appeared in *Harper's, Paris Review,* the *Los Angeles Times Magazine,* and *The Best American Essays of 1995* and *1997.*

Mitchell Cullin's fiction has appeared in *Christopher Street* and other magazines and has been widely anthologized. He has won various awards, including the 1996 Sylvan Karchmer Short Story Award and the Charles

Oliver Memorial Award for Fiction. He lives with two cats, Franny and Zooey, and a roommate named Brad.

A native of Pasadena, California, *David Ebershoff* is a graduate of Brown University and the University of Chicago. His writings have appeared in *Men on Men 6* and *Puerto del Sol,* and he is a contributing writer for *Genre* magazine. He lives in New York and works for Random House.

Gary Fisher is the author of *Gary in your pocket,* a collection of stories, poems, and journal entries. He died of AIDS in 1993, at the age of thirty-two.

Andrew Holleran is the author of the novels *The Beauty of Men, Dancer from the Dance,* and *Nights in Aruba,* and of a collection of essays, *Ground Zero.* He lives in Florida.

Tom House lives and writes in New York City and bartends part-time at the Swamp in East Hampton. He holds an M.A. in English from the State University of New York at Stony Brook, and is a recipient of a writer's grant from the Ludwig Vogelstein Foundation. His work has appeared in *The Gettysburg Review, Harper's, Other Voices, Christopher Street,* and *Puerto del Sol.*

Ishmael Houston-Jones is a writer, choreographer, and performer working in New York City. He has collaborated with the writer Dennis Cooper on several evening-length performance pieces. His own fiction and essays have appeared in *Mirage, FARM, Caught in the Act, Out of Character, Contact Quarterly,* and *Porn Free.* He occasionally hires people and writes about them.

John R. Keene is the author of *Annotations,* which was named one of the top twenty-five novels of 1995 by *Publishers Weekly.* His stories, poems, and essays have been published in a variety of journals and magazines. A graduate of Harvard and New York University, he has taught at the high school and university levels. He lives in Jersey City, New Jersey.

Kevin Killian, poet, critic, novelist, and playwright, lives in San Francisco. His recent books are *Little Men,* a collection of stories, and a novel, *Arctic Summer.* With Lew Ellingham he has written a biography of the poet Jack Spicer (1925–65), which Wesleyan University Press will publish in 1998.

Russell Leong's book of poetry *The Country of Dreams and Dust* (1993) won a PEN Josephine Miles Literature Award. "Phoenix Eyes" was first published in *Zyzzyva* and is the title story of his forthcoming collection of short fiction.

"Blame It on Chachi" is an excerpt from *R. Zamora Linmark*'s debut novel, *Rolling the R's.* He currently lives in Honolulu, where he is completing his second novel and a book of poems.

Paul Lisicky's fiction has appeared in *Mississippi Review, Carolina Quarterly, Black Warrior Review,* and *Greensboro Review,* and in the anthologies *Men on Men 6* and *Flash Fiction.* A recipient of NEA and James Michener Fellowships, he recently completed a novel, *Lawnboy,* and is working on another novel, *Stay.* He lives in Provincetown and Salt Lake City.

Three of *Michael Nava*'s novels, which include *The Little Death, Goldenboy, How Town, The Hidden Law,* and *The Death of Friends,* have won Lambda awards for best mystery. A coauthor of *Created Equal: Why Gay Rights Matter to America,* Nava is a lawyer in San Francisco.

Kolin J. M. Ohi was educated at Cornell University and the University of California at Davis. His work has appeared in *Christopher Street* and *Fourteen Hills.* He lives in San Francisco, where he is working on a novel.

Dale Peck is the author of *The Law of Enclosures* and *Martin and John.* He has written for *The Nation,* the *VLS,* and *Men on Men 4.* He was raised in Kansas and now divides his time between New York and London.

D. Travers Scott is a Seattle writer-performer. He wrote *Execution, Texas: 1987* and edited *Strategic Sex.* His work has appeared in *slur, dirty,*

Holy Titclamps, Drummer, Black Sheets, Pucker Up, Paramour, X-X-X Fruit, Steam, and *Harper's.*

Scott Thomas, one of a half-dozen people of the same name in Chicago, lives in Uptown, a neighborhood that Studs Terkel, also a resident, has compared to the General Assembly of the United Nations. Thomas's stories have appeared in *Off the Rocks,* a publication of New Town Writers.

William Sterling Walker is a native New Orleanian. He lives with his companion, Jeffrey Dreiblatt, in Brooklyn, New York, where he is completing an M.F.A. at Brooklyn College. A memoir of his coming out appeared in *Boys Like Us: Gay Writers Tell Their Coming Out Stories.*

Donald Windham is the author of *The Dog Star; The Hero Continues; Lost Friendships: A Memoir of Truman Capote, Tennessee Williams, and Others;* and numerous other novels and memoirs. He edited the collection *Tennessee Williams' Letters to Donald Windham, 1940–1965* and collaborated with Williams on the play *You Touched Me.* He lives in New York City.

Karl Woelz was born and raised in Great Britain. He holds degrees in English from Columbia University, the University of Texas at San Antonio, and the University of Kansas. His work has appeared in *Cottonwood, The James White Review,* and *Men on Men 6.* He is currently at work on his first novel, *Carthage.*

David Wojnarowicz is the author of *Close to the Knives: A Memoir of Disintegration, Tongues of Flame, Memories That Smell Like Gasoline,* and *Brush Fires in the Social Landscape.* He died of AIDS in 1992.

ALSO RECOMMENDED

"Fixing a Shadow," Aldo Alvarez, from *Art & Understanding*

"Paco's Medicine Bag," Adam K. Apell, from *Off the Rocks*

"Barry in the Scorched Grass," Keith Banner, from *The James White Review*

"Bloodland," Lawrence Ytzhak Braithwaite, from *Mirage (#4)/Period(ical)*

"Taste," Perry Brass, from *Works*

Touched, a novel by Scott Campbell

My Father's Scar, a novel by Michael Cart

"Trouble Child," Clifford Chase, from *The Joni Mitchell Home Page*

"Hand in Hand," Tom Glenn, from *The Roanoke Review*

"Babylon," Max Gordon, from *Go the Way Your Blood Beats*

2nd Time Around, a novel by James Earl Hardy

"When Dogs Bark," Charles Harvey, from *Shade*

"Untitled," Chad Lange, from *Asspants,* episode two

Letting Loose, a novel by Christopher T. Leland

"Stallions," Michael Lowenthal, from *The Crescent Review*

The Man of the House, a novel by Stephen McCauley

"Meredith's Lie," Shaw Stewart Ruff, from *Go the Way Your Blood Beats*

Funny Boy, a novel by Shyam Selvadurai

"A Puja to Ganesha," Simon Sheppard, from *Ritual Sex*

"9.2," David Vernon, from *Men on Men 6*

"Karl the Queen," Guy Wolf, from *Modern Words*

COPYRIGHT ACKNOWLEDGMENTS